POLITICS OF MODERN IRAN

POLITICS OF MODERN IRAN

Critical Issues in Modern Politics

Edited by
Ali M. Ansari

Volume IV
International Relations

Routledge
Taylor & Francis Group

LONDON AND NEW YORK

First published 2011
by Routledge
2 Park Square, Milton Park, Abingdon, OX14 4RN

Simultaneously published in the USA and Canada
by Routledge
711 Third Avenue, New York, NY 10017

Routledge is an imprint of the Taylor & Francis Group, an informa business

Editorial material and selection © 2011 Ali M. Ansari; individual owners
retain copyright in their own material

Typeset in Times New Roman by Glyph International Ltd.
Printed and bound in Great Britain by MPG Books Group, UK

British Library Cataloguing in Publication Data
A catalogue record for this book is available from the British Library

Library of Congress Cataloging in Publication Data
A catalog record for this book has been requested
Politics of modern Iran / edited by Ali M. Ansari.
p. cm. – (Critical issues in modern politics)
Includes bibliographical references and index.
ISBN 978-0-415-40911-7 (set) – ISBN 978-0-415-45278-6 (v. 1) –
ISBN 978-0-415-45279-3 (v. 2) – ISBN 978-0-415-45814-6 (v. 3) –
ISBN 978-0-415-45281-6 (v. 4) 1. Iran–Politics and government.
I. Ansari, Ali M.
JQ1785.P66 2011
320.955–dc22   2010034051

ISBN 13: 978-0-415-40911-7 (Set)
ISBN 13: 978-0-415-45281-6 (Volume IV)

Publisher's Note

References within each chapter are as they appear in the original
complete work

CONTENTS

ACKNOWLEDGEMENTS

The publishers would like to thank the following for permission to reprint their material:

Ithaca Press for permission to reprint Ali M. Ansari, 'Iranian Foreign Policy under Khatami: Reform and Reintegration', in A. Ehteshami and A. Mohammadi (eds.) *Iran and Eurasia*, (Reading: Ithaca Press, 2000), pp. 35–58.

I. B. Tauris for permission to reprint S. Bakhash, 'Iran's Foreign Policy under the Islamic Republic, 1979–2000', chp. 12 in L. Carl Brown (ed), *Diplomacy in the Middle East: The International Relations of Regional and Outside Powers*, (London: I. B. Tauris, 2001), pp. 247–258.

The Middle East Journal for permission to reprint S. Chubin, 'Iran's Strategic Predicament', *Middle East Journal*, 54 (1): 10–24, (2000).

Taylor & Francis for permission to reprint Ali M. Ansari, 'Iran and the US in the Shadow of 9/11: Persia and the Persian Question Revisited', *Iranian Studies*, 39 (2): 155–170, (2006).

Shaffer, Brenda, ed., The Limits of Culture: Islam and Foreign Policy, pp. 241–262. © Massachusetts Institute of Technology, by permission of The MIT Press.

Chatham House (The Royal Institute of International Affairs) for permission to reprint Ali M. Ansari, 'Cultural Transmutations: The Dialectics of Globalization in Contemporary Iran', in T. Dodge and R. Higgott (eds.), *Globalization and the Middle East: Islam, Economy, Society and Politics*, (London: RIIA, 2002), pp. 132–150.

Zentrum Moderner Orient for permission to reprint H. Fürtig, 'Universalist Counter-Projections: Iranian Post-Revolutionary Foreign Policy and Globalization' in K. Fullberg-Stolberg, P. Heidrich & E. Schone (eds.) *Dissociation & Appropriation: Responses to Globalization in Asia and Africa*, (Berlin: Zentrum Moderner Orient, 1999), pp. 53–74.

University of Washington Press for permission to reprint G. Sick, 'Iran's Foreign Policy: A Revolution in Transition', in N. R. Keddie and R. Matthee (eds.) *Iran and the Surrounding World*, (Seattle: University of Washington Press, 2002), pp. 355–375.

Cambridge University Press for permission to reprint Khosro Fatemi, 'The Iranian Revolution: Its Impact on Economic Relations with the United States', *International Journal of Middle East Studies*, 12 (3): 303–317, (1980).

Yale University Press for permission to reprint M. Atkin, 'Myths of Soviet-Iranian Relations', in N. R. Keddie and M. J. Gasiorowski (eds.) *Neither East nor West: Iran, the Soviet Union, and the United States*, (New Haven/London: Yale University Press, 1990), pp. 100–114.

University of Minnesota Press for permission to reprint A. Milani, 'Narratives of Modernity: Perspective of an Oriental Despot', in M. J. Shapiro and H. R. Alker (eds.) *Challenging Boundaries: Global Flows, Territorial Identities*, (Minneapolis: University of Minnesota Press, 1996), pp. 219–232.

Taylor & Francis for permission to reprint S. Chubin, 'The Last Phase of the Iran–Iraq War: From Stalemate to Ceasefire', *Third World Quarterly*, 11 (2): 1–14, (1989).

Wiley for permission to reprint E. Karsh, 'Military Power and Foreign Policy Goals: The Iran–Iraq War Revisited', *International Affairs*, 64 (1): 83–95, (1987–88).

Disclaimer

49

DOUBLE DEMONS

Cultural impedance in U.S.-Iranian understanding

*William O. Beeman**

Source: *Iranian Journal of International Affairs* 2(2–3) (1990): 319–34.

Introduction: the process of demonization

The decade from 1978–1988 marks one of the most remarkable chapters in the history of international foreign relations – the era of troubled and difficult relations between the United States and Iran. The period is remarkable first, because of the extraordinary degree to which the two nations lacked perspective on the cultural basis for each other's political motivations and strategies in the international arena, and second for the degree to wich each side was able to use vilification of the other as a political stratagem for domestic political purposes.

For both nations this was the longest period of direct wrangling each had experienced with a nation outside of their own immediate geographical sphere in the 20th Century. The difficulties the two nations faced went beyond simple misunderstanding or conflict of interest. The differences both experienced were essentially cultural. Each nation, led by their governmental leaders, constructed a mythological image which served to "demonize" the other party.[1] Paradoxically fulfilled the worst expectations of the other, playing true to the image being created for it.

For Iran, the United States became the Great Satan, an external illegitimate force which continually strove to destroy the pure, internal core of the Islamic Revolution. For the United States, Iran took on another demonic form – that of the "crazy outlaw" nation whose activities were illegal, unpredictable, and irrational.

This "mythology of the other" was complimented by each nation's mythology of itself and its role in world affairs. For Iran the Revolution of 1978–79 assumed this mythic status. For the United States, a more complex structure which I term the "U.S. Foreign Policy Myth" held sway.

U.S. myths

The "U.S. Foreign Policy Myth[2]" is an extremely powerful and pervasive American belief system about the nature of foreign policy, how it is conducted, and how it affects American life. This belief system is troublesome because of the hold it has in shaping political strategy and defining "normalcy" in foreign affairs, even when it falls far from the mark in reflecting reality. At best foreign policy and military strategy based on this system of belief is ineffective. At worst it is detrimental to American interests.

The United States is not alone in espousing such a system. Indeed, virtually every nation operates in the foriegn policy realm from an equally inaccurate base of beliefs. (I will deal with Iranian myths below). It is natural for this to be so. Nations, like individual human beings develop habits of thinking, often based on real short-term experience or shaped by a particularly powerful leader, which are difficult to break. When these habits are institutionalized in the bureaucracy they become especially pervasive. In this case, the U.S. foreign policy myth is narrowly applicable. It works fairly well when dealing with Western industrialized nations, including the Soviet Bloc. It may also have been serviceable in dealing with the rest of the world in the immediate post World War II period. However, it has become woefully outdated for dealings with the global community in the past two decades, and will become even more outdated as mankind moves into the 21st Century. As a further point of contrast, those who have memories of earlier periods in United States history will be able to see how the current belief system differs from that of previous periods.

The five principles of belief

The five principles are, briefly as follows:

1   *The world consists of nation-states.*
    It is not surprising that the United States should come to believe that the world consists entirely of nation states with basically homogeneous populations whose primary identity (and homogeneity) derives from identification with their common nationhood. The United States was, after all, the first great nation founded on this principle.
    Of course, there are very few nation states in the world. One can think of a few European countries, Japan perhaps, a few of the new Pacific island states, but that is about the extent of it. The majority of the people of the world do not identify primarily with their nationhood, and certainly not with the central governments that rule the nations in which they happen to live. The notion that one would sacrifice one's life for one's president or prime minister is a patent absurdity in virtually every nation on earth.
2   *The East-West power struggle is the most important event in world politics. All other political relationships must be ranked in terms of it.*

2

Before World War II, even the United States accepted the belief in a multi-polar world structure. Now the United States has accepted a basically bi-polar model, and tends to structure the entire world order within this framework.

Of course, for most nations on earth the East-West struggle is very nearly irrelevant for the conduct of everyday life, except as an enormously bothersome obstacle which they must confront at every turn. The possibility of nuclear destruction is of course a paramount concern for thinking people everywhere, but it is the height of bitter irony that the bulk of the people who will be destroyed and suffer in a nuclear holocaust have absolutely no interest in the ideological struggle that will be the basis for the holocaust.

Few nations would accept the American belief that all nations must eventually assign themselves to one camp or another, and some, like India, have had to work very hard to stake out an independent position.

3   *Economics and Power are the bases of relations between nations.*

Power politics as a philosophy has been with the United States only a short time. It was articulated in an extremely effective way by Hans Morganthau, perhaps the principal teacher of the current crop of United States politicians exercising executive power in the United States foreign policy community. Former Secretary of State and National Security Avisor Henry Kissinger was perhaps its most celebrated practitioner.

For anthropoligists of all shades it is particularly galling to see that in the United States conduct of foreign policy, almost no attention is paid to cultural differences between nations. It is assumed that wealth and military might are universal levellers, and that little else matters. Occasionally it is recognized that religious feeling, ideology, pride, greed, or altruism may be factors in the course of human events, but such matters are often dismissed as unpredictable factors.[3]

4   *Nations are ruled by a small group of elite individuals.*

It is difficult to understand why the United States, with a strong internal ethic supporting democracy and broad-based, grass-root participation in public affairs finds it so difficult to take these same broad-based processes seriously in other nations.

Yet again and again, one finds that the conduct of United States foreign policy is based on identification and support of narrow elite political structures: elite elected officials, elite dictators, elite religious officials.

Clearly, power is thought to inhere in these narrow structures, An office is the chief sign of this power, perhaps reflecting the earlier stated belief that the world consists of nation states.

Thus the United States cannot easily see underlying cultural processes which contribute to social change, or, seeing such processes, feels them to be automatically negative in nature because they threaten the established order.[4]

5   *The Normal Conduct of Foreign Policy thus consists of the elite leaders of nation states meeting in seclusion discussing matters of power and economics presumably in the context of the East-West conflict.*

This final point is not a separate belief, but rather the congruence of the preceding beliefs into an image – a scenario which in fact, describes much of the conduct of foreign policy carried out by the United States in recent years.

Normalcy

As mentioned above, the U.S. foreign policy myth is a definition of normalcy – of expectations about how actors in the world behave and are motivated to act. Nations and actors that do not fit this mold are relegated to residual cognitive categories: "irrational," "crazy," "criminal," "unpredictable," and "deviant."

The United States had indeed become accustomed to pursuing serious foreign policy negotiations over economic and military conflict exclusively with other Western industrialized nation-states. "Third-world" and "developing" nations were traditionally dealt with in offhand, summary fashion. The legitimate needs and desires of the peoples of these countries, especially when they were in conflict with the recognized elite leadership structures were never a part of U.S. foreign policy considerations. Indeed, such factors were regularly ignored or seen as directly opposed to U.S strategic interests since they were viewed as "destabilizing forces."

The "Kissinger doctrine" in U.S. foreign policy, which still pervades the policy community, was opposed to attempts to understand the needs of other nations, feeling that it was their job to represent their own needs to the United States. Policy was often carried out with the aid of elite leaders – plumbers – who had been co-opted through a combination of economic and military force.[5] Indeed, until the conflict in Vietnam in the 1960s and early 1970s it had been possible to deal with conflict in these nations almost exclusively through co-optation, military threat or economic pressure.

The Vietnam conflict should have been a warning to Americans that basis for international relations in the World was changing. Unfortunately Vietnam was treated as an aberration – a defeat to be ignored and forgotten as soon as possible. The basis for U.S. involvement in the conflict was unqualified U.S. support of a dictatorial regime that was out of contact and out of favor with its own population. That support arose from U.S. need to carry out its own foreign military strategies, based on a popular domestic political posture of containment of Communism.

Iran filled a similar role in U.S. foreign policy sphere to that of pre-conflict Vietnam. It was one of the "twin pillars" of U.S. defense in the Persian Gulf region (the other being Saudi Arabia). In the immediate post-war period oil supplies from the Gulf region were critical for the United States, and the spectre of Gulf oil falling under the domination of the Soviet Union, however unrealistic that scenario might be, was enough to justify a massive foreign policy effort aimed at shoring up friendly rulers in the region – more plumbers – who could be counted upon to carry out U.S. foreign policy with little need for U.S. officials to involve themselves in great depth with the nations in question.

Shah Mohammad Reza Pahlavi was an ideal plumber in U.S. eyes. He was restored to his throne in 1953 through the efforts of the U.S. Central Intelligence Agency after a coup d'etat engineered by Mahammad Mossadeq which American officials feared would allow greater Soviet influence in Iran. Thereafter the shah became one of the United States' chief political and military clients. He purchased billions of dollars of advanced military equipment from the United States and provided a fertile economic climate for Western investment in the Iranian economy.

The shah was an extremely clever client. The money for all of his purchased and economic improvements came from the sale of oil to Western nations, the price of which was jacked up some 400 percent in 1973 by the Organization of Petroleum Exporting Countries (OPEC) largely due to the shah's influence. Thus the United States and its allies were actually paying for economic improvement and arms purchases by Iran through the increased price of oil.

Iran's pattern of dealing with the United States during the post-war period was a continuation of a century of similar dealings with other great powers. Iran had been in conflict with other industrialized nations – Great Britain and Imperial Russia in the 19th Century and the Great European Powers in this century. However, it had always been powerless to resist them either militarily or economically in any significant way. The Pahlavi shahs, like the Qajar shahs before them were alienated from their own populations. Strapped for ready cash, they decided that cooperation with Western powers and Russia in economic and military matters was far more prudent – and profitable – than defiance. They sold concessions to foreigners on almost every national resource: agricultural, industrial, mineral and commercial and transportation. In the process they became wealthy themselves.

It was possible for them to do this by establishing a very special kind of foreign relationship with the United States and other Western nations – a state of cultural insulation whereby the West was largely prevented from coming into close contact with Iranian culture and civilization. The United States, being Iran's chief ally in the West was most affected by this policy in the post-World War II years. Mohammad Reza Pahlavi insisted that all U.S. military and commercial dealings with Iran be passed through Iranian internal affairs back to the U.S. government of which the shah did not approve. Embassy staff members with few exceptions did not speak Persian until the period immediately following the revolution, and were, in any case, kept from meeting with the bulk of the Iranian population.[6]

The Iranian Revolution marked a dramatic watershed in this state of affairs. After a brief six-month period of secular nationalism, the government was taken over by religious forces. The secular nationalists were out of power and Iran became an Islamic Republic. Suddenly the rules for interaction between Iran and the United States changed. Iran's leaders adopted an independent set of international relations goals, summed up in the phrase "neither East nor West". They expressed the desire to establish a true Islamic Republic based on religious law. They became deeply suspicious of U.S. motives, fearing that, as in 1953 the United States would attempt

5

to reinstate the monarchy in order to regain the economic benefits enjoyed during the reign of the shah.

More disturbing for American politicians was the attitude of the new Iranian leaders. They assumed an air of moral superiority, and were not interested in cooperation with Western nations on Western terms. Moreover, they seemed comfortable committing acts which outraged the United States with no apparent thought as to the possible consequences. This kind of behavior was inexplicable for most Americans.

To add to the difficulty, in the immediate post-Revolutionary period, the Iranian leaders were not in full control of their own nation. Though identified by U.S. policy makers as elites, they had very little capacity for independent action on the foreign policy scene.

In short, post-Revolutionary Iran violated every tenet of the U.S. policy myth. Iran looked like a nation-state, but its political structure was – both under the Shah and today – far more tenuous than that of any Western nation. After the Revolution it was not concerned with the East-West struggle, preferring to reject both sides. Its national concerns transcended matters of military and economic power; it was often far more concerned about questions of ideology, morality and religious sensibility. Its elites were and continue to be informal power brokers and balancers of opinion rather than powerful actors able to enforce their will directly on the population. Moreover they have had to be extremely careful about contact with foreign powers, since their offices do not protect them from political attack as a result of such contact.

All of this has given U.S. leaders fits. Iran does not conform to the set model of international behavior with which the foreign policy community is prepared to operate. As a result the Iranians are "crazy outlaws".

Iranian myths

For American citizens one of the most difficult aspects of the Iranian Revolution was comprehending the blanket condemnation levelled against the United States by Iranian officials and revolutionary leaders. The vituperative, accusatory rhetoric seemed to be aimed at indicting all U.S. leaders since World War II for unacceptable interference in Iranian internal affairs, and destruction of the Iranian culture and economy.

For most Americans it seems incredible that such a blanket condemnation of the United States could have any substance in fact. Didn't the United States want to help Iran develop in the 1960s and 1970s? Weren't American industrial firms invited by the Iranian government to engage in joint economic ventures for the ostensible benefit of the Iranian people? Was'nt the U.S. interest in developing Iran's military strength during this period also in Iran's best interest? From an American standpoint it seems that the United States could be accused of no worse than wanting to make an honest dollar in a fertile market.

In the light of disinterested hindsight, however, it seems that there was indeed real justification for the complaints of Iran's revolutionary leaders. At the time of the revolution, Iran was left with a demoralized population, an economy sprawling and out of control, and a repressive, autocratic government that allowed its citizens no influence whatsoever in policies that affected them directly – not even the right to complain.

But, by the assessment of its own members, a far more serious development had taken place in Iranian society; the civilization had lost its spiritual core. It had become poisoned – obsessed with materialism and the acquisition of money and consumer goods. For pious Iranians, hardships can be endured with the help of one's family and social network; and through faith, *tavakkol*, ultimate reliance on the Will of God. But to lose one's own sense of inner-self – to be a slave to the material world is to be utterly lost.

Understanding why Iranians came to feel this way about themselves, and why the United States came to be blamed for causing this state requires a close analysis of Iranian cultural and ideological structures. Iranian ideology was expressed during the revolution and after in religious terms.

However, using "religion" *or* "religious fervor" as a label for Iranian opposition to the United States is far too simplistic. Anti-American feeling was widespread during and after the Revolution, and was not confined to people who followed the clergy. It was also acutely felt among secularized members of the middle and upper classes, who cared not a fig for the mollahs and ayatollahs. More significantly, it was expressed by many highly religious persons who actually opposed the clerical leadership of Iran, and who were convinced that the United States was supporting that leadership.

The reason for the violent expression of anti-American sentiment which wreaked havoc on relations between the two countries and eventually led to the taking of a whole embassy full of American hostages in November 1979 lies in the symbolic role which the United States played vis-a-vis the Iranian nation in Iranian eyes.

Taking their clue from Ayatollah Ruhollah Khomeini, the Iranian revolutionaries delighted in referring to the United States as the "Great Satan" in public street demonstrations. Although this epithet seems to be hyperbole on the part of the mob, such names give important clues as to the symbolic conceptions being invoked. In this case it is significant that the term "Great Satan" was used, and not another.

In order to understand the full significance of this seemingly straightforward linguistic usage, a thorough look at Iranian inner symbolic life must be pursued.

Internal and external – the moral dimension

Religious doctrine often serves as the most tangible concretization of the core symbols of society. In so doing, religion both makes statements about the truth of the conceptual world in which society exists; and prescribes for society's members what they should do, and what they should avoid doing. Furthermore, religion serves as a formal statement of symbolic categorizations in cultural life. It helps man regulate his life by placing certain aspects of it at the core of his value and action systems, and relegating other aspects to the periphery.

Religious systems, like all systems of patterned symbolic elements, are not merely static arrangements of idealizations – they are dynamic, and occasionally make their dynamic nature explicit. Such is the case with Iran.

The central symbolic pattern in Iran, which renders human actions both great and small as meaningful for Iranians, is the struggle between the inside (the internal, the core) to conquer the outside (the external, the periphery).[7]

The contrast between the pure inner core and the corrupt external sphere in Iranian ideology is explored in depth in a recent study by M.C. Bateson, et. al.[8] This paper discusses the differences between the exemplary traits of *safa-yi batin*, "inner purity" and the bad traits of the external world which lead one to become *badbin*, "suspicious, cynical, pessimistic". The bad external traits, epitomized in adjectives such as: zerang "shrewd", forsattalab "opportunistic", *motazaher* or *do-rou* "hypocritical", *hesabgar* "calculating", and *charbzaban* "obsequious", "insincere", are qualities which Iranians feel they must combat in themselves as well as in the external world.

Iranians during the Pahlavi era, especially during the final ten years would often express regret at behavior which they felt was unduly at odds with the good qualities desirable for one with a pure and uncorrupted inner core. A doctor of the author's acquaintance in a village outside of the city of Shiraz once went into a long disquisition on the difficulties of living in what he assessed as a corrupt world:

> They are all corrupt, all of my superiors. They are stealing all the time, and not just for the government – they also steal from the poor people who come to them for medicine and treatment. God help me, in this system they force me to be dishonest as well. They will give me medical supplies, but only if I pay them some bribe. When I ask them how I am to get the money, they tell me to charge the patients. So you see I have no choice, I must steal too if I want to carry out this job. I hate myself every day of my life for being dishonest, and I wish I didn't have to be, but I can't help it.

Iranian concern with this problem is reflected extensively in expressive culture. One of the principal themes of Iranian literature, films, and popular drama shows characters caught between the drive toward internal morality and the external pull of the corrupting world. This is, in fact, one of the central concerns in the doctrine and practice of Sufism, where the killing of one's "passions", (*nafs*), is one of the prerequisites to achieving mystic enlightenment. Display of one's concern for the depth of feeling that accompanies the drive toward the pure inner life is highly valued throughout Iranian society. This leads individuals to disdain that which is superficial or hypocritical. One of the highest compliments is the tension between the internal drive toward morality, and one can pay another person is to say: "his/her inside and outside are the same". (Bateson, et. al. 1977:269–70)

Internal and external – the legacy of history

The struggle between the pure forces of the inside and the corruption of the external exists not only in the idealization of individual morality; it also is a principal theme in the popular view of the history of Iranian civilization.

For ordinary Iranians the waves of external conquest which have buried their land over the centuries; Alexander and the Greeks, the Arabs, Ghengis Khan and the Mongols – are as alive as if they happened yesterday. The British/Russian partition of the country into two spheres of influence in 1907 continued the pattern of cycles of conquest. Finally, as will be argued below, the economic domination of Iran by the United States in the post-World War II period seemed to extend the age-old pattern into the modern period.

Nevertheless, every time Iran was conquered by one of these great external powers, the nation subsequently rose like a phoenix from the ashes and re-established itself. The times between these conquests were peak periods in Iranian culture. They were the periods of the flowering of the greatest literature, art, philosophy, mathematics, artisanry, and architecture.

Thus the struggle between inside and outside, when painted on the canvas of Iranian history, is seen as a struggle between the destructive forces of external invading conquerors and the reproductive growing forces of the internal core of Iranian civilization. The internal core has thus far been the victor.

The struggle between inside and outside has also been encapsulated in the central myth of Shi'a Islam – the martyrdom of Imam Hosain, third Imam of Shi'a Moslems, and significantly, grandson of the Prophet Mohammad.

Hosain's father, Ali was the only caliph to be recognized by both Shi'ites and Sunnis. Following his death, his son Hasan was convinced to resign his claim to leadership by Sunni partisans, who then usurped the caliphate, bestowing it on the ruler of Damascus, Mo'awiyeh. On his death, it passed to his son, Yazid.

Hosain was called upon to recognize the leadership of both Caliphs of Damascus, but he refused – and this act set the stage for his subsequent martyrdom. In this legendary act of refusal, Hosain came to represent for Shi'a Moslems the verification of the truth of the spiritual leadership of Ali and his bloodline (also the bloodline of Mohammad), through his willingness to be martyred when his own right to succession to leadership of the faithful was challenged.

Thus Hosain has continued to provide Iranians with a concretization of the struggle between internal and external forces. In death, he became an eternal symbol of the uncompromising smuggler against external forces of tyranny, the defender of the faith, the possessor of inner purity and strength, the great martyr in the name of truth.[9]

Yazid and his henchmen, on the other hand, become the supreme symbols of corruption. They not only are murderers, but they also represent false doctrine – imposed from without. The sufferings of the family of Hosain, who survived the slaughter of their patriarch, are laid to Yazid's account, as are, by extension the sufferings of all Shi'ite followers in subsequent history. To this day, a cruel, corrupt individual who brings ruin to others is labelled "Yazid".

From this exposition, it should be clear that in Iranian society the source of corruption is external to the individual, and to society itself. If civilization or individuals become corrupt, it is because they do not have the strength to resist forces from without that are impinging on them at all times. This particular directionality gives a specific bias to Iranian political psychology. As internal conditions within the country become more and more difficult, the tendency on the part of the population is to search for conspiracy from an external source. This was a distinct feature of the Pahlavi regime, which saw opposition to the central government as a Marxist-inspired plot. The same bias inspired the efforts of the oppositionist forces, who saw the central government policies as inspired by non-Iranian considerations. The confrontations which led to the revolutionary events of 1978–1979 and the ouster of the shah took place in an ironic context: both the shah and his opposition viewed themselves as defending the inner core of the civilization against the external forces of corruption and destruction. Thus, the battle of the Revolution can be seen as a battle of definitions: he who could make his vision of the inner core valid for the population as a whole, could control the nation.

The duty of a righteous Muslim is to resist corruption and promote the good. Any action is justified against a corrupting force. Thus the ouster of the shah was presented as a religiously justified action, and persecution of those who supported the shah was likewise seen as justified.

The United States for post-revolutionary Iran fit perfectly into the cultural mold reserved for corrupt forces. It was an external, powerful, secular force. It supported a regime which revolutionary leaders designated as corrupt. It gave the shah refuge and refused to allow verification of his claim of illness, thus raising the possibility that it was plotting against the Revolution.[10] When the Iran-Iraq war began, the United States seemed to "tilt" toward Iraq, a second corrupt external force, and demonstrated again and again in its actions in the Persian Gulf region that it was working against Iran's interests in the course of the war. It was thus easy for Iran's leaders to apply the epithet "Great Satan" to the United States and make it stick.

The United States for its part should realize that this period of stress in dealing with Iran constitutes an invaluable lesson for the international relations of the future. Most nations in the world do not conform to the narrow U.S. mythology of foreign relations. As world politics becomes more multi-centered in the next decades, it will be increasingly necessary for American politicians to deal with the nations of the world on a one-to-one basis, taking their cultural sensibilities into account. Labelling nations and their leaders "criminal", "outlaw" or "crazy" because the cultural underpinnings for their actions are difficult to understand does nothing to promote real solutions to political differences creating problems in the world today.

Notes

* William Beeman is Professor of Anthropology at Brown University. This paper was presented to the "Seminar on Iran," University of New Brunswick, Canada, Oct. 1989.

1 I borrow this term from Professor R.K. Ramazani in his insightful book *The United States and Iran*. See also his insightful book, *Revolutionary Iran* and James Bill's remarkable account of U.S.-Iranian relations, *The Eagle and the Lion*. See also Beeman 1987, 1986c.

2 I have elaborated on the U.S. foreign policy myth at greater length in other publications (Beeman 1986b, 1986d).

3 Nowhere is the structure of this belief so clearly seen as in the composition of United States embassy staffs. There are always economic attaches, and political attaches but in no embassy in the world is there a single officer whose primary duty is to interpret cultural differences which could cause misunderstandings between nations. This lack is reflected in mistake after mistake in the conduct of U.S. diplomatic personnel everywhere – events I hardly need to detail for readers here.

In fairness, I must note that the United States is hardly alone among nations in having some unskillful diplomats and foreign policy advisors, or being unable to analyze cultural differences. I should further note that the sensitivity that is demonstrated by talented, diligent persons at the working levels of the foreign policy community is often obscured in the United States when recommendations and observations reach the White House, where action decisions are made by persons with minimal direct experience in dealing with the cultural realities of the non-Western world. As an anthropologist I cannot resist stating that I think the world could use many more anthropologically trained individuals in foreign policy positions everywhere to compensate for those who believe that money and guns are the only bases for international understanding.

4 Of course, as the world knows, if broad social movements prove to be important in terms of the United States' interpretation of the East-West struggle, then great significance is attached to them.

5 Given the United States' extraordinary economic and military resources compared to the developing world, especially in the immedite post World War II decade this "superpower" mentality was perhaps understandable, but increasing sophistication of the education of world population (many of whom were educated in the United States) has made this view seem naive and anachronistic.

6 James Bill (1988) documents this isolation extremely effectively.

7 The account of the opposition between the internal (*baten or batir*) and the external (*zaher*) is somewhat simplified for the purposes of this discussion. See also Beeman 1982, 1986 for a much fuller discussion. It should be pointed out that Iran is by no means unique in maintaining a distinction between "inside" and "outside" dimensions in symbolic culture. Javanese and Japanese are two other cultural systems with this distinction, but the particular content of the two cultural arenas in those societies is very different from that of Iran. For additional discussion on this point see Beeman 1986a. Nikki Keddie points out that the *zaher* need not be identified merely as the locus of evil. It also can be seen as a zone which contains and excludes those evil forces which may attempt to intrude on the pure *baten* which should not be open to outsiders. Cf. Nikki Keddie, "Symbol and Sincerity in Islam", *Studia Islamica* 19 (1963): 27–64.

8 Cf. Bateson, M.C, J.W. Clinton, J.B.M. Kassarijian, H. Safavi, M. Soraya, 1977: 257–273.
9 Cf. Michael M.J. Fischer, *Iran: From Religious Dispute to Revolution*. (Cambridge: Harvard University Press, 1980) pp. 147–156; for an account of the meaning of the figures of Hosain and his father, Ali in present day politico-religious discourse. Fischer terms the cultural symbolic complex of Hosain and his death the "Karbala paradigm."
10 This was, of course the immediate cause of the capture and holding of U.S. embassy personnel for 444 days in 1979–80.

IRANIAN FOREIGN POLICY UNDER KHATAMI

Reform and reintegration

Ali Ansari

Source: A. Ehteshami and A. Mohammadi (eds) *Iran and Eurasia*, Reading: Ithaca Press, 2000, pp. 35–58.

This chapter explores the various influences that have helped deter-mine Iranian foreign policy since the inauguration of President Mohammad Khatami in August 1997, looking in particular at the role of the president himself in the determination and shaping of that policy. Ansari argues that, contrary to common assessments and per-ceptions, President Khatami not only plays a key role in formulating policy, but he also accords it a high priority such that it is arguably central to his vision of a reconstructed and reformed Iran, reinte-grated within the global economic and political system. Far from seeing foreign policy as a secondary sphere of activity determined by domestic considerations – in some ways an extension of domes-tic politics – President Khatami, it is argued, sees foreign policy as integral to domestic development, with both enjoying a recipro-cal relationship whose consequences may have a beneficial effect on local attitudes and the direction of socio-political development within the country.

The background

Since the election of Seyyid Mohammad Khatami to the presidency of the Islamic Republic in May 1997, Iran has moved energetically to consolidate and expand its foreign relations, not only with its regional neighbours but also further afield with its more traditional antagonists in Europe and North America. Concrete steps have been taken to consolidate relations with Iran's Arab neighbours and to reiterate Iran's stance that it poses no threat to the stability and security of the region. In particular relations have been solidified with Saudi Arabia, invoking memories of an earlier regional axis which saw the two OPEC giants seek to cooperate and if possible coordinate policy on both economic and political issues. While obvious differences remain the tenor of the relationship is markedly different. Crown Prince Abdullah attended the Organisation of Islamic Conference meeting in Tehran in December 1997, the highest ranking Saudi visitor to Iran for almost two decades, while the chairman of the Expediency Council, former President Rafsanjani, spent almost two weeks in the kingdom in early 1998. Since then senior ministerial visits between the two Gulf powers have been regular and the language has moved from one of suspicion and confrontation to one of support and constructive dialogue. Relations have similarly warmed with Egypt, another Arab state consistently vilified by the revolutionary regime in its heyday. While not condoning Egypt's peace treaty with Israel, Iran now appears to be willing to re-establish diplomatic relations. As if to prove a point, Iran has also taken concrete steps to build bridges with Iraq, although in this case, while pilgrimages may be seen as a stage in the road map to better relations, it would be fair to point out that the road map is a long and twisted one. A key indicator of Arab–Iranian relations, the Abu Musa dispute has also taken something of a back seat in the past year, reflecting perhaps its status as a consequence rather than a cause of Arab–Iranian mistrust.

However, by far the most interesting developments have been in Iran's relationship with its key protagonist, the West, and particularly the United States. In the 18 months since Khatami's election, there has been a dramatic transformation in attitudes encouraged not only by constructive statements by leaders on both sides, but also by the orchestration of 'events' intended to facilitate a 'crack in the wall of mistrust'. These have included sporting events, in particular wrestling, and a fortuitous meeting at the World Cup in France, but have also been extended to conversations and meetings between former hostages and hostage takers finally leading, during the anniversary of the US Embassy takeover in November 1998, to an invitation by hostage takers to their former captives to visit Iran. That radicals in the establishment have dismissed the idea and a newly discovered *Fedayeen-e Islam* have sworn to assassinate any returning hostages may serve to remind us not to get carried away with the rhetoric of *rapprochement*, but neither should it deflect from the fact that a wide range of individuals generally considered *persona non grata* by hardliners have already visited Iran, including Anthony Cordesman, Geoffrey Kemp, and most peculiarly, Rupert Murdoch. While critics may protest that in practical terms there has been little progress on US–Iranian relations, and that sanctions indeed remain in place, it would be erroneous to suggest that developments have been insignificant and superficial. On the contrary, a change of tone and methodical deconstruction of the distrust is an essential prerequisite to the construction of better relations in the future, if these relations are to be built on firm foundations, above and beyond the immediacy of short-term economic interest or political expediency.

Indeed I will argue here that President Khatami, and the political establishment supporting and encouraging him, employ a conception of political development of which foreign policy occupies an integral and pivotal aspect – one that operates within a strategic perspective and depends upon the construction of a legitimate basis from which to conduct and implement policy. This chapter seeks to show this by first exploring some of the key determinants of President Khatami's foreign policy articulation, and then investigating the strategy by which he seeks to pursue and impose his agenda.

The dynamics of determination

Any foreign policy is determined by a variety of different influences and events, many of which have been comprehensively elucidated by other authors.[1] It is clear for instance that, since the inauguration of the 'era of reconstruction' in the aftermath of the war and during the presidency of Hashemi Rafsanjani, one of the key influences on the increasingly constructive and pragmatic foreign policy being pursued was the need for economic reconstruction and development. Broadly speaking, policymakers in Iran, recognising the urgent need for economic development, argued that foreign policy should serve those needs more constructively than they had done in the past. More stable political relations, particularly within the region, were seen not only as a way of encouraging investment, but also providing Iran with a local market to sell its goods. Europe was also courted as Iran's main trading partner, and in the import boom which characterised the first Rafsanjani administration, European companies were only too eager to reciprocate. There were of course critics within Iran, and while the development of foreign policy relied in part on forging a consensus within the political establishment, more extreme critics were by and large dismissed as ignorant of the realities of international relations.[2] However, Iranian foreign policy-makers soon came to appreciate the flaw in their analysis of the international situation and in particular of attitudes towards the Islamic Republic.

The flaw was basically that, although countries both within the region and further afield were willing and often eager to pursue economic relations, in particular trade with Iran, and on occasions were willing to cooperate on political matters, the underlying strategic political environment remained negative. The level of distrust of Iran's intentions was so great by the turn of the 1990s that even the blatant aggression of Iraq against Kuwait could not be decisively exploited by Iranian diplomats. To policy-makers within Iran, emerging from the relative isolation of the Iran–Iraq war, and with President Rafsanjani at the helm, the realisation that they had lost the initiative during the first decade of the revolution and that the international environment was in effect ideologically reconstructed against them was a bitter pill to swallow. In the first place, the image of the Islamic Republic in the outside world, firmly established during the traumas of the early revolution, and not countered by anyone within the regime (indeed in some cases encouraged), was at odds with the image many policy-makers held within the country. A self-consciousness developed and, nurtured within the ideological cocoon of the early revolution, found itself confronting an image of itself it could not easily comprehend. Thus the surprise expressed by many officials when their apparent 'goodwill' in ensuring the release of the hostages in the Lebanon was not immediately reciprocated, or when Iran stood aside during the Kuwait War in 1991, and stuck resolutely to sanctions. Indeed, arguably, the Iranian reaction reflected a somewhat naive assumption in the certainty of a realistic conception of international relations. For them, the goalposts were constantly being moved, confirming perhaps the perfidy of the West and the fickleness of the Arabs.

But for others, some of whom had increasingly served in diplomatic missions in the West, other lessons were being drawn. One catalyst for this re-articulation of foreign policy may have been the resurrection of the Abu Musa and Tumbs dispute with the United Arab Emirates. Iranians found that, far from being able to reap the rewards of their prudent policy during the liberation of Kuwait, they were now being subjected to accusations of military occupation, and the speed with which the international media seized upon the issue came as something of a shock. As Deputy Foreign Minister Abbas Maleki said at the time, 'The volume of press coverage on Abu Musa is bigger than the island itself.'[3] Immediately the Iranian government found itself defending the foreign policy of the Shah, as it sought to argue that the 1971 occupation of the islands was in fact legitimate; and for the first time Iranian academics and policy-makers, while noting that the Shah had made mistakes domestically, publicly conceded that this did not at all reflect on his foreign policy, which had been on the whole well conducted.[4]

While such an admission was anathema to the radicals and hardliners, it did signal a return to strategic depth in foreign policy analysis and development. This cannot but have been helped by the existence of numerous 'retired' members of the imperial diplomatic corps within Iranian think-tanks and universities who were able to contribute to the radical rethink.[5] A number of key historical lessons had to be learnt, and these, it is argued, while not unchallenged, have helped determine Iranian foreign policy to this day. Indeed, while such an outlook had proponents, it has only really come to fruition following the inauguration of President Khatami, whose election success not only provided a window of opportunity for an ideological re-assessment and readjustment, but also provided a man with the credible conviction to pursue this shift energetically.

The logic of defending the Shah's foreign policy led inexorably to an analysis of why it could be considered a success. One of the first reasons recognised was the Shah's ability to integrate Iranian political and economic development and historical purpose into an essentially Western narrative framework. Thus it was recognised that the relationship between the Shah and the United States was not simply one of disinterested patron–client, but incorporated an essential ideological dimension which ensured that, whatever eccentricities were exhibited by the Shah, his allies always 'understood' him. It was this 'understanding' that allowed the Shah to seize the islands and to dominate the Persian Gulf with Western acquiescence and encouragement, and while the Shah might berate the West for laziness (for some a tactical blunder), such an understanding remained a strategic pinprick.

Indeed, so intimate was this 'understanding' that the departure of the Shah radically inverted the relationship.

There can be little doubt that the revolutionary regime, eager to distance itself from its predecessor, sought to encourage the new 'misunderstanding', and it was only, as noted above, during the Rafsanjani administration that the extent of the chasm became apparent. The immediate response was unsurprisingly somewhat crude as analysts sought to imagine how this situation could be reversed. Noting that the Shah used the threat of the Soviet Union to integrate himself and Iran within a burgeoning US Cold War narrative, Iranian policy-makers now sought a way in which the West could once again depend on Iran as a bulwark against Russia. This attempted re-creation of the past was however confounded by the new relationship between post-glasnost USSR/Russia and the United States, and the fact that the geopolitics of the region was irreversibly altered by the collapse of the Soviet Union. There was simply no 'red threat' anymore. The increasing volatility and instability of the FSU however did allow another resurrected policy to emerge – the presentation of Iran as a centre of stability. While some countries would remain sceptical, it was a theme that was to be emphasised with increasing success in the 1990s, as the international environment became correspondingly less stable and commercial pressures began to make themselves felt in the form of oil companies seeking viable routes for exporting Caspian oil. One key aspect of this ideological dimension to foreign policy was a growing appreciation of the role of the international – in particular Western – media organisations, and the role they could play in the manipulation of public opinion. Again, while some argued vociferously for a more coherent strategy towards the Western media, the learning curve was a steep one and it has only been since the election of President Khatami that the government can be said to have enjoyed some measure of success.

Historical determinants

In sum, during the first decade of the revolution, foreign policy always came a poor second after domestic considerations and in many ways was simply an extension of domestic rivalries. As such there was rarely enough attention given to the development of a coherent foreign policy, and criticisms from abroad were ignored, if not in actual fact considered a virtue. During the second decade, the period of the 'second republic',[6] there was an increasing awareness that this could only be rectified through the development of a more coherent strategy, independent of though not separate from domestic considerations. Indeed in some circles the sphere of foreign relations was seen not only as serving domestic needs and as such reactive to them, but as an aspect of political activity which could be expanded, explored and utilised in such a manner that positive results could he brought to bear on domestic developments. As such the value of foreign policy as an aspect of government was raised as the relationship between domestic and foreign policy was increasingly reciprocal and potentially mutually beneficial. As this view gained prominence the traditional revolutionary dogmas of isolationism retreated, but throughout much of the second decade tensions existed, stemming from those who wanted to maintain revolutionary purity through isolation, but also from the prevarications of those who supported economic relations in order to service domestic needs but were ambivalent about taking the next step. Indeed vacillation and ambiguity may be said to have been the hallmark of the Rafsanjani administration, increasingly aware of the need for a more professional focus but hesitant and awkward about the practical steps required to achieve it.

This revision in attitudes towards foreign policy determination reflected the political and philosophical debates which had permeated much of domestic Iranian intellectual and political discourse for the better part of a decade,[7] and mirrored the emergence and pre-eminence of supporters of what may best be characterised as the moderate or progressive wing of the Islamic revolutionary movement. Any political movement carries with it a broad range of opinions reflecting varied historical experiences and socio-economic backgrounds, but within the limitation of ambiguity some broad ideological characteristics can be discerned. Most members of this movement share a particular interpretation of recent Iranian history and of the course of the Islamic revolution itself, along with an integrative approach to relations with the outside world, in particular the West. In short, the revolution of 1979 is the latest and greatest of Iranian popular movements this century aimed at securing freedom, independence and security for the people and state. As such it is a worthy successor to both the Constitutional Revolution of 1906 and the National Movement of 1951–3 led by Dr Mosaddeq.

Reflecting on the failure of both these movements to achieve their aims, there is less inclination to blame foreign powers, but instead greater introspection and concern that the social and political framework had not been sufficiently prepared and that consequently anarchy became an all too convenient stepping stone for renewed autocracy. In order to avoid this happening again there must be sufficient social and political preparation; in other words, a concerted effort to re-align the political culture and mentality of Iranians away from a fatalistic submission to autocracy. In analysing the failure of the Shah, many commentators in Iran similarly argue that the Pahlavi experiment failed because sustainable economic development must be founded on a platform of political legitimacy – something which the Shah quite clearly failed to achieve.

It is quite apparent from this brief sketch that their interpretation of the cause and aims of the Islamic revolution differs quite markedly from many of the revolutionaries, who either from a belief in structural determinism or from religious conviction do not see political and economic pluralism as a possible or indeed desirable consequence of the revolution. The moderates on the other hand are emphatic that the aims of the revolution were to promote economic and political plurality, and in support of their vision have added to the familiar totems of 'freedom' and 'rule of law' the concept of 'civil society'. As such they have inclined to the argument that the revolution was diverted from its true course – a reality most obviously revealed by the stark contrast between political realities and the covenant between state and people expressed in the Constitution of the Islamic

Republic of Iran – although the reasons for this diversion vary from problems caused by the war with Iraq to the regrettable consequences of internal rivalries. The revolution is therefore a continuing dynamic and as a political project awaiting completion is *hegemonic* in its conception.[8]

An appreciation of this domestic dynamic, that is the historical interpretation and philosophical outlook it encapsulates, facilitates an understanding of the gradual transformation of foreign policy determination outlined above. The concept of hegemonic competition derived from historical experience was relatively easily transferred to the sphere of foreign policy. But the 'moderates' brought with them further distinctive ideas. While most revolutionaries found little difficulty in the application of a hegemonic contest – indeed the concept of the 'Great Satan' or preoccupation with the threat of a 'cultural onslaught' revolved around it – the moderates refused to countenance a purely antagonistic relationship. For them, the competition was not a one-dimensional confrontation, Manichean in its crude categorisation, but a multifaceted dialectic in which a dynamic synthesis was the key to a progressive integrative development. One of the clearest indications of this integrative approach is reflected in the continuing work of Abdolkarim Soroush, who has argued that a rejection of the West is too short-sighted and that Iranians must count among their intellectual inheritance the legacy of the West, as well as pre-Islamic and Islamic Iran.[9] Thus while most would agree that the international system was 'unjust' and favoured the economic and political interests of the Great Powers,[10] the moderates provided a distinctly different solution which increasingly came to be seen as more compatible with Iran's position in the international order. While many influential hardliners rejected this approach, as they rejected the domestic agenda, the election of Seyyid Mohammad Khatami on 23 May 1997 with an overwhelming majority was a significant victory for the moderate movement.

Khatami and the strategy of legitimation

Khatami's inauguration was a significant turning point heralding the increasing ascendancy of the moderate conception of political development and the role of foreign policy in that development. It would be erroneous to believe, however, that the victory was total. On the contrary, Khatami's election, while significant in the hegemonic contest and indicative of a trend with deep social roots, reflects a continuing dynamic; as such, foreign policy is still determined through negotiation and consensus with other parties and factions in the Iranian political arena. It would however be equally erroneous to suggest, as some have attempted to do, that foreign policy determination is beyond the control or influence of President Khatami and his allies, or that the Leader, Ayatollah Khamenei, represents an ideological pole inflexibly at odds with the moderates. Such a confrontational model of Iranian politics, often extended to encompass foreign relations as well, is just as crudely Manichean as the hardline philosophical world view outlined above. As the following will show, the reality is considerably more complex, and as President Khatami and his allies seek to pursue and implement their political agenda they have frequently resorted to negotiation and compromise with their domestic enemies in order that the strategic goals can ultimately be achieved.

President Khatami believes in the Islamic revolution, but is also aware that it has fallen short of its lofty ideals. For him, history, in a Hegelian sense, is the progress of consciousness of freedom,[11] and it is precisely in this area that the revolution in particular, and modern Islamic interpretations in general, have failed to deliver. Indeed, for him, Islam without freedom is not Islam at all.[12] Elected on a platform of civil society, freedom and the rule of law, President Khatami has been consistent in his reiteration of a desire to see a more pluralistic economic and political environment within the country. Like his predecessor, Khatami is faced with an ailing, 'sick' economy which urgently needs an injection of capital, preferably foreign. However, unlike President Rafsanjani, Khatami is more acutely aware of the complementary nature of the economic, political and ideological aspects of this process and arguably better placed to exploit it. Thus while there is a need for foreign capital, President Khatami not only recognises the need for a stable political and regional environment to secure this investment, but crucially also recognises the potential of the benefits of positive foreign relations on domestic political development. The logic of pluralism at home is greater plurality abroad and the relationship is reciprocal. And just as the domestic agenda must be constructed on firm foundations, so must the reintegration of Iran into the international order. Thus dialogue and reintegration are the hallmarks of Khatami's foreign policy, while his strategy is one of communication and co-option targeted towards the three main vehicles or communication and ideological dissemination: expatriate Iranians, the international media and the foreign intelligentsia.

An excellent example of the reciprocal effects of foreign policy on the Iranian domestic agenda and a key influence in the attempted realignment of Iran within the international order was the rise of the Taleban in Afghanistan. Ever since the withdrawal of the Soviet Union from Afghanistan, Iran had been competing with other regional powers, in particular Pakistan, to ensure a favourable resolution to factional fighting and the establishment of a sympathetic government in Kabul. The emergence of the Taleban was a significant reversal as this radical Sunni organisation increasingly imposed an extreme form of Shariah law in Afghanistan, thus promoting rather than reducing the flow of refugees, but also adopted a vehemently anti-Shia and, by extension, anti-Iranian disposition. While the cautious welcome afforded to the emergent Taleban by the US State Department on the occasion of their conquest of Kabul was viewed with some embarrassment in US academic circles, and may indeed have prompted serious reflection as to how far US policy would go to 'punish' Iran,[13] the impact of the Taleban on the direction of domestic political development was far more significant. Its significance was recognised by the moderates and singularly misunderstood by their opponents, as was to become apparent in the election campaign which brought Khatami to power. For Iranians, the rise of the Taleban and their extreme brand of Islam provided them with a barometer and reference point with which they could measure and assess their own Islamic government. What they saw not only horrified them, but also caused them to draw comparisons with the social and cultural zealots within Iran.

In successfully encouraging the view that Ali Akbar Nateq Nouri represented the vanguard of a Taleban style of Islamic government, and in identifying their fear with his person, Khatami's supporters inflicted the coup de grâce to the campaign of Nateq Nouri, who only recognised the potential damage of this unfortunate association extremely late in the day. It would not be too far to argue that it represented a political stroke of genius.[14] In protesting his innocence Nateq Nouri simply confirmed his guilt in the eyes of the electorate and effectively condemned himself to electoral oblivion.[15]

At the same time, Seyyid Mohammad Khatami was portrayed as the antithesis of the Taleban, epitomising in his person the qualities of rationality, moderation and intellectual rigour. He was in effect the model of progressive Islam, modest in both demeanour and wealth, while dignified and respected; intellectually vital and knowledgeable not only in Islamic philosophy but also in Western philosophy, a key ingredient in his appeal to the intelligentsia. This domestic distinction was not lost upon an increasingly inquisitive international audience, for whom Khatami's electoral triumph was similarly unexpected. The importance of the Taleban and the image they represented for the intelligentsia is convincingly shown by the attitude they took during the growing confrontation in the summer of 1998, when contrary to expectations it was the moderate intelligentsia who advocated a full scale assault on the Taleban against the advice of most army and Revolutionary Guard commanders. Despite the obvious practical reasons against such an intervention, it would seem that they had themselves fallen victim to their own myth.

So convincing has this identification of President Khatami been that his domestic opponents have been consistently frustrated in their attempts to blame Khatami for the economic difficulties which continue to mount during his first term in office.[16] Khatami for his part, it is argued, is acutely aware of the impact favourable international events may have on his consolidation of power within Iran. That is not to say, of course, that the emergence of the Taleban has not caused President Khatami distinctive problems – an unstable eastern frontier goes counter to Khatami's desire for a stable and secure environment for economic development and investment – but it shows how their presence has been used to good effect in the development of the Khatami myth both within and outside Iran.

On the whole, President Khatami has been fortunate in that international events have provided him with opportunities to promote his agenda and encourage a gradual shift in international attitudes towards Iran. Persistent problems with both Afghanistan and Iraq, personified in the American psyche by Osama bin Laden and Saddam Hussein, have allowed Iran to push with greater success than previously its identification as an island of stability, while the detonation of nuclear weapons in India and Pakistan has deflated US accusations of Iranian pursuit of weapons of mass destruction. More importantly within a regional environment was the continued intransigence of the Netanyahu government in Israel over the peace process and the disaffection this caused among America's Arab allies. Indeed, Israeli intransigence was by default making Iran's stated position about the injustice of the peace process seem realistic, if not true. The international environment has thus been favourable to a realignment, but the opportunities presented had to be seized.

The first major opportunity presented itself within the first few months of the new administration. While the next Organisation of the Islamic Conference (OIC) meeting was scheduled to be held in Tehran in December 1997, there was considerable anxiety among Iranian officials about the level of attendance and an eagerness to use the event as a showcase in which to market the new Iran. Great efforts were therefore made to ensure that senior representatives from each country would attend, and to complete the conference facilities in time for their arrival. Success however was assured by Arab frustration with the Netanyahu government, which meant not only that the previous Mena (Middle East and North Africa) meeting at Doha was poorly attended, if not boycotted, but conversely that the OIC meeting in Tehran was well attended. The contrast was a stark one. For Iran the arrival of dignitaries such as Crown Prince Abdullah of Saudi Arabia, referred to earlier, symbolised the return of their country to international recognition and respectability, while for the United States it was a clear reminder that Iran was not isolated. However, the meeting also allowed President Khatami to make his mark on the international stage, although his immediate audience was a regional one. Thus, while Ayatollah Khamene'i opened the conference with a speech many considered harsh, vitriolic and antagonistic to the West,[17] President Khatami rather pointedly opened his talk with these words, 'I do not know if I should begin my speech with the bitter issues that are, or the joyous issues that should be.'[18] Recognising that his audience was composed in part of representatives from 'moderate' Arab states, Khatami then proceeded to deliver a much less confrontational speech with a good deal of reflection on self-inflicted wounds in the Islamic community. In both its tone and nature it was characteristic of the moderate intellectual movement that had propelled him to power. In place of Khamene'i's, 'The materialistic Western civilisation encourages everyone to become materialistic', Khatami urged a better understanding of the West:

> We should know that between the Islamic civilisation – or more correctly the civilisation of the Muslims – and our lives today, there stands a phenomenon known as Western civilisation whose positive achievements are not few, and its negative effects are also manifold, especially for non-Westerners. Our age is one of domination of Western civilisation and culture. Understanding it is necessary. An effective understanding goes beyond the frills of that civilisation and reaches the roots and foundations of its values and principles.[19]

Indeed the speech is quite significant in highlighting a number of themes which were to become the hallmarks of Khatami's hegemonic project. Moving on from a reassessment of the past, and the failures of an Islamic civilisation to retain its cultural and scientific dominance, Khatami argued that in order to recreate such a vitality, a careful study of past strengths, stripped of anachronistic weaknesses which may have been relevant to a specific historical period, but were no longer valid, had to be pursued. This historical reassessment, and the replacement of dogma with vitality, was a quintessentially 'ideological' project, and the creation of a 'modern' Islamic civilisation required the 'materialisation of an Islamic civil society'.

Clearly with his audience in mind, President Khatami then drew on the conceptual imagery of Medina, arguing that just as 'Western civil society was primarily inspired by the Greek city states ... the historical and theoretical essence of the civil society that we have in mind is rooted in the esteemed Prophet's Medina'.[20] Furthermore, the changing of the name of Yathrib to Medina was 'not merely a change of titles'. The change signified that 'a spiritual, historical and geographical entity was created in the world that was essentially the harbinger of the dissemination and spread of a particular type of culture, world view and ethos ...' The international dimension is revealed when it is argued that real peace and security can be achieved when one has a deep understanding of the culture and thoughts of others, for which a dialogue is necessary. But this dialogue cannot achieve anything if one is insecure in his own identity.

> True dialogue will only be possible when the two sides are genuinely aware of their roots and identity, otherwise, the dialogue of an imitator who has no identity with others is meaningless and is not in his interest.[21]

The relationship is therefore ideally dialectic, in which each gains from interaction with the other, and development in one sphere must proceed and sustain development in the other. The centrality of 'thinkers and scholars' to the project is stressed, indeed they are described as 'the pivot and axis of this movement'. At the conclusion of his philosophical framework he alluded to the discourse on the clash of civilisations and described it as arising from 'hegemony-seeking relations' which had to be countered through 'dialogue'. On the sidelines of the Conference he suggested that he might initiate this dialogue by submitting a message to the great American people. He did not say when, nor suggest what he might actually say, but it was sufficient to whet some appetites.

In due course he was to agree to submit his message and begin his dialogue with the American people in an interview with CNN on the 7 January 1998. President Rafsanjani had conducted interviews with US television companies before, but what made this exercise different, it is argued, was President Khatami's acute recognition of the power and influence of international media organisations (in particular television) and their potency as a vehicle for ideological communication and dissemination.[22] In 1995, as the head of the National Library of Iran, Khatami delivered a paper at a conference on information science, entitled, 'Observations on the Information World'.[23] His comments are revealing.

In its contemporary, complex forms, information technology represents one of the highest achievements of modern culture which uses its control over information to solidify its domination of the world. Thus, inquiry into the nature of the information world is inseparable from uncovering the nature of modern civilisation itself. And until we address this important question we will not be able to muster the confidence and wisdom to understand our relationship to modern civilisation. Otherwise, we will live in a world whose rules have been set by others, at the mercy of circumstance, not as masters of our fate ... The flood of information in our age saturates the senses of humanity so extensively that the ability to assess and choose is impaired even among Westerners who are producers of information, let alone us who have a peripheral role in the information world. Electronic information is the brainchild of modern civilisation. Thus, the power of today's information-based mass culture is tied to the legitimacy of the values of Western civilisation for which the information revolution counts as the most prominent achievement.

There can be little doubt therefore that President Khatami was fully aware of the opportunity afforded to him by CNN, and it is significant that he opened the interview with a prepared statement which revealed both his understanding of Western civilisation and his strategy for reintegrative legitimation. In other words, not only did he indicate his knowledge of American history, and indeed his respect for the 'great American people', but he also suggested an ideological symbiosis through which Iranian political development was associated and integrated, and thus legitimated in the eyes of Western observers. At one level, the Iranian president impressed his audience with his comments on the Pilgrim Fathers and Plymouth Rock, and importantly, his 'regret' for the US Embassy take-over in 1979. He also expressed disapproval of the burning of US flags, and noted revealingly that anti-US slogans were not intended as insults against the American people or to undermine the American government, but that, 'these slogans symbolise a desire to terminate a mode of relationship between Iran and America.'[24]

These concessionary comments were the ones most readily picked up by the pundits in the United States, along with his now famous urging that 'there must be a crack in this wall of mistrust in order to prepare for a change', but they were not, it is argued, the most significant aspects of the speech. These were reserved, in the main, for the American intelligentsia, and it is worth noting that the initial reaction scarcely commented on them. In the first place he reminded his audience of the shared history between the United States and Iran and the regrettable consequences of that relationship when viewed in a deeper historical context.

There is a bulky wall of mistrust between us and American admin-istrations, a mistrust rooted in improper behaviour by the American governments. As an example of this type of behaviour, I should refer to admitted involvement of the American government in the 1953 *coup*

d'état which toppled Mosaddeq's national government, immediately followed by a $45m loan to strengthen the *coup* government. I should
also refer to the capitulation law imposed by the American government
on Iran.[25]

In emphasising these incidents, well known by most Western students of Iran,
and regretted by a few, Khatami sought to redraw the historical map and include
events which would make what happened subsequently more understandable. His
statement also reiterated the importance of these events within Iranian political
culture, which was finally recognised by Secretary of State Albright in a speech to
the Asian Society in New York several months later, a not insignificant concession
in itself. But more important than all this was President Khatami's assessment
of American democracy and his reference to de Tocqueville's 'Democracy in
America', which he noted, with no little irony, most Americans had obviously
read. This was a clear signal to the Western intelligentsia that there existed a
common language and interactive space. In his analysis of de Tocqueville the
parallel he wished to draw with the Iranian experience was clear.

> In his view [de Tocqueville], the significance of this civilisation
> [American] is the fact that liberty found religion as a cradle for its growth,
> and religion found the protection of liberty as its divine calling. Therefore
> in America, liberty and faith never clashed, and as we see, even today
> most Americans are religious people. There is less war against religion in
> America. Therefore, the approach to religion, which was the foundation
> of Anglo-American civilisation, relies on the principle that religion and
> liberty are consistent and compatible ... We feel that what we seek is
> what the founders of American civilisation were also pursuing four cen-
> turies ago. This is why we sense an intellectual affinity with the essence
> of American civilisation.[26]

In combining the myths of the founding fathers with the rational intellectual analysis of de Tocqueville, and associating it with developments within Iran, President
Khatami sought to integrate the Iranian historical experience with that of the West
and to weave a complex integrative narrative into a single text. Rather than a
hegemonic clash, the case was being made for a hegemonic synthesis. The tools
of this synthesis were not governments, but 'thinkers and intellectuals', the most
obvious immediate vehicles being the employees of CNN itself. Indeed while
US government officials debated the importance of the interview and generally
expressed disappointment at the limited initiatives on offer, there was little room
for doubt at CNN headquarters, where an 'historical conjuncture' was already
being manufactured.[27]

Combined with a generally sympathetic response from US academics eager to
make use of new opportunities for renewed contact, the US government was forced
within a week to reverse its initial caution, and in fact welcome the opportunity

for exchanges. Arguably, President Khatami, through CNN, had out-manoeuvred the inertia of the US foreign policy establishment and forced the pace. In the information age, the big battalions were on the airwaves, and if anything, President Khatami underestimated the ideological punch of the modern mass media in the West.

Over the next six months the trickle of exchanges, beyond the high profile sports encounters, which saw not only the Stars and Stripes hang in Tehran but the singing of the US national anthem, grew, as more journalists and academics flew to Tehran to 'rediscover' Iran. Far from simply being the 'Cleric who charmed Iranians', it was increasingly apparent that Khatami had succeeded in charming key sections of the Western intelligentsia as well.[28] The accelerated change in the tone of the relationship between Iran and the West and the implications this would have on policy, in particular the many vested interests on both sides which had thrived on the 'double demomsation',[29] became an increasing cause for concern.

The gathering momentum of the foreign policy sphere appeared to be losing touch with domestic political realities and as a consequence invoking a reaction which would be counter-productive to the process President Khatami wished to initiate. Whatever the excitement among the media therefore, both sides sought to put on the brakes. President Khatami found his administration under attack from a number of fronts and in the summer of 1998 he lost both his trusted ally, the Mayor of Tehran, and his lieutenant, the Interior Minister Abdullah Nouri. While these developments caused some unease and could have forced a retrenchment, the consensus seems to have been that the broad direction of policy had to be maintained and pursued, though with less haste.

Several conclusions could be deduced from this decision. First, it was clear that the administration and some members of the political establishment did not feel that the new foreign policy initiatives were unsustainable in the domestic environment and its continuing dynamic. Furthermore, this dynamic, with its occasional reverses, could indeed be harnessed and managed in such a way as to benefit itself; and this could be achieved precisely because the tectonic shift in attitudes towards the Islamic Republic of Iran was already providing foreign commentators with an ideological cushion with which to explain and understand, if not ignore altogether, the vagaries of domestic politics in Iran.[30] Iran was once again a potential 'island of stability' in an otherwise unstable region and there can have been few who did not recognise the coincidence of interests in both Iraq and Afghanistan, especially in the aftermath of the US missile strike against the Taleban.

Efforts to provide a common ideological framework within which to locate these interests continued with President Khatami's visit to the United Nations General Assembly in September 1998. During his brief trip he had the opportunity not only to address the General Assembly, but more importantly to talk to expatriate Iranians in the United States and also to discuss his ideas with foreign reporters, two groups who arguably have formed the vanguard of the ideological project. In his address to the expatriate Iranians, President Khatami showed his mastery of political discourse and his ability to tailor his talks to his audience in an effort to co-opt them,[31] but also revealed the depth of his theoretical literacy in the importance of both ideologies and myths. As such, his focus on Ferdowsi's *Shahnameh* and the 'spirit of Iranians' showed his ability to communicate with ordinary Iranians, while his attention to the mythic foundations of the nation was quite clearly addressed to the intelligentsia both within and outside the hall, declaring in no uncertain terms that he spoke *their* language. Thus, he said,

> mythology is a highly vast and complicated subject, which has received much respect, analysis and research in our time. Mythology describes the spirit of various nations. And there is no nation or people whose history is free of myth. Of course, in conformity with the weight of civilisation and the history of a nation, the myth of a nation is deeper and more complicated. And civilised nations usually have myths. The ethical myth and the myth epic indicate the spirit of the Iranians.[32]

Arguably, President Khatami's emphasis on the philosophical foundations of his political thought and his desire to explore these with a wider audience, while generally considered impressive, was also creating an impression of detachment. There was certainly some concern in Iran that this 'philosophical' approach was missing the target, as when, at the end of a press conference in New York, President Khatami decided on an impromptu elucidation of the problem of justice in human history and Plato's analysis of it.[33] There can be little doubt that much of the audience were somewhat bewildered by the digression. Indeed his presentation to the General Assembly, while more circumspect and cautious, was not averse to a brief digression on his philosophy of history, which as 'the glorious history of truth and the realisation of justice' was effectively Hegelian in its conception. At the same time during the press conference he revealed the historical influences on his determination of the importance of ideology in Iran. When asked by a Western journalist whether political parties would soon be part of the Iranian political landscape, Khatami answered emphatically that parties could be established, 'right now'. He then explained:

> Unfortunately, it is not up to the government to establish parties; the people must do this themselves. The experience of civil society is a new one for us. Although we embarked on this one hundred years ago [the Constitutional Revolution of 1906], we did not succeed in practice. The constitutional system was a system that could have formed the basis of an acceptable civil society for our culture and nation. Unfortunately internal disputes and intervention by foreigners meant that an oppressive dictatorship emerged from the heart of our constitutional system [ie Reza Shah]. After World War II ... again there was a good opportunity for freedom. In view of the lack of maturity of our domestic forces, we turned on each other with such ferocity that we failed to institutionalise

27

this freedom in the country. With the *coup détat* of the 28th Mordad [against Dr Mosaddeq], that period also came to an end.[34]

Such comments serve to remind us that his philosophical and ideological outlook do relate to a historical reality and that President Khatami recognises the dialectic which exists, in the same way as he recognises the relationship between foreign and domestic policy and, he would argue, the relationship of the West with the East. Arguably, he conceptualises both relationally and dynamically[35] and the momentum of the dynamic must be maintained and indeed sustained, through initiatives both ideological and practical.

Faced with mounting pressures at home, President Khatami, in agreement with the main members of the political establishment, decided to deliver another ideological *coup de grâce* – this time directed at foreign critics – and solve the Salman Rushdie issue, which had plagued Iranian–EU relations for nearly a decade. It was a bold stroke and a skilful exercise in diplomatic crisis management by both the main governments involved, with both effectively selling it as a triumph to critics at home. While criticism mounted in Iran, it has remained marginal and the restoration of diplomatic relations has not been stalled. In publicly confirming once again that the Iranian government would not send assassins to kill Salman Rushdie and disassociating themselves from the bounty offered by the 15th Khordad-Foundation, the Iranian government could justifiably argue that the honour and dignity of the nation had been maintained. In return Britain recognised the religious inviolability of the fatwa and its permanence, as well as the insult caused to Muslims, thus maintaining its credibility among its Arab and Muslim constituents. In other words, Iran had confronted Great Britain (the great bogeyman of modern Iranian history) and had emerged unscathed, pride intact, if not a little enhanced. Henceforth Iran could treat Britain on equal terms and as such a new Anglo-Iranian relationships could be constructed on firm and legitimate foundations, free from either fascination or hatred.[36]

There was a heavy price to pay for this move, however, as concessions had to be made to domestic opponents. Neither was the legitimation complete, but it was a significant step, and overnight President Khatami removed the one serious obstacle to the intellectual rehabilitation and reintegration of Iran. While differences would remain, it was the condemnation of a writer which had prolonged the antagonism of much of the Western intelligentsia. Seemingly oblivious to the reality of the compromise solution in the days and weeks after the resolution, media coverage of Iran became overwhelmingly sympathetic and above all 'understanding'. All this despite a concurrent crackdown on the press within Iran. The resolution of the Rushdie affair, however, represented an excellent example of the multifaceted continuing dynamic at work, with progress in foreign policy complementing and occasionally compensating for developments at home. In this case, it may be conjectured, the long-term rewards abroad far outweighed the immediate losses at home, and arguably would in time help reverse those losses.

Conclusion

President Khatami's success in presenting himself, both at home and abroad, as a champion of progress, justice and democratic plurality continues unabated and represents one of the most rapid and dramatic shifts in ideological perception and interpretation in recent years. The image of the turbaned mullah, fanatic and dogmatic, which permeated Western perceptions has been transformed in the space of a year. Arguably President Rafsanjani sowed the seed and President Khatami has reaped the harvest, and there is undoubted truth in the fact that the rapidity of this transformation was in part due to a receptive political will nurtured over the previous decade.

But it is worth remembering that under President Rafsanjani positive movements were being consistently undermined by an overwhelmingly negative undercurrent, which made constructive relations between Iran and her neighbours, to say nothing of the West, erratic and tenuous at best. Interest might remain in economic cooperation but could only be institutionalised through ideological integration and a recognition of an integral commonality. While President Rafsanjani appealed to Iranians abroad not to relinquish their identity, Khatami went further and explored the nature of that identity. In adding further dimensions to the discourse he facilitated entry by groups that previously remained suspicious or excluded. Thus he targeted the foreign intelligentsia as well as the media and made it clear that he 'understood' their language, even if at times it appeared he knew it better than they did.

Antagonistic isolation, while useful for the reconstruction of Iranian identity and confidence, had now to be replaced by dialogue and synthetic integration. Ironically the strategy is in many ways similar to that pursued by Mohammad Reza Shah when he sought to integrate Iran within a burgeoning Cold War myth and make Iran indispensable to the Western project – a truly strategic partner. The critical difference was that, while the Shah consolidated and indeed expanded his foreign relations, he did so from a domestic foundation of illegitimacy, and as his attempts to legitimise his rule at home foundered he increasingly compensated abroad, further alienating himself from realities at home. The Shah's strengths began abroad and remained abroad. Khatami's election has provided him with an altogether different basis for legitimacy, founded within the domestic political environment and which must now be expanded abroad. In so doing, he must retain a balance in this development and remember that foreign policy can complement and occasionally compensate, but must always be rooted in the firm foundations of domestic political legitimacy.

Notes

1 See for example A. Ehteshami and R. Hinnebusch, *Syria and Iran: Middle Powers in a Penetrated System* (London: Routledge, 1997), Chapter 3, pp. 27–57.
2 See Larijani's comments reported by IRNA dated 2 May 1997; BBC SWB ME/2910 MED/13 dated 5 May 1997. There has been continuing tension between those who believe contact is both useful and necessary and others who insist it can only pollute

the Islamic revolution. One of the more notorious cases was that of Larijani, whose visit to London in 1996 and discussion with the then head of the Middle East section of the Foreign Office effectively destroyed his political career.

3 Deputy Foreign Minister Abbas Maleki, 11 October in *Iran Focus*, November 1992.

4 'This is not the Shah's policy, it is Iran's national interest and a matter of Iranian sovereignty. Whether it is a monarchy or republican or any other type of regime is irrelevant. The Shah did not come from Mars, he was an Iranian.' Farhang Rajaee of Tehran University, responding to criticism that the Islamic Republic is defending the Shah's policy; quoted in *Iran Focus*, November 1992.

5 Views were also garnered from exiled officials.

6 A. Ehteshami, *After Khomeini: The Iranian Second Republic* (London: Routledge, 1995).

7 See for example M. Boroujerdi, 'The encounter of post-revolutionary thought in Iran with Hegel, Heidegger, and Popper' in S. Mardin (ed.), *Cultural Transitions in the Middle East* (Leiden: E.J. Brill, 1994), pp. 236–59; also A. Matin-Asgari, 'Abdolkarim Sorush and the secularisation of Islamic thought in Iran', *Iranian-Studies*, 30:1/2 (Winter/Spring 1997), pp. 95–115.

8 'Hegemony, relations of force, historical bloc' in D. Forgacs (ed.), *A Gramsci Reader* (London: Lawrence & Wishart, 1988), Part 2, Chapter VI, pp. 189–222.

9 Boroujerdi, 'The encounter', p. 243. The roots of this thinking can be found in the conception of the Iranian revolution as a worthy successor to the French and Russian revolutions, thus conveniently integrating Iranian and European histories, despite the apparent rejection of the latter.

10 Iranian attitudes are possibly best summed up in the note by Karl von Clausewitz: 'The aggressor is always peace-loving ... he would prefer to take over our country unopposed.' See his *On War* in Paret & Howard (eds.), p. 370. Hence the dictum, 'The conqueror always loves peace.' In this understanding, the world system is engineered to support the West, which of course promotes peace in order to maintain the status quo. As a consequence this must be opposed.

11 See for example, President Khatami's speech to the United Nations General Assembly, New York, 21 September 1998: '... one can discern the trajectory of history towards liberty. The history of humankind is the history of liberty.'

12 See President Khatami's inaugural address at the Majlis on 4 August 1997. Also BBC SWB ME/3346 MED/9 dated 1 October 1998: 'President Khatami addresses Tehran students at the beginning of the academic year', dated 29 September 1998. For a discussion of the concept of freedom, see M. Khatami, *Fears and Hopes*, trans. A. Mafinezam in *Hope and Challenge: The Iranian President Speaks* (Binghamton University, Institute of Global Cultural Studies, 1997), pp. 35–7.

13 In appearing to support the Taleban the US administration effectively sent the message that radical Islamic ideology was not the problem; being Iranian was. Such logic proved distinctly unpalatable to many US intellectuals on moral grounds let alone the consequence of inevitable confrontation it implied. While the characteristics of Islamism may change, Iranian identity could not.

14 G. W. F. Hegel, 'The German Constitution' (1802) in *Hegel's Political Writings*, trans. T. M. Knox (Oxford University Press, 1964), p. 216.

15 Nateq Nouri's loss of the political initiative is indicated by his campaign speeches in May 1997, the first of which dealt with his revolutionary qualifications. Increasingly aware of electoral disaffection, he then hastily sought to deal with more concrete issues such as women and the prospect for multi-party politics, both issues Khatami had made his own. See BBC SWB ME/2917 MED/3–11 dated 13 May 1997; ME/2920 MED/7 dated 16 May 1997; and ME/2926 MED/7 dated 23 May 1997.

16 Much to the consternation of the hardliners, Khatami's popularity has been consistently high after a year in office.

17 SWB ME/3099 S1/1 dated 11 December 1997; Khamenei's speech to the OIC conference dated 9 December 1997: 'The materialistic Western civilisation encourages everyone to become materialistic. Money, gluttony and lust have become recognised as great efforts, and in vast parts of this world purity, honesty and the spirit of sacrifice have been replaced by deceit, conspiracy, greed, jealousy and other ugly characteristics.'

18 SWB ME/3099 S1/4 dated 11 December 1997: Khatami's speech to the OIC conference dated 9 December 1997.

19 Ibid., S1/5.

20 Ibid., S1/5.

21 Ibid., S1/6. See also BBC SWB ME/3339 MED/2 dated 23 September 1998: 'President Khatami addresses Iranian expatriates in the USA', dated 20 September 1998: 'The first rule of dialogue … is to know yourself and identity. The second rule is to know the civilisation with which you want to maintain a dialogue.'

22 See J. Thompson, *Ideology and Modern Culture: Critical Social Theory in the Era of Mass Communication* (Oxford: Polity Press, 1990), pp. 163–272; see also A. Gramsci, *Selection from Cultural Writings*, ed. D. Forgacs (London: Lawrence Wishart, 1985), pp. 386–427.

23 See Khatami, 'Observations on the Information World' in *Fears and Hopes*, pp. 61–71.

24 BBC SWB ME/3120 MED/4 dated 9 January 1998: CNN interview dated 8 January 1998.

25 Ibid., MED/5.

26 Ibid., MED/2. President Khatami also drew parallels with America's fight for 'independence' much as Dr Mosaddeq had done 46 years earlier. (It is worth noting that de Tocqueville's discussion of the role of religion in American democracy is absent from many modern abridged editions.)

27 The reasons for this are of course multifaceted and while they may include genuine interest in dialogue, they surely also reflected the network's desire to fully exploit its 'exclusive'.

28 E. Sciolino, 'The cleric who charmed Iranians', *New York Times*, 1 February 1998; see also 'On the virtues of the West by Mohammad Khatami' in *Time* magazine, 19 January 1998.

29 W. Beeman, 'Double demons: cultural impedance in US–Iranian understanding', *Iranian Journal of International Affairs* (Summer/Fall 1990), pp. 314–19.

30 Khatami's success is well indicated by the attempt by Iranian hardliners to utilise the Western media in their favour by purchasing advertising space in *The Times* in which to publish a speech by Ayatollah Khamene'i on the occasion of the Hajj. It was a very crude attempt at media manipulation and showed a clear misunderstanding of the nature of the Western media. However, as far as Khatami's strategy was concerned there could be no better example of imitation being the sincerest form of flattery.

31 Unusually, this encounter was broadcast on CNN.

32 BBC SWB ME/3339 MED/1 dated 23 September 1998: 'President Khatami addresses Iranian expatriates in the USA', dated 20 September 1998.

33 BBC SWB ME/3344 MED/11–16 dated 29 September 1998: 'President Khatami's press conference at the UN', dated 22 September 1998.

34 Ibid., MED/13–14.

35 K. Mannheim, *Ideology and Utopia* (London: Routledge & Kegan Paul, 1960), p. 135.

36 BBC SWB ME/3339 MED/2 dated 23 September 1998: 'President Khatami addresses Iranian expatriates in the USA', dated 20 September 1998.

51

IRAN'S FOREIGN POLICY UNDER THE ISLAMIC REPUBLIC, 1979–2000

Shaul Bakhash

Source: L. Carl Brown (ed.) *Diplomacy in the Middle East: The International Relations of Regional and Outside Powers*, London: I. B. Tauris, 2001, pp. 247–58.

The impact of the 1979 Islamic revolution on Iran's foreign policy has been the subject of considerable debate among scholars and analysts. Some have discerned a post-revolution foreign policy dominated by ideological considerations. Others have argued that Iran is no exception to the rule that the geostrategic interests of states determine foreign policy; and that, inevitably, Iran's foreign policy has continued to be characterized by the same geostrategic considerations and priorities that defined foreign policy under the monarchy. In fact, the Islamic revolution and the ideas and ideology to which it gave birth have significantly reshaped Iranian foreign policy. There are continuities across the watershed of the revolution, but the transformations in foreign policy orientation are also striking.

Under the monarchy, the United States was a close ally, and the shah took pride in his close relations with Western Europe. Iran had excellent relations with Israel. In the Middle East and the Persian Gulf, Iran identified most often with the Arab monarchies and the conservative Arab states, including Saudi Arabia, the Gulf amirates, Jordan, Morocco, and Sadat's Egypt. Relations with the radical Arab states—Syria, Iraq, and Libya—were generally strained. Iran under the shah was, in essence, a status-quo power and served as an element of stability in the Persian Gulf.

By contrast, under the Islamic Republic, the United States has come to be regarded by Iran as the "great Satan" and an enemy of the Islamic Republic. Diplomatic relations were broken in 1979, and the rupture continued two decades after the revolution. Diplomatic relations with Britain, France, and Germany were frequently disrupted by minor and major incidents that derived primarily from the political and foreign-policy attitudes generated by the revolution. On the Arab-Israeli conflict, Iran took the position that Israel was an illegitimate state that had

32

no right to exist. After 1990, Iran remained intractably hostile to the Oslo peace process. For a decade after the revolution, diplomatic relations with Egypt, Morocco, and Jordan remained broken, while Iran moved closer to the Arab radicals. Syria became its closest Arab ally, Libya was considered a friend, and Iran acted with alacrity to support the radical Islamic regime that seized power in Sudan in the early 1990s. In the first decade after the revolution, Iran was with good reason seen as a disruptive element in the Persian Gulf region rather than a source of stability. At the very least, Iran adopted a rhetoric against Saudi Arabia and the Gulf amirates that these states viewed as an attack on their legitimacy. Iran saw itself, and behaved, as an anti-status-quo power.

Revolution and foreign policy

Several elements contributed to these altered directions in Iran's foreign policy. Iran's new rulers saw their revolution as a model and catalyst for Islamic revolutions throughout the region and sought, at various times, to advance such revolutions by example, word, material support, and action. Even after hopes for a wider upheaval in the Persian Gulf and Arab Middle East began to wane, Iran's new leaders continued to treat Islam as the preeminent weapon for the world's exploited peoples to use against the great powers. In the Iranian view, for centuries the great powers had been exploiting Muslims, looting their resources and threatening their culture.

Iran's leaders, moreover, claimed for the dominant figure of the Iranian revolution, Ayatollah Khomeini, a kind of spiritual leadership for Muslims everywhere. Khomeini took his role as spiritual leader and spokesman for the Muslim world with utter seriousness. His words and actions implied a transnational Islamic responsibility that extended beyond Iran's borders. In January 1989, for example, Khomeini addressed a letter to Mikhael Gorbachev in which he applauded the Soviet leader for abandoning the false god of communism, urged him to avoid the equally false god of capitalism, and advised him to return to God, read the Qur'an, and study the Islamic mystics and philosophers. Again, it was as a defender of the world's Muslim community against the supposed insults and blasphemous content of the novel *The Satanic Verses* that Khomeini condemned the author, Salman Rushdie, to death. Khomeini addressed his last will and testament not only to the people of Iran but also "to all the Muslim nations and the oppressed of the world."

Khomeini and his lieutenants felt little compunction in publicly denouncing other Muslim heads of state, arguing it was an Islamic duty to denounce the tyrant, the corrupt leader who had strayed from the Islamic path. In his last will and testament, a document intended as a guide to policy for his successors, Khomeini described King Husayn of Jordan as a "criminal peddler" and King Hassan of Morocco and President Mubarak of Egypt as American lackeys and associates of "criminal Israel." He called for the public cursing of the rulers of Saudi Arabia for their alleged "treachery" against the house of God.

33

Khomeini's successor, Ali Khamenei, aspired to a similar role as spokesman for the world Islamic community. He championed the cause of Muslims in Bosnia and the West Bank, Somalia and Lebanon. He argued that the Palestinian question and the ultimate disposition of Jerusalem were "an Islamic matter" on which presumably all Muslims, not just Palestinians, must have a say. He repeatedly urged the Islamic world to unite and gird itself for a struggle with the exploitative, threatening West. In these ways he sought to assert Iran's primacy among Muslim states, to capture for himself the prestige and authority that he believes Khomeini enjoyed among Muslims worldwide, and also to bolster his position at home.

This universalistic streak in Iran's postrevolution ideology was strongest in the first decade following the revolution, but its influence on foreign policy continued well into the 1990s. Iran's leaders supported Islamic movements beyond their own borders out of both conviction and calculation. The support that Iran lent to these movements by word or deed was a token of Iran's own Islamic credentials and helped boost the regime's standing, or so the leadership thought, with constituencies at home. It served as a means of projecting Iranian influence abroad and allowed Iran to create for itself a presence in Lebanon or to become a player, if only briefly, in Bosnia or in the politics of the Arab-Israeli conflict. As such, Islam served the same purpose for Iran as Arab nationalism had for Egypt under Nasir. Supporting Islamic causes abroad was also an attempt to secure leverage against countries like the United States and Israel that were hostile to Iran. Iran used the Shiite Hizbullah party to drive American marines out of Lebanon, to harass Israeli troops in that country, and to take American hostages who were then used (not necessarily successfully) to influence American policy toward Iran.

Resistance to Western cultural hegemony, suspicion of Western motives, and unease with even the appearance of friendly traffic with the West was another element in the revolutionary legacy that impacted on foreign policy. The revolution, after all, defined itself in part against what was seen as the shah's excessive deference toward the United States and his excessive zeal for Westernization. The revolution, by contrast, stressed Islamic authenticity and identity. The postrevolution period was characterized by repeated attacks on Western cultural influence and the liberal intelligentsia that were its presumed agents. In 1993, the Supreme Leader, Khamenei, revived a campaign against Western cultural influence. The term he employed, "cultural onslaught," was added to the revolutionary lexicon; it was a code word for the supposedly corrupting influences of the West fostered by liberals and reformers. In the 1996 parliamentary elections and the 1997 presidential elections, Khamenei tried to rouse public opinion for or against various candidates or political factions by asserting that the people would not vote for "an American Islam" or for those who would be "soft" on America. Twenty years after the revolution, conservatives were still trying to taint their opponents with the "American" or "Western" brush. Such rhetoric, used in part for domestic political advantage, nevertheless bred an environment hostile to normal relations with European countries and America.

34

The propensity for "revolutionary" posturing and action also remained a legacy of the revolution and exacerbated Iran's relations with the Arab states of the Persian Gulf, the United States and the Western European countries. In the months immediately following the revolution, clerical propagandists fanned out in the Gulf amirates to preach the need for Islamic revolution. One senior cleric warned the amir of Bahrain that he would call on the Bahrainis to overthrow him if he did not treat his people with greater consideration. Ayatollah Montazeri, a senior cleric who at one time was expected to succeed Khomeini as Iran's leader, in the early 1980s denounced the Saudi ruling family as "a bunch of pleasure-seekers and mercenaries," and asked, "How long must Satan rule in the house of God?" For years, Iranians on the annual *haj* pilgrimage to Mecca acted on Khomeini's instructions to "disavow the infidel" by organizing demonstrations against Israel, America, and the "world-devouring" great powers. These demonstrations almost invariably led to clashes with the Saudi authorities. Iran changed tack only after inept handling of the demonstrators by the Saudi police in 1987 led to riots in which over 400 pilgrims, 270 of them Iranians, were killed. Diplomatic relations between the two countries were broken as a result and not resumed for three years.

In addition, there existed a plethora of government organizations that acted independently, sometimes with and sometimes without government sanction. The security agencies felt free to pursue policies which, even if officially sanctioned, did not always coincide with government policy. The government often appeared to be pursuing contradictory policies. For example, after 1990, Iran actively sought better relations with the countries of the European Union. Yet in these years, Iranian agents carried out a string of assassinations of Iranian dissidents in European capitals and cities, including Paris, Berlin and Vienna. Well into the second decade after the revolution, it was often difficult to know whether such operations were the result of decisions taken by the government, by its agencies acting independently, or by rogue elements within the regime.

The examples are legion. In 1982, following the Israeli invasion of Lebanon, Muhammad Montazeri, the senior cleric's son, flew armed Iranian volunteers to Lebanon to fight the Israelis. He prevailed in his enterprise although the government was opposed and tried forcibly to stop him. Shapour Bakhtiar, a former prime minister and opposition figure, was assassinated in Paris by Iranian agents on the eve of a long-planned state visit to Tehran by French President François Mitterrand. The Mitterrand trip, the first by a European head of state to the Islamic Republic and therefore of considerable importance to Iran, was canceled. In May 1987, the second-ranking British diplomat in Tehran was pulled out of his car and beaten after an Iranian consular officer was arrested in Manchester on shoplifting charges. In June of that year, the French embassy in Tehran was surrounded by a mob, and French diplomats were prevented from leaving the embassy or the country, after the French police tried to question an Iranian embassy employee in Paris in connection with a series of bombings that had taken place in the French capital the previous year. These incidents led to a rupture of diplomatic relations with both Britain and France. In 1996, the German federal prosecutor issued a warrant for the arrest of Iran's minister of intelligence for involvement in the 1992 assassination in Berlin of the leader of the Kurdish Democratic Party of Iran and three others. The trial of the Iranian agents charged with the assassination was underway when Belgian officials in Antwerp boarded an Iranian ship bound for Germany. They found on board mortar shells, a rocket launcher, and 250 kilos of TNT.

The consequences for foreign policy of a government impelled by conflicting priorities and impulses and competing power centers is well illustrated by the politics of the Rushdie affair. In 1988, Ayatollah Khomeini had endorsed an annual budget for 1989–1990 and a five-year development plan that authorized the government to borrow abroad and to permit foreign investment. Both had been taboos in the revolutionary lexicon. The development plan itself was to mark a new era of economic reconstruction and engagement with Europe. The foreign ministry moved to repair relations with half a dozen countries, including Britain, France and Germany. Yet in February 1989, Khomeini wrecked months of careful Iranian fence mending in Europe by issuing his "death decree" against Rushdie. Countries of the European Community withdrew their ambassadors from Iran, and discussions on industrial projects with West Germany, France, and other countries were suspended.

The Rushdie affair continued to bedevil Iran's relations with the European states for several years. Although Khomeini himself died in 1989, it was considered unthinkable to declare void a decree issued by the revered founder of the Islamic Republic. In the early 1990s, Rafsanjani, as president, tried to find formulas by which he could explain away the decree. But he backed off under attacks from clerics looking for domestic political advantage or convinced that an abandonment of Khomeini's ruling amounted to a betrayal of Khomeini and the revolution. Discussions between Iran and European states in 1992 led to a declaration by Iran that it would respect international law in this matter, implying that Iran would not attempt to assassinate Rushdie. Almost immediately, 180 deputies in the 270-member Majlis signed a letter affirming Khomeini's edict. In 1994, Iran promised the Europeans that it would put in writing an undertaking not to kill Rushdie. But at the last minute, at a meeting with E.U. officials, Iran's representative refused to put his signature to the document. It was not until September 1997, following the election of Muhammad Khatami to the presidency, that Iran's foreign minister handed the Europeans an undertaking that they found acceptable, declaring that Iran would not attempt to carry out Khomeini's decree. Only then did the E.U. ambassadors return to Tehran.

Postrevolution foreign policy was obviously characterized by a strain of pragmatism, as well. Iran, for example, did not allow President Asad's harsh repression of the Muslim Brotherhood to influence the close relations with Syria, its one reliable Arab ally. During the Iran-Iraq war, Iran was careful to maintain correct relations with Abu Dhabi—a principal transit port for imports into Iran—despite the fact that it joined other Gulf states in siding with Iraq in the war.

There were numerous deliberate attempts to reshape foreign policy in a more pragmatic direction. One such attempt was made in 1984, following criticism of a spate of visits abroad by the foreign minister and the speaker of the Majlis, Rafsanjani, who was beginning to play an increasingly important role in shaping foreign policy. The visits were designed to secure Iran arms and greater international support in the war with Iraq; but to the guardians of the revolutionary flame, these visits and the quest for help abroad smacked of pandering. Khomeini had to step in to defend the new policy. In widely publicized remarks, he attributed the criticism of the foreign visits to Iran's enemies. He noted that the Prophet had sent emissaries to all parts of the world, and that for Iran not to do so now meant courting defeat and annihilation. This came to be known as Khomeini's "open window" policy. It was clearly controversial, and Khomeini had to invoke the example of the Prophet to justify it. In the following months, Khomeini's lieutenants tried to use his remarks to diminish Iran's international isolation; but, as already noted, the "open window" policy was undercut by the actions and rhetoric of officials, government agencies, and Khomeini himself.

Postrevolution foreign policy, then, was the product not only of traditional Iranian geostrategic interests but also of a worldview and of Iran's place in it that was born out of the revolution. Its principal themes included a belief in the worldwide relevance, especially to Muslims, of the Iranian revolution; a belief in the revolution's exportability; a commitment, at least in the early years of the revolution, to altering the nature of regimes in the Persian Gulf and the regional balance of power; a conviction that certain aspects of Western culture were threatening to Iran's cultural and national identity; a suspicion of Western, and particularly American, intentions toward Iran; a revolutionary ideology that attached value to a truculent, muscular posture in international relations, and that considered friendship with the West a sellout of revolutionary principles; and a willingness to use unconventional means, including assassination and hostage taking, to achieve foreign-policy ends. Foreign policy was also significantly influenced by domestic politics and rivalries; by the conflicting agendas of different government agencies or quasi-independent groups acting with only partial government sanction; and by the propensity of the government itself to pursue several conflicting foreign-policy goals at the same time. Again and again, the government seemed unable to agree on priorities aimed, for example, at securing the goodwill of both conservative regimes in the Middle East and the Islamic radicals who wished to overthrow them; and at catering both to domestic constituencies committed to export the revolution and to technocrats who argued that Iran must secure foreign investment to rescue its deteriorating oil industry.

Postrevolution foreign policy is thus best understood as the result of a dialectic between what, in shorthand, can be described as pragmatic and ideological considerations, between traditional Iranian foreign-policy orientations and a worldview generated by the revolution. The relative strength of ideology and pragmatism has tended to wax and wane, depending on domestic and international factors, personalities, and the nature of the issues involved. Most often, foreign policy

37

has run on parallel tracks: it has been both ideological and pragmatic in temper, both revisionist and traditional in intent. The pragmatic strain in foreign policy has tended to be more in evidence in the second decade following the revolution, but the worldview generated by the revolution has continued to exert an influence, and the trend toward pragmatism has resembled a bumpy road rather than a smooth progression.

Pragmatism in the post-Khomeini era

A more concerted attempt to mute the ideological and reinforce the pragmatic strain in foreign policy came with the election of Rafsanjani as president in 1989. Several factors made a new foreign-policy initiative possible. Perhaps most importantly, Iran's devastating war with Iraq had come to an end in 1988. This removed a major irritant in Iran's relations with the Persian Gulf states and the Western European countries. The eight-year war left the country physically and emotionally exhausted, and considerably drained revolutionary fervor. It was ready to devote its energies to repairing war damage and reviving a much-battered economy. Khomeini's death in 1989 removed a powerful, domineering presence, and allowed his lieutenants more flexibility in domestic and foreign policy. Rafsanjani, the new president, had a reputation as a pragmatist and deal maker. He put together a team of technocrats focussed on economic development, launched what he described as the "era of reconstruction," and set about repairing Iran's foreign relations.

The 1990–1991 American-led war to expel Iraq from Kuwait also proved favorable to Rafsanjani's initiative. Iran acted out of national interest when it refused to acquiesce in the Iraqi annexation of Kuwait, but Rafsanjani enhanced his reputation as a pragmatist by siding, in effect, with the aims of the American-led alliance. He consolidated his position at home and confirmed that more moderate men were at the helm in Tehran by facing down a faction in the Majlis that urged an alliance with Iraq against the United States. Rafsanjani used the cover of the war to reestablish diplomatic relations with Egypt, Saudi Arabia, Jordan, and Morocco—all controversial measures. After the war, he used Iranian influence to help secure the release of American hostages being held by Iranian-supported groups in Lebanon. He launched a major effort to repair relations with the Arab states of the Persian Gulf and with the European countries.

The policy yielded results. Although relations with Egypt remained difficult, relations with the Persian Gulf states, Morocco, and Jordan markedly improved. The E.U. countries, led by Germany, conducted a substantial trade with Iran. When Iran ran into balance-of-payments difficulties in 1993–1994, foreign creditors, primarily Japan, Germany, and other European states, agreed to reschedule about $12 billion in Iranian debt. American pressure limited but failed to stop arms sales and technology transfer to Iran by China and Russia. In 1995, the American oil firm Conoco signed a $1 billion agreement to help develop Iranian offshore oilfields. The deal proved abortive when a presidential order banned American companies from investing in Iran's oil industry and forced Conoco to cancel the agreement. Nevertheless, Iran's to Conoco indicated a new willingness to deal with the American companies. Moreover, the French firm Total promptly signed the deal that Conoco canceled—the first of its kind since the revolution. Iran then went on to sign a number of agreements with French, Russian, and other companies to develop Iran's oil and gas resources.

The success of the Rafsanjani initiative was limited by opposition at home, the government's own actions, and persistent problems with the United States abroad. Hardline clerics and parliamentarians frustrated Rafsanjani's attempts to explain away Khomeini's edict against Rushdie. The assassination of Iranian dissidents in Europe eventually seriously strained relations with at least some European countries. There continued to be reports of Iranian involvement either directly or through surrogates in terrorist acts. Argentina claimed evidence that linked the Iranian-backed Hizbullah of Lebanon with the 1992 bombing of the Israeli embassy in Buenos Aires, in which twenty-nine people were killed, and the 1994 bombing of a Jewish Center in the capital, in which eighty-six people lost their lives. Some reports blamed agents trained in Iran for the 1996 bombing of Khobar Towers outside Dharan, Saudi Arabia, in which nineteen American servicemen were killed. The bombing took place in the seventh year of the Rafsanjani presidency. The anti-American and anti-Israeli rhetoric out of Tehran continued unabated.

Moreover, America continued to express concern over Iran's weapons programs, its opposition to the Arab-Israeli peace process, its support for groups like Hizbullah in Lebanon and Llamas on the West Bank that used violence to undermine the Arab-Israeli peace process, and evidence of Iranian support for terrorist groups. The United States blocked World Bank loans to Iran. American opposition was decisive in excluding Iran from pipeline projects to carry oil and gas from fields in Central Asia and Azerbaijan to markets abroad. America also pressured its European allies and Japan not to invest in Iran or extend to Iran loans, credits, and significant trading privileges. Such pressure did not stop, but did reduce the extent of European and Japanese involvement in the Iranian economy.

The Clinton administration tightened America's own sanctions against Iran. President Clinton, as noted, signed an order in March 1995 that barred American firms from investing in Iran's oil industry. In April, he signed an order that banned all American trade with Iran. In April 1996 he signed a bill that required the president to impose a range of sanctions against foreign firms investing more than $40 million in Iran's oil and gas industry. By the end of Rafsanjani's second term, his foreign initiative appeared to have lost steam. Nevertheless, he had begun a process that his successor as president, Muhammad Khatami, was able to continue.

In his 1997 election campaign, Khatami ran on a platform of political liberalization at home and "friction-reduction" or détente abroad. His message resonated with the electorate. Nearly 80 percent of eligible voters cast ballots; 70 percent of them voted for Khatami. He thus came to office with a strong public mandate. Unlike Rafsanjani, who perfected a style that was ambiguous and shifting in both tone and gesture, Khatami articulated clear and consistent domestic and-foreign policies, and seemed far better able to win trust both at home and abroad. The rapid improvement in Iran-Saudi relations in the Khatami period was largely attributable to a meeting between Khatami and Saudi Crown Prince 'Abdallah during the Islamic summit in Tehran in December 1997. 'Abdallah came away from this encounter persuaded that Khatami was sincere and would keep his word regarding foreign-policy moderation.

Khatami moved in the first few months of his presidency to deal with at least three of the issues of greatest concern to the United States. At the Islamic summit in Tehran in December 1997, he privately told Yasser Arafat that Iran would acquiesce in any agreement with Israel acceptable to the Palestinian people. In January of 1998, in a now famous interview with CNN, he condemned terrorism and attacks on innocent civilians, and he also invited Americans to join in a "thoughtful dialogue" with the Iranian people. The invitation to a "dialogue" led to a program of exchanges between Iran and America that involving scholars, filmmakers, artists, and athletes; there was an expectation that government-to-government exchanges would eventually follow. In an address to the U.N. General Assembly in September 1998, Khatami called for a "dialogue of civilizations." He also declared the Rushdie affair "completely finished," and his foreign minister, as noted, gave the Europeans a written commitment that the Iranian government would not enforce Khomeini's death edict. Hardliners in Tehran tried to generate the usual uproar regarding this supposed retreat from revolutionary principles, but the government remained firm, and the protests against its "neutral" stance on the Khomeini edict had little effect.

The pattern observable in previous years, of pragmatic intentions undercut by the legacy of the revolution, domestic politics, and competing priorities, reasserted itself. For example, the Supreme Leader, Khamenei, who almost certainly had endorsed the idea of a "dialogue" between the Iranian and American people and the assurance Khatami gave to Arafat, very soon reverted to harsh attacks on the United States, and adamantly ruled out negotiations or diplomatic relations with America. Khamenei also began to suggest that Arafat did not represent the will of the Palestinian people (thus implicitly absolving Iran of the undertaking to be guided by whatever agreement with the Israelis the Palestinian people endorsed). He strongly attacked both the Wye Plantation accords signed by Arafat and the Palestinians, and the resumption of negotiations between Syria and Israel in 1999. This was an indication of unresolved tensions in the shaping of foreign policy, although by the end of 1999 the pragmatic strain in Iranian foreign policy appeared stronger, the ideological and "revolutionary" strain weaker, than at any time under the Islamic Republic.

Foreign policy fundamentals

By the end of 1999, it was also possible to identify a number of consistent and fundamental principles in Iranian foreign policy.

First, like the shah's government, the Islamic Republic came to attach primary importance to stability along its own borders and good relations with neighboring states. It reserved support for radical Islamic movements for the "far abroad," for places distant from Iran's borders like Lebanon, Sudan, or the West Bank. Along its own borders, it no longer supported militant Islamic groups against their own governments. For example, Iran did not allow sectarian conflict and attacks on the Shiite community in Pakistan to mar relations with that country. It expressed sympathy with fellow Muslims in Kashmir, but was careful not to take sides in the India-Pakistan conflict over Kashmir. Iran continued to support one of the warring factions in Afghanistan, but once the Taliban gained substantial control over the country, it resisted the temptation to get deeply mired in Afghanistan's civil war. It did not try to stir up Islamic sentiments in the newly independent republics in Central Asia and the Caucasus. It stood on the sidelines in the civil war in Tajikistan in which 20,000 to 50,000 persons—largely Muslims—lost their lives. Most often, Iran sought to cast itself in the role of peacemaker among Muslims and between Muslims and their neighbors. At one time, or another, it tried to mediate disputes between warring factions in Afghanistan and Tajikistan; the rival Kurdish parties in Iraq the governments of Azerbaijan and Armenia; and even the amir of Bahrain and his Shiite subjects.

After Iraq was expelled from Kuwait, Iran showed restraint in the limited aid it extended to fellow Shites when Saddam Husayn brutally crushed an uprising in southern Iraq. It stood back even as Iraqi troops bombarded Shiism's holiest shrines. In stark contrast to the 1980s, when Iran pursued its war into Iraq with the aim of toppling Saddam Husayn and installing an Islamic government in Baghdad, the regime had grown chary of military or open-ended entanglements along its own borders. Concerned lest the autonomous enclave the United States helped create in Iraqi Kurdistan lead to the breakup of Iraq, Iran joined Syria and Turkey in affirming a commitment to Iraq's territorial integrity. Occasional friction in relations notwithstanding, Iran appeared dedicated to maintaining good relations with Turkey—a policy that has survived growing (and, for Iran, alarming) military cooperation between Turkey and Israel. President Khatami continued a policy of strengthening ties with the Persian Gulf states. For example, while highly critical of the American military presence in the Persian Gulf, Iran refrained from criticizing Kuwait for permitting Americans to be based on Kuwaiti soil. Iran strongly opposed the Oslo peace process, but its criticism of Oman and Qatar for recognizing Israel was muted.

Second, Iran's foreign policy is shaped by overriding security concerns. Iraq's invasion of Iran in 1980, the eight-year war with that country, and the sense that Iran received virtually no support from the international community in the face of naked aggression have left deep scars on the national psyche. Moreover, Iran with good reason feels it lives in a dangerous neighborhood. Instability is endemic along its border with Afghanistan, and constantly possible along the borders with the former Soviet republics in Central Asia and the Caucasus. Iraq remains an unpredictable and menacing presence, and there is no certainty concerning Saddam

Husayn's regional ambitions and weapons capability. Given America's hostility to Iran, huge military presence in the Persian Gulf and uncertainty about its intentions another source of concern. Military cooperation between Israel and Turkey, and the possibility that Arab-Israeli peace might lead to an Israeli diplomatic, commercial, and perhaps military presence in the Arabian Peninsula, reinforce Iran's perpetual fear of encirclement.

Third, Iran has deliberately sought to foster relations with other great or regional powers as a counter to the United States. If the 1980s were characterized by tension between Iran and the Soviet Union over Afghanistan, the suppression of the Iranian Tudeh (Communist) Party, and the anti-imperialist rhetoric generated by the revolution, the 1990s were characterized by care on Iran's part to reinforce ties with Russia. Iran, for example, did not seriously try to compete with Russia for influence in the newly independent republics in Central Asia and the Caucasus; its criticism of the war Russia conducted against Muslim militants in Chechnya was strikingly muted. Iran also cultivated China, an important source of weapons and weapons technology; the E.U. states and Japan as important trade partners; and regional powers like India.

Historically, Iran dealt with the great powers either by seeking to secure some room for maneuver by balancing one against another or by invoking one to check the other, more threatening one. In the nineteenth century, a weak Iran attempted to maintain its independence by playing off Britain and Russia against one another. At times, it also sought protection from an expansionist Russian through closer alliance with Britain. In the 1950s, Prime Minister Muhammad Musaddiq coined the term "negative equilibrium," to describe the manner in which Iran would avoid falling under the influence of either Britain or the Soviet Union. The shah in the 1950s sought protection against a perceived threat from the north by tying Iran closely to the United States. In the later 1960s and 1970s, he felt strong and stable enough to seek good relations with the Soviet Union even as he maintained his close, informal alliance with America. The shah also made it a practise in his later years to develop close trade and diplomatic ties with a host of other powers, including the European states and China.

The Islamic Republic's great-power diplomacy in the 1990s was therefore a return to a well-established tradition, with some difference. The United States, considered a friend and potential ally since early in the twentieth century, was uncharacteristically cast in the role of potential enemy (although this view could change); and no single country (like Britain in the nineteenth and early twentieth centuries or the United States in the mid-twentieth century) emerged as Iran's principal great-power partner.

Fourth, beginning with the Rafsanjani presidency in 1989, and in sharp contrast to the first decade following the revolution, Iran has been seeking substantial foreign investment, particularly in the oil sector. Iranian officials are well aware that the huge sums required to repair and expand the neglected oil and gas industry cannot be generated at home and must come from abroad. This goal, however, has encountered formidable obstacles, some historical, many the result of the revolution.

The revolution reinforced a deep historical fear among Iranians of rulers willing to "sell" the country to foreigners, and of control and exploitation of Iran's valuable natural resources by foreign firms or governments. The tobacco monopoly protests of 1890–1891, the constitutional revolution of 1905–1906, and the oil national-ization movement of 1951–1953 were all partly reactions to a sense of foreign domination and exploitation. The Islamic revolution was also, in part, a response to what many Iranians perceived to be the excessive role of foreign firms and multi-nationals in the Iranian economy. After the revolution, there was a massive exodus of foreign firms and personnel, and the government took steps to take over or nationalize numerous large foreign-related enterprises, including oil operations—either as a matter of policy or because it felt compelled to do so as a result of the disorders following the fall of the monarchy. Revolutionary rhetoric subsequently stressed economic independence and autarchy, and reinforced sentiments against foreign borrowing, foreign investment, or a foreign economic presence in Iran. The question of foreign involvement in the Iranian economy carries with it pow-erful historical and revolutionary baggage. Provisions in the 1985 budget and the first development plan that allowed for foreign borrowing and investment were, as noted, controversial. In the 1990s, Iran began to permit foreign participation in developing oil resources; but, significantly, foreign participation was confined to offshore fields. Until the end of 1999, the government still felt it could not risk permitting onshore foreign involvement in the energy industry.

In addition, the legal framework was not conducive to large-scale foreign invest-ment. Red tape, overlapping jurisdictions of government departments, labor laws overly protective of the labor force, a court system easily manipulated by poli-tics, the continued insecurity of property, weak guarantees for private investment, and conflicting government policies all discouraged significant private investment, whether domestic or foreign. The hold on the economy exercised by the Founda-tion for the Disinherited and other para-statal foundations that controlled hundreds of expropriated and nationalized enterprises discouraged competition and a larger role for the private sector. The pursuit of foreign investment and the integration of Iran into the international economy, like some other elements of foreign policy, therefore remained tied to major and controversial issues of domestic politics and policy.

Finally, Iran continued, as under the shah, to view itself as a regional power and to aspire to a large regional and even international role. The shah had cultivated a sense of the greatness of Iran by virtue of its size, population, history, and imperial past. The Islamic Republic cultivated a sense of the greatness of Iran on the same basis, but rather than the imperial past it stressed the centrality of the revolution itself and of Iran's Islamic credentials. But as the second decade of the Islamic Republic was coming to an end, the concept of that role was changing. Iran was no longer in the business of exporting the revolution or, with a few exceptions, appealing over the heads of governments to the Islamic masses. The government, rather, took pride in its role as president of the Islamic Conference Organization, and in speaking for the community of Muslim states, Iran still aspired to a leadership role among the Persian Gulf states. It argued, for example, against the American military presence in the Gulf, and for a Gulf defense system maintained by the regional states themselves. But such a leadership role for Iran was not on the cards, given the Shiite-Sunni divide, lingering Arab suspicions of the country, and its diminished military and economic clout. The Islamic Republic, like the monarchy, entertained a sense of Iran's weight, its rightful role, in the region and on the international scene. But unlike the shah's government, or even the Islamic Republic in the early years, Iran at the beginning of the twenty-first century no longer seemed certain what that role should be, or how it could fulfill it.

IRAN'S STRATEGIC
PREDICAMENT

Shahram Chubin

Source: *Middle East Journal* 54(1) (2000): 10–24.

Iran is fortunate in its strategic situation. It has no historical enemies, no irredenta, no source of permanent tensions on its frontiers.
It is well endowed with resources, material and human and well-
situated. Iran has a distinct identity and culture and a unity denied
many of its neighbors. It has failed to capitalize on these assets due
to an excessive cultivation of past grievances and an ideological
view of current challenges. It has thus squandered the country's
potential. A more pragmatic approach to the greatest challenge of
the day—globalization—would be in Iran's interest. The problems
accumulating in the Islamic republic are not solved by invocation
of slogans and the attribution of blame to past or current scapegoats.
Whether Iran can make the adjustment that this implies and whether
some elements in the leadership are prepared to be judged by their
performance and be accountable to the public remains uncertain
though central to the chances of the Islamic Republic being able to
assume its rightful place in the family of nations.

Iran has evolved considerably over the past decade, but it still has some way to go
before it becomes a "normal" state, defining and pursuing its national interests dis-
passionately. This article focuses on the challenges which remain for Iran before
it accomplishes that goal. It emphasizes the strategic slumber that has characterized the country's external relationships. This slumber stems from a complex of
ideological blinders, and a cultivation of historical grievances, which, combined,
serve to distort Iran's appreciation of its environment, and hence are an obstacle
to the country's coming to terms with that environment.

While it can be argued that Iran has changed since its revolutionary days, is more
pragmatic, and less inclined to pursue ideological interests divorced from Iran's
national interests, this hardly disposes of the issue. There is still a struggle within

Iran over how to define those interests and promote them. Many of the mistakes which Iran has made in the past are culturally determined, the result of a mindset, and thus persistent, and need to be grappled with comprehensively.

Finally, recent mistakes *do* matter. Nations build reputations (status and prestige) only with difficulty, yet can destroy them relatively easily. The excesses of the revolutionary period need to be acknowledged by Iran itself, if it is to deal with the rest of the world on a realistic basis.

Strategy may be defined as the integration of a broad set of means (instruments) in the service of a desired end. It implies one or more goal(s); a meshing of multiple means to the desired end(s) and a relatively long-term perspective.[1] Iran's approach differs in each case. Its national style has been to adopt contradictory goal(s); to fail to co-ordinate the means; to take a short term view, tactical at best; and to strike a position of part moral superiority and part outrage, in place of a workable policy. Iran does not have an enviable record in strategy, in understanding the context and adapting means to ends. The entire record of its conduct of the war with Iraq (1980–88) reads like a primer in how *not* to conduct war:

- It cancelled $11 billion in arms on order from the United States, and purged the military while provoking Iraqi President Saddam Husayn with threats of destabilisation;
- By seizing US diplomats as hostages in 1979 it ensured that there would be little sympathy for Iran in Washington if Iran became embroiled in a war;
- In adopting the strategy of "people's war", which China was just abandoning, Tehran recycled a fashionable strategy of doubtful utility to a state which had its prime assets located near its adversary's border;
- It politicized its armed forces, eliminated ranks, and insisted that faith could do what technology and expertise could not. It then pursued a strategy in which it assessed victory by the degree of its own commitment rather than the attainment of battlefield objectives.
- In continuing the war for six years (June 1982–July 1988) Iran swapped victory for defeat, and exhaustion for undoubted supremacy of the region. (As then speaker and later President Ali Akbar Hashemi-Rafsanjani wryly put it in 1988: "we bit off more than we could chew"[2]).
- In expanding the war to the Gulf states in the "tanker war" (1987–1988), thus provoking US protection of the Kuwaiti tanker fleet, Iran played into Iraq's hands: internationalization did not favor Iran.
- The use of non-conventional means for strategic purposes, specifically the use of subversive groups to destabilize states in the Gulf and the Levant, was costly and unproductive. It forfeited Iran the moral high ground, and sympathy as the victim, which it apparently craves.

The list of blunders is long and by no means exhausted by these illustrative examples. They reveal a not very brilliant record of strategy: too little understanding of context; a preference for making a point, rather than adopting a successful policy in the service of an achievable end; and a tendency toward self-indulgence, to "feeling good".

The context: global

Two primary characteristics of international relations today are globalization and the increasingly visible gap between those states that are moving, through economic reforms and political development, into the class of states associated with prosperity and the democratic peace, and the others, which are not.[3] Despite, or because of, the globalization of markets, ideas etc. the chasm between those states that have emerged from history [4] ("post-modern" states in Robert Cooper's terms[5]) and those—modern and pre-modern—mired in history, has grown. The latter confront problems of anarchy (as described by Robert Kaplan[6]), legitimacy, and wars. They are the "rest", opposite a richer, more pacific and expanded "West". The "rest", or residual "South", are destined to be outsiders suffering from war, penury, and perpetual disorder. This condition, perhaps not unusual in some parts of the world, may come to engulf other states unable to handle the multiple challenges of globalization. The "winners and losers" (to quote Paul Kennedy[7]) in coming years will be determined by the ability of states to adapt to prevailing challenges and to surmount them. This requires reading these challenges correctly.

Mobility of capital (and to a lesser degree, labor) and the advent of a globally integrated market subject to its own rules (not those of government dictates), pose a range of challenges for all states. Not least, they impose a discipline on the conduct of national economic policies, and require a degree of competitiveness, transparency and the clear application of the rule of law, which challenge traditionally opaque and often arbitrary dealings of governments, hitherto unaccountable to anyone.

Globalization also blurs domestic and foreign policies. These domains can no longer be insulated; each affects the other and foreign perceptions of creditworthiness and calculations of risk. Since Foreign Direct investment (FDI) vastly outstrips the amount of assistance and credit on offer from governments, countries seeking access to foreign capital must address the markets and market requirements or demands.

Another dimension related to, but not a result of globalization, is exemplified by the explosion of the communications revolution, from computers, to fax and the Internet, to satellite television. Advanced economies are increasingly dominated by the information sector, the "knowledge economy." Information systems (and the service sector) are the dynamic areas of economies. With this shift has come a different estimate of what constitutes "power" on a day-to-day or usable basis. Nowadays, Joseph Nye's idea of "soft" power,[8] the power of attraction and inducement (versus that of coercion), the attractiveness of a culture, is widely accepted as an important dimension of power. The confusion of globalization with US domination often comes from the fact

47

that much of the content of global entertainment and the hyping of market-only solutions originate in the US, which has (typically) embraced globalization most enthusiastically.

Globalization implies interdependence, competitiveness, and transparency. This will not inevitably lead to democracy in a linear fashion, but it may increase its chances. Similarly democracy may in time lead to the creation of zones of stability and security communities. The enlargement of areas associated with democracy may, in this view, expand the "democratic peace."

How does all of this affect Iran? If the changes in international politics are as momentous as depicted here, Iran has a simple choice: to join the states adapting to change, or resist it with all the resultant implications. For our purposes, it is important that the issues are at least posed this way, so that the stakes are clear and decisions (and non-decisions) are made in full cognizance of their likely costs.

Iran's preoccupations, if its slogans are anything to go by, have been with achieving independence and self-reliance. What possible meaning can these phrases have for a state that receives over 90 percent of its revenues from oil sales, the demand for which, and price of which, are determined by a global energy market? Independence is a chimera for a state tied to a classically interdependent market. It is even more of an illusion for Iran, which hopes someday to sell its gas and transport that of others to the global market. It is an historical irony that some states seek independence precisely when it has become a mirage. Those that seek a type of autarky, hesitant to relinquish power to others, or afraid to join the global economy and adapt to its needs, consign themselves to the ever-thinning ranks of the marginalized: the Burinas, North Koreas and Cubas.

Another theme is Iran's preoccupation with "cultural threats". These are depicted not as nuisances but as a "scourge", as mortal threats:

"Audio and visual waves which are worse than warships and warplanes are being used to disseminate a rogue culture aimed at reasserting the domination of the enemies of Islam, paving the way for the imposition of unethical values and Westernized ideas to captivate and humiliate Muslims."[9]

On the face of it, there is a striking disjunction between the preoccupations ("discourse") of Islamic Iran and the dynamics of current global politics. Yet, on a more profound level, Iran's problems and concerns reflect those of many societies ill at ease with the consequences of globalization. Most states would share the view that globalization is a mixed blessing; it has the potential to link economic crises as much as to spread prosperity. It also threatens to homogenize and impoverish the world by flattening local cultures and traditions.

To these "threats", most thoughtful people respond by seeking to ensure that there are firebreaks to stop a spreading economic meltdown, and encourage selectivity in the embrace of the culture disseminated by global media empires, to prevent the relentless "dumbing-down" of culture. There is no reason why globalization has to mean the Americanization of culture or even, in some respects, of values. Iran has distinguished itself (if that is the word) by harping on cultural irreconcilability and by seeking to prevent globalization and the "internet-ization" of society.

This is a futile pose: it does Iran's leaders little credit and history suggests it is doomed to end in failure and disappointment. Opting-out is a strategy for losers and fighting the inevitable is nonsense: the alternative of embracing it selectively and seeking to direct its course in the cultural domain is the only rational policy. Iran has sought to depict the problem as a huge conspiracy directed at the Islamic Republic, as if the erosion of sovereignty in international affairs, whether in the European Union, or elsewhere, is not the daily stuff of contemporary international relations. In personalizing the problems of globalization, as if others do not face comparable challenges, (witness the Asian states' attempt to identify a notional "Asian" way), Iran typically casts itself into the role of victim, as the target of some conspiracy to undermine its independence, rather than as part of a world-wide phenomenon, a challenge which confronts everyone and calls for rational responses. Self-absorption limits Iran's capacity to understand its context, and react to it.

The context: regional

Iran is, in some respects, a blessed country: It faces no urgent or existential threats; it has a strong sense of identity, a notable culture and ancient civilization from which it takes inspiration; it is endowed with resources, including a location at a strategic crossroads; it has a capable, resilient, gifted, spirited, and generous people, a population not too small, and large enough to constitute a significant market and power.

Admittedly with reference to traditional security concerns, Iran is not without problems. Two recent wars and their legacies color the politics of the region. The proliferation of weapons of mass destruction cast their shadow over the region. Iraq retains access to some of the full spectrum of weapons of mass destruction (WMD) that it developed. There is a massive infusion of advanced conventional arms into the region. India and Pakistan have now overtly nuclearized their conflict and still engage in conventional hostilities. Iran and Iraq still engage in border skirmishes and low-level proxy wars. The entire region in an arc from Iraq, with the Shia in the south and the Kurds further north, through to the Kurdish regions of Turkey and the conflict between Azerbaijan and Armenia, on through Afghanistan and Tajikistan, is one of conflicts and overlapping ethnic disputes. Iran has been the host to large numbers of refugees (some two million) from its immediate neighbors to its west and east.[10]

Two issues potentially affect Iran's security directly. One is the vexed question of Iraq. The border issue is not settled and Iraqi vengeance directed at Kuwait could cause problems as could the retention of WMD by Iraq. Another concern is Iraq's potential disintegration into ethnic or confessional enclaves. In periodic crises Baghdad tests the waters and seeks to intimidate the Gulf Cooperation Council (GCC) states.

Another issue is the developing link between Turkey and Israel, which offsets Iran's ties with Syria. This could lead to problems between Tehran and Ankara which would otherwise be manageable. The linking of these two sets of relations cannot be in Iran's interests, especially as it ties Iran to Syria's hostility toward Ankara, and emboldens Turkey to throw its weight around.

These two sets of issues aside, Iran is basically without enemies. Unusually, in a region of turmoil, Iran is relatively secure. Its core security as a nation state is not threatened. It is not about to disintegrate. It is not a failed state, threatened by ethnic dissension or secessionism.

On another level, it is a different story. The Middle East is slipping behind in the new economic context of competition for markets and capital. States have interfered arbitrarily and ineffectively too often, created lop-sided, uncompetitive, state sectors, extended subsidies and entitlements which are difficult to withdraw or reduce, and depend too much on rising oil revenues. Economies are not diversified enough or integrated regionally. Population growth has raised a host of problems for states, from education and job creation to the need to trim subsidies and welfare systems. Most of the remedies for a more efficient private sector have important political implications, notably more transparency and greater rule of law.

Iran, like most of its neighbors, has choices to make, which boil down to: adapt or be left behind. If the revolution is to survive it must adapt to the society's needs. Iran has a population of whom some 65 percent are under 25, who need to be educated, fed and employed.[11] They will not take slogans on faith, or forever be content with a government, however well-intentioned, that is incompetent and/or repressive. For this generation also demands more freedom, not as a favor but as a right.

Iran thus faces the "new security issues as much as, if not more than, any other Middle Eastern state."[12] Together with the environment and water issues, these domestic concerns will challenge all governments. Iran will have to reconsider its priorities accordingly. It will need to move from the legitimacy it gained from the fact and aftermath of the revolution to something more demanding and fragile: performance legitimacy.

Iran's strategic aims

Any state with a margin of choice seeks more than the attainment of a minimum of security as a goal. Most such states seek security *plus* influence. Influence can be seen as a desire to see a congenial environment or milieu around the country, one in which its interests are taken into account, and in which it has a say on the broader issues that concern it. Many states seek to "punch above their weight". These may be ex-great powers, aspiring great powers, or revolutionary states.

Iran has few advantages here. It has no "natural" constituency, no Iranian world or commonwealth, no ex-colonies. Facing in several directions with extended borders, north, south, west and east, it has no historic or dependable allies. At the same time, as a revolutionary state, it assumes that its model has wider relevance and applicability, regionally and further afield. Iran sees its revolution as embodying its "values": independence and self-reliance certainly, but also authenticity and spirituality, a model society of social justice. What does this mean concretely? Iran seeks to pursue and promote its own values. It wants to be free to practice its own religion and culture, free from threats from others. The respect and equality it strives for, and the reciprocity which it demands, are commendable and understandable. However, often it appears that these demands are one-way: freedom to practice its own values has been interpreted as freedom to interfere in the affairs of neighboring states, notably in the Persian Gulf.

There is another side to Iran's aims which has become distorted in practice. Iran, like many states, has a set of grievances which animates it and sets limits to its policies. Where Iran has become unusual is in its un-natural, morbid inflation and cultivation of this set of grievances. The sense of victimhood, exploited by an unscrupulous leadership, can have very deleterious consequences. It can lead to the unhealthy kind of self-absorption and assumption that it holds a monopoly on injustices, which can itself lead to excesses. Several observers have noted this mix of self pity and sense of historical grievance has led to nihilism and barbarity in the case of the Serbs.[13]

Iranians have wallowed in their sense of grievance with little consideration for that of others, and their own responsibility, in some cases, for self-inflicted wounds. While this predisposition to blame others is in part historically conditioned, due to the constant interference of outside powers in Iran and Iranian politics, it is also culturally congenial as it plays to the Iranian Shi'i sense of being wronged. Nevertheless, there is something profoundly cynical in the attempt by Iran's current leaders to shift the blame for their incompetence (and worse) to others, not least in an era when Iran is for the first time in modern history truly responsible for its own destiny.

In summary, while Iran seeks space for the propagation of its values abroad, it is not always as fastidious in allowing others to pursue theirs untrammeled. Reciprocity apparently is to work in one direction only. Although Iran has a legitimate set of historical grievances, it has been selective in their employment against the West rather than Russia; has exaggerated them, especially in seeing them as historically unique; and has been oblivious to its own excesses (hostage-taking and terrorism), while cultivating them in a manner that can only be called perverse and potentially dangerous. Insofar as its leadership has nurtured and promoted this culture of complaint and victimhood as a diversion or excuse for its own failures, Iran has made this issue part of the ideological baggage of the regime. The regime thus responds to global forces as conspiracies directed at Iran, rather than as part of the changes accompanying the spread of technology. (Hence the egregious failure in dealing with globalization.)

This ideology based on confrontation and a sense of grievance thus becomes a source of distortion, and weighs heavily on the performance of the regime, constraining adaptation to the real world. It is one thing for states, especially revolutionary states, to insist on their singularity and the continuing validity of their message, quite another to claim and act upon an assumed monopoly on historical injustice.

Defense and security policy

It was mentioned earlier that from the view of security, traditionally defined, Iran is in a privileged position. It faces potential serious threats only from Iraq and possibly Turkey. In the case of Turkey, potential conflict is likely to arise not from any direct bilateral dispute: there is no border or equivalent unresolved issue between the two neighbors. Between 1945–1979 the two non-Arab states were on friendly terms, aligned to the West and very much in step on Middle East politics. What changed besides Iran's post-revolutionary attempts to agitate and revive religion as a political factor in Turkey? Iran's recent support for the Kurdish Worker's Party (PKK), sanctuary, arms and possibly training have begun to appear more intolerable to Ankara. Turkey's entente with Israel may also have emboldened the Turkish military to flex muscles on this issue after the successful resolution of a similar problem with Syria in autumn 1998 (when Turkish pressures forced Syria to expel PKK leader Abdullah Öcalan). At the least Iran's "strategic alliance" with Syria risks bringing Iran into conflict with Turkey on issues which, at best, are peripheral to Iran's national interests. Iran would do well to consider whether good relations with Turkey do not outweigh any dubious 'strategic' benefits from alliance with Syria.

Iraq is a different case. The border dispute, the ostensible cause of the war 1980–88, has yet to be resolved. It has been superseded by the legacy of the war itself: the surprise attack, the use of chemical weapons, the destruction of Iranian cities, which now figure among the lessons of the war and make reconciliation and normalization harder. Moreover, the problems on the Iraqi side have hardly been addressed, namely Iraq's access to the Gulf's waters and more broadly its role in the Persian Gulf and Arab world. Weak or strong, with or without Saddam Husayn, Iraq will pose manifold challenges for Iran. Any foreseeable Iraqi government can be expected to seek strong military forces, possibly including WMD, not least to deal with its fractured society and to strengthen its own coercive powers. Any Iraqi government will want influence in the Gulf and access to its waters. Any Iraqi government will distrust Shi'i Iran's potential for influence in an Iraq with a predominant Shi'i population. Any Iraqi government may be tempted to use Iranian opposition elements as leverage against Tehran. And anyone in charge in Baghdad may be tempted to fuel an economic recovery by flooding the oil market.

Iran will have to consider how to deter Iraq and defend Iran. Some sort of strategic dialogue will be necessary if only to establish the kinds of "red lines" between the two states that will reduce misunderstanding and strategic folly. Iran needs to devise a strategy for Iraq, strong or disintegrating, that balances between purely military and exclusively political: that deters and engages, warns and reassures.

These two cases apart, Iran's defense planners have to consider a number of general issues which build not only on the lessons of the conflict but on their own resources, security requirements and available technology. The questions include:

1. *With respect to defense: national borders plus?* How much emphasis on defense of borders only, how much on power projection? Defense of borders by forward defense or by "people's war" (i.e., defense in depth)? Deterrence by denial and/or retaliation (especially in the case of WMD)? In regard to maritime borders: sea denial or sea control?

2. *What kind of defense doctrine?* Independence and self-reliance do not give very useful guidance here. This requires careful detached strategic planning (regularly updated) as opposed to improvisation. It requires the integration of manpower, procurement policies and force structure. At the least, Iran needs mobile forces to deal with its far-flung borders and a number of specified contingencies. Its exercises could emphasize this need for mobility. Combined arms operations need to be improved if defense capability is to improve.

3. *Force structure and manpower.* With a large, under-employed population, is universal conscription necessary? What are the (military, social, economic) benefits of a more professional army? What mix of conscripts and professionals would be indicated from a purely military (technical) standpoint? Is equipment or technology a consideration? What about the tradeoff between quality and numbers?

4. *Should "self-reliance" drive procurement policies?* Indigenous production has undoubted attractions: it can reduce the leverage of external suppliers (e.g. by manipulating spare parts or follow-on deliveries); reduce dependence on "foreign" technology which may not be appropriate for the needs of the consumer (especially given manpower differences), and therefore may slow assimilation; imports may reflect the supplier's emphasis on high technology rather than the importer's interest, where possible, in substituting manpower-intensive technology. Imported equipment (especially in its sophisticated variants) is costly to buy, use and replace. Domestic production has obvious political attractions as well. But it has less to commend it from an economic or military standpoint.[14] Domestic production, due to the significant capital investment required, is often costlier than equivalent imports and less reliable. There is much to be said for reliance on robust, effective technology but not for technology that is outdated or inflexible.

While most states suffer from a gap between resources and needs, it is important that ideological distortions not drive procurement policy. In practice for Iran, necessity has been the mother of invention. Poor relations with the Western states have made imports of arms impossible even if it were decided that it was desirable. Generally in Iran the issue has been wrongly formulated: it is not a matter of absolutes but rather of degrees. What kinds of mixes of weapons-systems would be cost effective and meet Iran's military requirements? Technology is not a "fix" for other deficiencies: it is not a shortcut or equalizer, but it can serve as a force multiplier, when appropriately acquired and used.

5. *There is a clear relationship between manpower policies and the role of armed forces in society.* What Iran needs is not politically reliable "revolutionaries"

but Iranian nationalists. Above all, what Iran needs today is democratic (civilian) control of the armed forces. Like the totalitarian regimes of the former Eastern Bloc, revolutionary Iran has equated support for the regime with loyalty to the country. Also, it has allowed the mission of the armed forces to become obscured by political interference. On the one hand (again like China, which is now discarding it) Islamic Iran has involved the Revolutionary Guards (*Pasdaran*) in "reconstruction". In fact, through the para-statal foundations, which are beyond the control of the formal government, these military elements are now more entrepreneurs than soldiers.[15] While this may increase their loyalty to their paymasters, it does little to enhance Iran's defense capabilities. Worse is the explicit build-up of the Pasdaran as the pillars of the Islamic regime and an implicit control and rival of the regular military.

This development had a particularly chilling effect during the country's first steps toward democracy in 1998 and 1999, when Pasdaran and other military leaders made statements and issued warnings which are beyond the prerogatives of the armed forces.[16]

Military interference in domestic politics is not tolerable in societies professing to pursue democracy or even "the will of the people". The confusion of the mission of the military and their entanglement in business affairs and domestic and factional politics can only reduce the effectiveness of Iran's armed forces in national defense (as well as impairing the growth of democracy.)

6. *Defense and security policy is not simply a matter of doctrines, forces and equipment.* Arms control can be a useful adjunct of security policy. Iran should consider whether the proliferation of WMD in the region is to its advantage and whether it could play a positive role in stemming further proliferation, and establishing guidelines that would be regionally acceptable. At the least Iran has incentives to reduce the possibility of miscalculation in the use of WMD between itself and Iraq and Israel. Arms control implies restraint and reciprocity, characteristics rarely associated with contemporary Iran. Iran's recent (June 1999) SCUD missile attacks on *Mujahedin-e Khalq* (MKO) opponents in Iraq was ill-considered in light of the foregoing. Does Iran want to establish a norm in the region that missile strikes (or air attacks) on other states are permissible as a form of "hot pursuit"? While Iran condemns Turkey's hot pursuit actions in northern Iraq, can it be surprised that after its own strikes, Ankara reportedly used air strikes against PKK (Kurdistan Workers Party) elements in northern Iran? To deter a threatened Iranian invasion in the autumn of 1998, the *Taliban* in Afghanistan also threatened missile strikes on Iranian cities. Iran would do well to consider its actions carefully from the political standpoint and in terms of longer term interests when framing and implementing defense policy.

Iran's society and state

Iran's power as a revolutionary Islamic state peaked in the mid-1980s. Until then the revolution, still creating its own myths, was relatively unsullied. The population, politically mobilized, believed in the future. Iran was a model for the oppressed who, in the name of their faith and culture, could take their destiny into their own hands. Since then the story has been about the steady erosion of support for the system. Gone is the automatic support for the regime and the assumption of its good intentions. In part, this is the result of time and the graying of the original revolutionaries. In part, it is the result of the corruption, broken promises, and blame-passing by the regime's leaders, who hold everyone but themselves responsible for the regime's failures. The system *has* evolved, but not enough to accommodate the demands of society.

For whatever reasons/excuses (the reader may choose), the story of Iran's economy is one of constant decline: inheritance of a "dependent" economy; the privations of an "imposed" war; the shortages created by foreign sanctions and embargoes; the distortions arising from excessive state intervention, or the chronic mismanagement and corruption of the regime: Iran's economic problems can be attributed to all of these. What cannot be debated is that the rapid growth of the population and the decline in oil prices have only further contributed to this unhappy state of events. With resources declining, and with no visible substitutes, the Islamic authorities are presiding over the steady impoverishment of the nation. Soon, if it is lucky, Iran's greatest export, like India's and Egypt's, may be educated people. If it is unlucky, it may come to resemble Cuba or the Philippines. Like Argentina, Iran will belong to that category of states whose bright future, frequently invoked, recedes like the horizon before it is ever reached.

Can there be any doubt that a refusal or inability to face up to realities without invoking the usual foreign devils as excuses, has contributed to a failure to build a work ethic? Globalization, with all its attendant problems, enforces the discipline of the market which encourages innovation and competition, and requires transparency, a legal infrastructure, and the rule of law, all of which might be helpful for Iran at this stage.

In sum, the regime, no longer enjoying the unqualified acceptance of a credulous population, is now subject to "performance legitimacy." Today its legitimacy is bound up with what it can deliver, as opposed to what it can promise. Hence its legitimacy is conditional and brittle. The current turmoil in Iran represents a debate about the future and content of the Islamic republic. Many, perhaps most, Iranians would agree that insofar as Iran is an "exemplary state" today, this has more to do with its democratic credentials and the model of civil society that is being openly and courageously debated, than for any Islamic model it might constitute for other states in the region.

A few precepts for strategy

International relations are not zero-sum but positive sum   both or several sides can "win" simultaneously. It is possible for two potential adversaries to reach agreements that favor them both. Taking a long-term view helps, while geography cannot be changed, geopolitics can. Working on changing the geopolitics, and building predictability into regular encounters, can increase confidence and eventually security. Strategy, then, needs to consider the day after tomorrow.

Tactical thinking is not strategy Tactical expedients and ploys have a short shelf life. Policies reflecting the lowest common denominator are rarely productive.

Posturing is not policy and certainly not strategy Rhetoric and vituperation however satisfying, are not a substitute for a sustainable policy.

Emotionalism is not conducive to sound strategy A regime that seems to find it easier to talk to Saddam Husayn, who invaded the country and gassed its (and his own) citizens, than it does to the United States, shows a highly selective flexibility. A government that finds it difficult to acknowledge areas of overlapping interest with the United States (UNSCOM, Kosovo, Afghanistan) limits its own options needlessly. A regime that embraces the Palestinian cause as its own and embarks on a quixotic policy that undermines the Palestinians' legal representatives and its own interests, needs to reconsider its aims.

The costs of these policies accumulate.

Iran is self-regarding, obsessed, and narcissistic. Iran is unique neither in its sense of being historically wronged nor in the vague reeling that it has something positive to contribute to the world, in terms of spiritual values. Claiming a monopoly in both areas, Iran's relations with other states have been permeated by a sense of mission and revenge that has precluded a detached assessment of its own interests. Strategy requires a dynamic objective appreciation of the environment of operations, not simply the repetition of failed (and static) policies.

Ruses, tactical schemes, unconventional and deniable operations do nothing to embellish a state's claims to moral authority Reciprocity is not a one-way affair. A strategy that relies on the use of proxy groups, unconventional methods, the indirect approach and the clandestine, are poor substitutes for a more open and conventional strategy, based on diplomacy, dialogue and commerce.

Strategy is not likely to prosper unless it reflects the core interests of the nation and is supported by the people In Iran, thinking nationally rather than in terms of the regime's interests, could be cultivated with benefit to strategy.

"It's the economy, stupid"

Ayatollah Ruhollah Khomeini famously said: "the revolution was not about the price of watermelons.[17]" In the two decades since, nothing has destroyed the legitimacy of the regime as much as its failure to deliver the economic goods. No amount of excuses or diversions obscures this blunt fact. All the windy rhetoric about the revolution's virtuous aims bump up against the impoverishment of the nation. There is no distribution (just or otherwise) without production. There is no social justice without production. There can be no production without incentives, competition, and a "work culture". Ideology has several functions but one of its most deleterious and unintended is the degree to which it imprisons those who espouse it. As the recent example of the Soviet Union demonstrates, ideology colors and justifies actions and becomes the prism through which the world is seen, whether the ideology is genuinely believed or not. As a result, it blurs an understanding of the international context, leading as much to self-delusion as serving as a guide for action. The net result is a selective filter through which the world is apprehended and reality distorted.[18]

Being principled and standing up for core values are not an argument against flexibility, pragmatism or adjustment. To compromise is not (morally) compromising. In reality the Islamic Republic has been selectively pragmatic (consider Iran's interest in US arms in the Iran/Contra episode) or Tehran's reticence to raise Muslim issues that concern Russia (e.g. in Chechnya). Appeals to core values are made by the regime to avoid doing things that are necessary, but which threaten its grip on power. In the process it devalues what it describes as its "values."

Strategy and security

Strategy is the efficient match between resources and values (security, principles, wealth). One can distinguish between policies of "necessity" (territorial security, feeding population etc.) and "discretionary" policies, where leaders have choices and options as to what values, goals or desiderata to pursue, at what price. These may include the quest for influence, or support for "milieu" goals as described earlier. Little is pre-determined; politics can broaden what geography constrains. Technology and ideology act as variables. Technology can enhance resources and increase options. Ideology can act as a motivator and justifier as well as a constraint. Most states have considerable scope for choice. For most states, goals, especially those that are discretionary, must be fashioned to fit available resources. When these are declining, discretionary interests need to be reduced accordingly. Ideology may serve to justify such a cutback, but recent experience suggests the reverse: state ideology, through distortion, pushes for a more expansive definition of discretionary interests than are warranted by available resources.

Iran's strategic predicament, like that of other states, is to secure its interests (material and value) consistent with its resources, or to adjust them. Understanding the trade-offs and opportunity costs between the pursuit of discretionary interests (which can be reduced) and its other values, is the first step towards a realistic strategy. Either these discretionary interests must be redefined, or increased resources must be found.

Iran is in the happy position of facing no existential threat; it has no powerful predatory neighbor, no historic dispute ever-likely to erupt and escalate overnight. Thus it has broad scope in defining its discretionary interests: how much solidarity with Muslim peoples and the "oppressed", how much to invest in poorer Third World states, and how to give expression to the need for spiritual values in a changing, shrinking, multi-cultural world. Matching aims and resources requires a prior recognition that the real sources of power and status today, the prerequisite for any influence, are economic vitality and domestic legitimacy.

Today the greatest security threats in many non-Western states stem from a lack of domestic unity or political legitimacy. Political weakness and instability, as in the "failed states", reflects the failure of the state to represent society or to meet its needs. Domestic political legitimacy is the precondition for stability, development and security. No sustainable or effective strategy is possible without it. Strategy is increasingly dependent on society and on a settled domestic base. If Iran wants to play a more influential role in world affairs, it needs to concentrate on this. Giving definition to a modern and generally acceptable form of Islamic republic; reconciling individual and community rights and responsibilities; creating genuinely representative and accountable institutions; these are tasks that must take priority for Iran. Though they should preoccupy Iran, they do not preclude an opening to the world from which it can benefit. Iranians need to look forward, not backward, if they are to transcend the past.

Notes

This article is based on a keynote speech delivered at a conference on "Iran in the 21st Century" sponsored by the Center for World Dialogue in Nicosia 16–20 June 1999.

1　As John Lewis Gaddis writes about strategy, "Some principles of strategy are so basic that when stated they sound like platitudes: treat former enemies magnanimously: do not take on unnecessarily new ones; keep the big picture in view; balance ends and means; avoid emotion and isolation in making decisions; be willing to acknowledge error," John Lewis Gaddis. "History, Grand Strategy and NATO Enlargement." *Survival* vol. 40 no1 (Spring 1998), p. 145.

2　IRNA Tehran, Home Service 8 February in BBC SWB ME/0381/A/1–4, 10 February 1989.

3　The term refers to the notion that democracies do not go to war with other democracies. For a detailed discussion of this issue see Michael Brown, Sean Lynn-Jones and Steven Miller, *Debating the Democratic Peace: An International Security Reader* (Cambridge, MA: MIT Press, 1996).

4　Francis Fukuyama, *The End of History and the Last Man* (New York: Free Press, 1992).

5　Robert Cooper, *The Post Modern State and World Order* (London: Demos, 1996).

6　Robert Kaplan, "The Coming Anarchy," *The Atlantic Monthly* (February 1994), pp.44–76.

7　Paul Kennedy, *Preparing for the Twenty-first Century* (London: Harper Collins, 1993).

8　Joseph Nye, *Bound to Lead: The Changing Name of American Power* (New York: Basic Books, 1990).

9　Thus the *Rahbar* (Supreme Religious Leader), Ayatollah Sayyid 'Ali Khamene'i, addressing a conference of parliamentarians from Muslim states. Islamic Republic of Iran News Agency (IRNA), Tehran 15 June 1999, reported in BBC *Summary of World Broadcasts*, ME3562MED/1, 16 June 1999. Iran is not alone in seeking to hold back the flood. A more restrained criticism of the threat posed by the dominance of US culture often voiced in Europe (and especially France) came from the former head of the BBC, John Birt. He argued that national cultures could be degraded by the vulgar and sensational, that the global culture that was emerging was essentially American, and that it threatened to "undermine all national cultures." His answer was to encourage reason and rationality and to argue for the need for a civilising force like the BBC. See Gautam Malkhani, "Outgoing BBC Chief Warns of US threat to Culture" *The Financial Times* (London), 7 July 1999, p. 8. See the report from Human Rights Watch, which argues that the Arab states have tried and failed to battle against public access to the Internet. David Gardner, "Arab States Fail to Curb Internet" *The Financial Times*, 8 July 1999, p.5. The full Human Rights Watch report is available online at http://www.hrw.org/advocacy/internet/mena/index.htm. See also Howard Schneider, "The Arab World is Logging on Slowly and Ambivalently to the Internet" *International Herald Tribune* (Paris). 27 July 1999, p. 4.

10 See the author's paper on refugees and minorities in Iran presented to the conference "From the Indus to the Euphrates," St. Anthony's College, Oxford 23–25 April 1999. Also see the article by Bahram Rajaee in this issue.

11 Robin Wright, "The Iranian Revolution, Part II Comes into Focus," *Los Angeles Times*, 18 July 1999.

12 See Gary Sick, "The Coming Crisis in the Persian Gulf," *Washington Quarterly* (Washington, DC) Spring 1998.

13 Notably Michael Ignatieff on the culture of self-pity. See "The Bitter Men who Waited to Kill", *The Sunday Times* (London), 20 June 1999, p.26. Note Larry Hollingworth on the Serbs: "They are at their best when the odds are against them; often the odds are self-inflicted." "Time for Serbian Self-Examination", *International Herald Tribune* 6 July 1999, p.5. One Serb referred to the dangers of too much history: "But we learned that you cannot live from history. Americans have no history and they live wonderfully well." Roger Cohen, "Milosevic's Brutality in Pursuit of Greater Serbia Hastened its Downfall." *International Herald Tribune* 3–4 July 1999, p.5.

14 This has been borne out again and again in key developing countries. See Eric Arnett (ed.) *Military Capacity and the Risk of War: China, India, Pakistan and Iran* (Oxford: Oxford University Press for SIPRI, 1997).

15 For a recent discussion of the phenomenon in Asia, see "Armies in Business: Asia's Boardroom Brass" *The Economist* (London). 10 July 1999, pp. 78–79.

16 To take two recent cases, during the student demonstrations against hardline repression, the Guards Corps and a related foundation condemned the students while the Defense Minister, Admiral Ali Shamkhani, gave a gratuitous commentary on their origins and intentions. See IRNA, 13 July and 14 July 1999, in BBC/ME/3587MED/3, 15 July 1999. More serious was the veiled warning issued by 24 senior Pasdaran officers to President Muhammad Khatami expressing the limits to their patience in the face of his failure to "do his Islamic duty" before it was too late. The implied threat of a military coup shows how far the Islamic hardliners have politicized the military. See Mouna Naim: "*Les adversaires du président Iranien sont de plus en plus offensifs*" ("The Adversaries of the Iranian President are More and More on the Offensive"), *Le Monde*, 22 July 1999, p.3.

17 See Fred Halliday "The Iranian Revolution: Uneven Development and Religious Populism," *Journal of International Affairs*, (Winter 1983).

18 On the degree to which in retrospect the Soviet leaders became imprisoned by their ideology see John Lewis Gaddis, *We Now Know: Rethinking Cold War History* (New York: Oxford University Press, 1996).

53

IRAN AND THE US IN THE SHADOW OF 9/11

Persia and the Persian question revisited

Ali M. Ansari

Source: *Iranian Studies* 39(2) (2006): 155–70.

> 'The aide said that guys like me were 'in what we call the reality-based community,' which he defined as people who 'believe that solutions emerge from your judicious study of discernible reality.' I nodded and murmured something about enlightenment principles and empiricism. He cut me off. 'That's not the way the world really works anymore,' he continued. 'We're an empire now, and when we act, we create our own reality. And while you're studying that reality – judiciously, as you will – we'll act again, creating other new realities, which you can study too, and that's how things will sort out. We're history's actors ... and you, all of you, will be left to just study what we do.'[1]

In a recent trip to Europe, the new US Secretary of State, Condoleezza Rice, sought to heal the wounds which had emerged over the US decision to overthrow Saddam Hussein. She found a receptive Europe, anxious to avoid the rifts of the past and keen to accentuate the positive. In the aftermath of the elections in Iraq, there was even room for some agreement on how best to deal with Iran, and her ambitions for a nuclear programme. Everyone agreed that Iran was not Iraq, and by all accounts, the Bush Administration appeared content to allow the Europeans to pursue their negotiations with a view to resolving 'Iran' through diplomatic means. Indeed, it now seemed that far from sitting on the sidelines – waiting for the negotiations to fail – the United States had agreed to actively support the EU negotiations with offers of their own. Yet behind all the smiles, there was an air of discontent and barely disguised disagreement. The Americans were proving reluctant partners and their rediscovered faith in diplomacy, and the UN for that matter, seemed less a result of deliberate policy and more a consequence of its absence.[2] What the Bush administration lacked in detail it nonetheless made up with 'vision', and Rice's characterization of Iran as a 'totalitarian' state not only highlighted differences in appreciation between the US and her European allies of the reality of Iran but, perhaps more significantly, marked a distinct shift in emphasis within the United States itself. The State Department was clearly under new management, and the diplomatic ambiguity of the past, along with the flexibility this afforded, had been replaced with theological certainty.[3] It reflected a broader shift in US policy approaches since 9/11, away from 'traditional' realism and towards an ideological construction of international relations driven emphatically by myths.[4]

This paper is an investigation of the dialectical nature of US-Iran relations looking in particular at relations since the 9/11 terrorist attacks and the Iranian responses to President Bush's State of the Union address in January 2002, which classified Iran as a member of the 'Axis of Evil'. The paper argues that the events of 9/11 fundamentally altered the nature of US foreign policy making, away from the bureaucratic rationality of the past which had been understood under the rubric of a 'realist' interpretation of international relations, towards a charismatic justification with a revolutionary message.[5] This transformation of US attitudes stood in marked contrast to the tendency in Iran for a routinization of the revolution, and more towards rationalisation and international order. That this process of *normalization* was being encouraged at the very time that the founder and guardian of the global order was engaged in a radical transformation of its relationship with that order – with a view to changing it – resulted in a critical tension and a continued failure of communication which may be defined as an epistemological gap.[6] A gap which may only be overcome through the exercise of decisive leadership. Iranian policy makers, steeped in American international relations theory have been seeking to engage the 'realist', and have been disconcerted to discover the revolutionary.

Foundation myths

Throughout the 1990s, Iranian leaders had been grappling with the issue of the United States. Ever since the Hostage Crisis in 1979, diplomatic relations had been severed, and officially at least, the United States had imposed a series of embargos on the Islamic Republic with a view to bringing the revolution the heel. Nonetheless, in the absence of formal, 'real' relations, both Iran and the United States retained a very real presence in each other's political life, which took on mythic proportions. While American politicians may have been reluctant to indulge in the rhetoric of the 'Great Satan', there is little doubt that the experience of the Hostage Crisis and the subsequent Iran-Contra affair placed Iran in a category all of its own as far as US policy makers were concerned.[7] This emotive element within US attitudes towards Iran may have been vigorously denied by the bureaucratic rationalists within successive US administrations, but it was increasingly apparent to outside observers who were struck by the depth of the animosity. Indeed, this was not simply a popular antipathy but one which affected many members of the Washington elite and transcended party politics. Democrats bemoaned the fall of the Carter Presidency and noted with some bitterness that Iran's revolutionaries appeared determined to sabotage Carter's re-election prospects by very deliberately holding the hostages until after President Reagan's inauguration.[8] While Republicans were to prove equally unforgiving over the debacle of the Iran-Contra affair, which added criminal proceedings to the indignity of political embarrassment.

Indeed while American politicians were to emerge from the 1980s with their prejudices affirmed, in Iran the harsh reality of war was beginning to temper the ideological zeal of the revolution. The new President, Ali Akbar Hashemi Rafsanjani, seemed to be inaugurating a period of 'pragmatism', and it was apparent that a cadre of hitherto marginalised *ancien regime* diplomats and intellectuals were being reconciled to the Islamic Republic, with a view to encouraging a rational reconstruction of international affairs.[9] This was, to be sure, an incremental process which labored under the diplomatic fiasco that was the Rushdie Affair, but there is little doubt that Rafsanjani was seeking a routinization of the revolution. A number of institutes and think-tanks were established, with government support and funding, staffed in large part by International Relations experts trained in the United States, with a view to producing a rational (and 'realist') interpretation of the international order, and more specifically, the United States.[10] The conclusion they unsurprisingly drew, true to their training, was that the United States was a rational international player who pursued its 'interests'. These 'interests' were somewhat simplistically defined in economic and/or geo-political terms. Any sense of cultural or ideological determination in American foreign policy was dismissed as methodologically unsound, a view reinforced by those very bureaucratic rationalists who populated the US policy making establishment – ideology was quite obviously something *others* had. Thus, among the strategies to engage the United States which circulated in the early 1990s was one which sought to position Iran, ironically, as an 'island of stability' within a region that, after the fall of Soviet Union, was to all intents and purposes, increasingly unstable. This strategy was however unsustainable for the very reason that the Soviet Union was no longer a threat, so it was decided to seek engagement on economic terms. This suited the mercantile world view of the Rafsanjani administration which actively encouraged the notion that Iran was 'open for business'. While anticipating domestic criticism from hardliners in the regime, Rafsanjani was less prepared for the cool reception from the United States to the various economic enticements on offer.

Both offers lay in the oil sector, thought by many to be Iran's main source of economic leverage. In the first place, Iranian policy makers sought to capitalize on their geopolitical position as a transit route for oil and gas out of the Caspian basin towards the Persian Gulf, emphasising with much justification, the economic sense of running pipelines through Iran, as opposed to Turkey and/or Russia, a route which could take advantage of the extensive pipeline network already constructed throughout the country, and which it was argued, could be a force for stability throughout the wider region as countries became inter-dependent through the network. The second strategy was to target the United States directly by offering

US oil companies, in this case Conoco, a stake in Iranian oil development. Not only did these offers come to nothing, they resulted in a remarkable reaction, which saw on the one hand, the United States seek to circumvent the Iranian pipeline offer, by heavily underwriting the expensive alternative routes, including in this case, a dubious (on geographical as well as political grounds) route through Afghanistan, and the imposition of extensive sanctions through both Executive Order and legislation (the Iran Libya Sanctions Act – ILSA), which sought to introduce secondary sanctions on any foreign company investing in the Iranian oil and gas sector. There is little doubt that Iranian policy makers were somewhat perplexed by this reaction, but they were comforted by the fact that this was a Democratic administration and, as such, traditionally beholden to the Israeli lobby. President Clinton's decision to block the Conoco contract following intense pressure from the American-Israeli Public Affairs Committee (AIPAC) and his announcement of further sanctions at a meeting of the World Jewish Congress seemed to confirm this suspicion. Moreover the Clinton Administration's antipathy towards Iran had already been revealed by the imposition of 'Dual Containment', and of course the appointment of Warren Christopher as Secretary of State in 1993. It was an open secret that Warren Christopher, as a result of personal experiences during the Hostage Crisis, was no friend of Iran. Iranian 'realists' were therefore reassured that this was an anomaly born from Democratic prejudice, and that one had to wait for the Republicans to bring back pragmatic realism (a view reinforced by the Republicans in opposition). After all, in a curious effort to emphasise continuity over change (ie *normalization*), even the Shah had had difficulty with Democratic presidents. This was nonetheless a willful if convenient misreading of the political situation in the United States. Attempts to broker a deal with the first president Bush in 1991–2 had foundered on the potential embarrassment of the 'October Surprise' revelations, as well as the President's knowledge of the Iran-Contra affair, suggesting that the problem of Iran was not a party political issue in the United States. While the Clinton Administration's cautious initial welcome to the Taleban take-over in Kabul in 1995 hinted to those who cared to notice that America's problem was not with radical (revolutionary) Islam.

Khatami

One person who recognized the depth of the problem confronting Iran was Seyyed Mohammad Khatami, who understood that 'realism', far from representing the scientific objective reality its proponents proclaimed, was itself constructed by and a product of distinctive cultural values and prejudices. If Iran was unable to communicate its message, however tempting, to the United States, this was perhaps because the cultural assumptions were different and while the words may be the same, the meaning imparted was not:

> ... In its contemporary, complex forms, information technology represents one of the highest achievements of modern culture which uses its

control over information to solidify its domination of the world. Thus, inquiry into the nature of the information world is inseparable from uncovering the nature of modern civilization itself. And until we address this important question we will not be able to muster the confidence and wisdom to understand our relationship to modern civilization. Otherwise, we will live in a world whose rules have been set by others, at the mercy of circumstance, not as masters of our fate.... The flood of information in our age saturates the senses of humanity so extensively that the ability to assess and choose is impaired even among Westerners who are producers of information, let alone us who have a peripheral role in the information world. Electronic information is the brainchild of modern civilization. Thus, the power of today's information-based mass culture is tied to the legitimacy of the values of Western civilization for which the information revolution counts as the most prominent achievement....[11]

Khatami, a student of Western philosophy, was likewise seeking an engagement with the West, but the tool at his disposal, the means by which he intended to deconstruct the US hegemony,[12] was not the 'analytical' method of the Anglo-Saxon tradition, but the hermeneutic philosophy of the Continent:

True dialogue will only be possible when the two sides are genuinely aware of their roots and identity, otherwise the dialogue of an imitator who has no identity, with others, is meaningless and is not in his interest.[13]

In other words, material 'interest' could neither be communicated nor sustained outside a common cultural framework. Khatami's first systematic attempt to broach this problem was in his interview on CNN in January 1998, where he stressed the commonality of interests between the Islamic Republic of Iran and the United States while acknowledging areas of disagreement. It would be fair to say that the initial reaction from the United States was confused. They had been caught off guard, were unclear what it all meant, and consequently not sure how to respond. For all the discussion of the Pilgrim Fathers and Alexis de Tocqueville, Khatami nonetheless provided some distinctly practical suggestions about how to proceed:

There is a bulky wall of mistrust between us and American administrations, a mistrust rooted in improper behaviour by the American governments. As an example of this type of behaviour, I should refer to admitted involvement of the American government in the 1953 coup detat which toppled Mosaddeq's national government, immediately followed by a $45 m loan to strengthen the coup government. I should also refer to the capitulation law imposed by the American government on Iran.[14]

Tentative steps were taken to address this 'wall of mistrust' a few months later and, encouraged by different types of sporting diplomacy, there was a sense in some quarters that Khatami's dialogic offensive had made a modest breach in the wall. Nevertheless, despite the greater receptiveness to Khatami's message in Europe, there was little sign, beyond a sympathetic hearing, that the Western bureaucratic elites took him seriously. There is nothing to suggest for example that Khatami's proposition of a Dialogue of Civilizations was anything but a genuine attempt to engage and communicate meaningfully with the West. Unfortunately, the vast majority of his interlocutors regarded him as little more than a well meaning 'philosopher-president', whose intellectual meanderings were to be tolerated rather than understood. It is important to recognize that Khatami's detractors in this respect, were not only his ideological opponents, domestically and abroad (those, who it may be argued espoused a theological absolutism), but those for whom 'ideology' was a term of abuse and merely the consequence of an unkempt mind. This somewhat dismissive perspective was in some ways more damaging to Khatami, for while its proponents may have had much in common with Khatami with respect to the ends to be achieved, they disagreed sharply on the means to be used. Khatami's natural allies, both at home and abroad, therefore found it difficult to take him seriously, and his inability to secure his political agenda at home only served to confirm this view of him as wooly and ineffectual.

Indeed, by the time the Democratic Administration of President Clinton stooped to take up the gauntlet thrown down by Khatami in 1998, the political situation in both countries had taken a turn for the worse. Despite a triumphant election victory in the Majlis (February 2000), domestic pressures faced by Khatami were mounting and Iranian policy makers were becoming increasingly frustrated at the failure of his policy of engagement to yield concrete results. There were as yet no dramatic economic gains, despite a series of high profile visits to the EU, while in the US itself the campaign season had begun in earnest. The consequence of these developments was that the unprecedented apology by the new Secretary of State, Madeleine Albright, in March of that year for US involvement in the overthrow of Dr Mohammad Mosaddeq went largely unheeded in Iran.[15] Instead it was argued that it would be imprudent to negotiate with an administration which may not be in power following the November elections. In any case, pointed out the 'realists', a Republican administration would be easier 'to do business with.'[16]

The Bush administration and 9/11

This suggestion was of course not without its merits. Charting the developments in US-Iran relations throughout the 1990s, few would have disagreed with the view that the Clinton Administration had on balance done enormous damage to the possibility of rapprochement. It was under Clinton, after all, that the policy of Dual Containment had been developed and implemented; sanctions policy had been extended to include secondary sanctions; and crucially, US policy towards the Middle East had become intimately tied to the desires of Israel in a way that was inconceivable under the first President Bush. On the other hand, it was President Reagan who had explored contacts in what was to emerge as the Iran-Contra scandal, and there were tantalizing hints that had he won a second term, he would indeed have instructed his pragmatic Secretary of State, James Baker, to investigate an opening towards Iran. This was pure speculation of course, verging perhaps on wishful thinking, and it completely omitted to account for the fact that it had been a Republican Congress which had bound Clinton's hands with respect to the sanctions on Iran. Nonetheless, Iran's realists confidently predicted that a Republican victory in November 2000 would continue where Bush senior had left off, with a pragmatic 'interest' based foreign policy dominated by that most traditional of US interests, oil. The nomination as Vice President of Dick Cheney, with his links to the oil services company, Halliburton, which was rumored to have business interests in Iran, appeared to confirm this view, as did the comments of European businessmen and civil servants. Only one concern served to sour this generally rosy picture: the assumption that the Republicans would be so ruthless in pursuit of their vision of US interests that security and economic advantages would far outweigh any desire to see political reform in Iran. This, ironically enough, was a charge that the Democrats had leveled at the Europeans, accusing them of lacking principle in dealing with Iran and putting economic interests first. With a Republican presidency, such idiosyncrasies could be put aside, although some Europeans were undoubtedly worried at the potential competition American companies represented. From the Iranian perspective, a Republican victory would confirm the veracity of the realist methodology by removing the anomaly that was Clinton, provide an avenue for detente, which it could be admitted, Khatami's dialogue had facilitated if not opened, and by extension enhance the prestige of the 'pragmatists'.

However, much to Iranian consternation, the election of George W Bush in November 2000 did not provide the opportunities some had predicted, in large part because it took the Bush Administration some considerable time to settle into the job of government. The momentum of the last few years, however slow, was now halted while the new administration officials took up their posts. While Iranians waited to see what would emerge, the indications were proving less than auspicious. The President himself seemed disinterested in foreign policy, espousing what some considered to be the traditional conservative tendency towards isolationism, although the extent to which this was being taken was viewed with genuine concern in some European capitals, especially with respect to the Arab-Israeli Peace Process.[17] More seriously, however, were the people Bush was appointing to positions of importance on Middle Eastern affairs. Indeed, a number of officials had been involved and, in the case of Elliot Abrams, convicted for, their part in the Iran-Contra scandal, while others, such as John Bolton were noted for their zealous, even ideological adherence to a particular world view.[18] Still, the decision to host the Taleban in Washington with a view to developing an oil and gas pipeline from Central Asia through Afghanistan could be considered reflective of the new ruthless realism at work. If the Bush administration could work with the Taleban, went the recycled argument, then economic interests predominated over ideology. As noted above however, the decision to work with the Taleban, had previously been investigated by the Clinton administration, with a view to circumventing the economically rational choice of Iran, and could be more convincingly presented as an ideologically determined decision. In sum, the advent of a new Republican presidency did not fill the realist mould carefully crafted by Iranian analysts – however hard they tried.

Then the events of 9/11 took place. It is in periods of crisis that tensions expose themselves, and 9/11 was no exception. While Americans struggled to come to terms with what had happened and provide an explanation, the tensions between those who sought to 'judiciously study discernible reality', and those who wished to 'create' their own realities, came to the fore. What had hitherto been a trend (albeit a clear one where Iran was concerned) now sought to dominate. But it was by no means clear in the first months after the 9/11 attack that this particular world view would succeed in establishing its hegemony over US foreign policy. In Iran, on the other hand similar internal tensions were resulting in an unprecedented expression of sympathy which was greeted with some incredulity in the United States. Indeed, some US commentators noticed that there was considerably more public sympathy in Iran than in many of America's allies in the region. There was a moment, indeed, when it appeared that the ideological facade with respect to Iran was about to crack, especially when the rash attempt to blame the 9/11 attacks on radical Shias (the ubiquitous Hizbollah) was blatantly contradicted the facts.[19] Khatami sought to capitalize on this moment by delivering Iranian assistance to the emergent US war against the Taleban. He had assiduously cultivated the cultural framework in which trust could now be contemplated. Now it was time to convert this into a concrete reality by exploiting the obvious coincidence of interests in Afghanistan, and by all accounts Iranian assistance to the coalition both during and after the Afghan war, was not insignificant. Khatami was able to deliver because Reformists and pragmatists (conservative or otherwise) within Iran likewise enjoyed a coincidence of interests and real merits in pursuing this policy. Hardliners in Iran were less easy to convince.

Their counterparts in the United States were similarly less than enthralled by the tentative detente, and steps were taken to derail the potential rapprochement. As one Conservative commentator has noted, "from the perspective of Bush and the neocons, the US has been at war with Iran since 1979 and the time [had] come to settle the score."[20] A delegation of Israelis was dispatched to Washington to remind the Bush administration of the obvious dangers of the Islamic Republic, a perspective that was enthusiastically amplified by neo-conservatives within and around the government, who rushed to the airwaves to accuse Iran of harboring Al Qaeda operatives. There was indeed some confusion in Iranian circles about the presence or otherwise of Al Qaeda, and the final admission that Al Qaeda members had escaped across the border and were now in Iranian prisons did not do much to assuage suspicions of complicity and their conversion into fact in an American consciousness traumatized by 9/11.[21] More conclusive however, as far as the US administration and their Israeli guests were concerned, was the sudden and timely capture of the Karine A, a ship loaded with weapons for the Palestinian Authority. As the Israeli authorities and Prime Minister Sharon in particular made the most of parading the captured weapons, happily emblazoned with Persian lettering, they were initially confronted by an air of diplomatic incredulity. Not only was the timing of the find highly convenient, but even analysts ill disposed to the Islamic Republic, found it remarkable that a regime hitherto experienced in shipping arms and munitions overseas should choose to do this particular delivery via slow boat journey around the Arabian Peninsula. Caution was eventually thrown the wind when even the skeptics concluded that the source of the shipment was, at the very least, the 'rogue elements' in the regime determined to undermine Khatami. For those who had never been convinced by the 'totalitarian' description of Iran, here was the ready alternative: Khatami, the author of dialogue of civilizations, was not really in charge. Either way the explanation fits the prejudice, and by the beginning of 2002, Khatami's domestic and international policies were in tatters.

Much ink has been spilt debating the causes and consequences of Bush's State of the Union address on January 29th 2002, especially with regards to the inclusion of the theological motif 'axis of evil', a phrase which was to have political reverberations, particularly in Iran. Yet the speech is probably as interesting for what it did not include, and it is striking that 'al Qaeda' merited one, almost marginal mention, and Bin Laden, none at all.[22] It was as if the war in Afghanistan signaled the end of one chapter, and that now it was time to move on – to other targets. The reaction in Iran to this abrupt hardening of American attitude is revealing in both indicating the plurality and sophistication of views with respect to the United States, and the sheer bewilderment of many Iranian analysts who discovered that the real world did not match their *realist* assessment.[23] Even ordinary Iranians who could agree with Bush's criticism of the 'unelected minority' found it difficult to recognize themselves as part of an unholy alliance with Iraq and North Korea.

To be sure, there were some recognizable, if regrettable reactions. The Supreme Leader, Ayatollah Khamene'i immediately responded with characteristic rhetoric of his own, noting that, "The Islamic Republic of Iran is proud to be the target of the rage and hatred of the world's greatest Satan," while hardliners, particularly in the Revolutionary Guards, sought to exploit the event by imposing a state of emergency.[24] Despite the absence of formal relations, America had never left Iran. The 'Axis of Evil', ensured that it returned to center stage. The specter of America had been realized; regular politics, frequently subjected to douses of American interference (real or imagined), was now put on hold; the nation united against the 'foreign threat'; and conspiracies were amplified.[25] Politicians, meanwhile, became engrossed in the problem of 'who lost America'? Indeed, far from launching diatribes against the United States, Majlis deputies turned their attention to the alleged ineptitudes of the Foreign Ministry.[26] Others, in their eagerness to absolve the United States of such 'irrational' behavior, could see instead the hand of 'Perfidious Albion'.[27] According to the reformist deputy, Hojjat-ol Islam Alisaghar Rahmani-Khalili:

> By taking such a stance, George Bush is trying to test public opinion. And when the public opinion would correspond to his, he would then act. [The] European Union and a number of Asian and European countries have criticized Bush's position describing it as inappropriate and wrong. Only England has supported Bush. England is behind those crises created in our country and the outside movements that support them. England is the one who motivates America to act brutishly. We must discover England's footprint in these events. In truth, England is the one who fuels events.[28]

While hardliners relished the possibility of further antagonism, Reformist politicians along with their pragmatist allies, were desperate to discover the realist core at the heart of American rhetoric. Grasping at straws, they were encouraged by the apparent discomfort in the United States at the implications of Bush's comments. The 'realist' old guard in the State Department and Congress, clearly shaken, had sought to soften the rhetoric and even hinted at the possibility of dialogue, a prospect seized upon by reformists.[29] As one reformist journalist commented:

> There is no rational strategic explanation for refusing to hold talks with America. The sooner Iran begins to hold public and official talks with America, the sooner it will be able to further its own interests. However, the longer Iran postpones the talks, the greater the losses it will incur. In fact, if we had started to hold official talks publicly a few years ago, we would not have faced many of the problems in the bilateral relations between the two countries. Postponing the talks means that Iran has hardened its position. Eventually, Iran and America will have to negotiate. The longer such talks are postponed, the greater the losses Iran will incur and this will primarily serve America's interests.[30]

Ironically, efforts at a public dialogue were to be rapidly overtaken by news that a number of private initiatives appeared to be underway. The precise nature of these initiatives, secret and sensitive as they were, is likely to remain clouded for some time, but according to leaks in the Iranian press, it appeared as if the Chairman of the Expediency Council, Hashemi Rafsanjani, had been exploring the possibilities of a 'grand bargain' with the United States.[31] In retrospect, this may have been an attempt by the arch-realist in the Iranian establishment to broker a deal with like-minded ruthless realists in the United States. Rafsanjani's problem, however, was that this move was unlikely to win him friends among the hardline conservatives (who eagerly anticipated his failure), nor among reformists who suspected Rafsanjani's definition of 'interest' to be narrowly centered on issues of mutual security and stripped of any association with human rights and democracy. Indeed, Rafsanjani's gambit revealed a significant flaw in this particular realist conception. It failed to take into account the changes in political culture among Iranians (or for that matter within the United States). Neglecting the democratic imperative, it lacked a moral core and, with supreme irony, handed the moral high ground, on a platter, to the neo-conservatives. 'Realists', whether in the US or Europe, were quite clearly, unprincipled. In Iran, indignation was rife.[32] Their indignation was fuelled by calculated leaks from the hardliners, such as Ayatollah Jannati's unsubtle response to an apparently 'clever' question from an AFP reporter, "Rafsanjani is not involved in this, but a number of associates are involved in it."[33] To further muddy the waters, it was unclear who was involved in the negotiations, and which particular factions were represented. In the United States, despite initial rejections, it was later revealed that old Iran-Contra networks were being re-vitalized, along with all the usual suspects – leading some in Iran to conclude that the neocons were reassuringly realist to the core, while in Iran, Rafsanjani's association with the conservatives led people to conclude that despite all the harsh rhetoric, this was an initiative with widespread conservative backing. The more damning conclusion drawn by many reformists was that for all the rhetoric, America was quite happy to deal with Iran's 'unelected minority'.[34] Anti-Americanism, like anti-Iranianism, was rapidly becoming a bi-partisan affair.

Indeed, contrary to their political leanings, it was the reformists who were protesting that now was not the time to begin negotiations with the United States, while the conservatives increasingly stewed in the embarrassment of further revelations and sought to stifle debate.[35] Ultimately, each tried to outdo each other in their repeated denial of any desire to open a dialogue while public opinion reacted with characteristic irritation at the obvious lack of any progress.[36] The end to this steady debasement of political life came with an intervention from the Leader, Ayatollah Khamenei, urging all parties to desist from further debate. The comment proved highly counter-productive and took the public obsession with the United States to the point of ridicule. The head of Tehran Justice Office, Abbas Ali Alizadeh, a medium level cleric of moderate education, on apparently no authority or initiative but his own, abruptly announced, via a judicial decree broadcast on State television, that henceforth, any discussion about negotiations with the United States would be considered a criminal offence.[37] Quite apart from the insight it provided into the means by which Iran's 'autocracy' operated, this proved a highly unusual intervention – the Judiciary, let alone regional branches had not been in the habit of issuing decrees – which took many Iranians by surprise. Shock however, very rapidly gave way to ridicule as some conjectured that perhaps the decree applied only to Tehran, and that discussions could continue outside the province of Tehran. By the next morning however, farce gave way to anger as Majlis deputies lined up to lambast the hapless Alizadeh and his 'ignorance' of the law.[38] Even President Khatami was moved to condemn the Judiciary's actions:

> I am surprised with all the fuss made over a matter that has not yet happened. More or less all those who speak about talks with America

are either opposed to them or agree that now is not the time for such talks. Why must we create the impression that this is the time for talks? I follow the political system's overall policies. Let us not do anything that will threaten the country's interests and dignity and the system's overall policies. Then somebody announces that whoever negotiates has committed a crime, as if people are queuing in Iran to talk to America, and we have to stop them by force or through the judiciary. What kind of behaviour is this? We must be wise and run this country with intelligence, and God Willing, we are blessed with intelligence.[39]

Conclusion

For all the ridicule that mounted, the hardline conservatives were in effect able to close down any suggestions of a detente with the United States. Within months, the Judiciary moved, with great secrecy and to the ill-disguised frustration of the government, to arrest individuals involved in polling public opinion with a view to assessing the public reaction to any dialogue with the United States.[40] Despite the nuanced nature of the responses – Iranians remained on the whole distrustful of US intentions but thought dialogue a positive and worthwhile step – the hardliners dismissed the entire exercise as psychological warfare intended to weaken the revolutionary resolve of the Islamic Republic. Ayatollah Jannati reiterated the revolutionary dogma to a weary public, stressing that antagonism against the United States remained a *raison d'etre* of the state.[41] As an exercise in the status quo, it revealed a continued absence of decisive leadership in the Islamic Republic, and popular frustration was increasingly making itself felt.[42] Others openly directed their criticism at the Leader himself, lamenting his inability to seize the initiative on this issue, despite the urging of advisers.[43] Indeed, a sympathetic view of the United States and its policies remained among the general public and some reformist politicians all the way up to the Iraqi invasion, with few tears shed for the fall of the Baathist regime.[44] Even among intellectuals, articles discussing US policy continued to define it in terms of realism and rationality, whether in critiquing a prospective war in Iraq or explaining it.[45] Indeed, having absorbed one understanding of realism, Iranians were now digesting another which explained that the policy of regime change was simply an extension of the realist interpretation of international relations which regarded the world as essentially lawless.[46] Few, if any, commentators within Iran were willing to concede a cultural paradigm for the determination of what constituted US interests, in part perhaps because in acknowledging the ideological aspect of US foreign policy, one conceded ground to the ideological hardliners in Iran itself, and paradoxically fed the logic of structural determinism.[47] Iranian realists had all the difficulty of communication with the new American idealism, and none of the reassuring conviction of their ideological compatriots. Dismissive of Khatami, they had no alternative strategy to deconstruct the 'wall of mistrust', while Iranian hardliners relished its construction. The Bush administration for its part, settled into the political comfort of prejudice and myth, increasingly employing theological motifs which would unsettle their compatriots, but resonate with their opponents. As the current nuclear impasse indicates, neither side has been willing to recognize a cultural and ideological dimension to the construction of interest, or to see their positions as anything but real and rational. The focus on particularities has obfuscated the wider problem of cultural communication and disguised the reality that myth is just as important to US policy making as it is to revolutionary Iran. Perhaps Iran had exported her revolution after all?

Notes

1 Recounted by Ron Susskind, 'Without a Doubt', in *The New York Times*, 17th October 2004.

2 See for example National Security Council member, Bob Blackwill quoted in the *Financial Times*, March 16th 2004, 'Washington Hardliners wary of engaging Iran', Guy Dinmore: "Bush has a vision for the Greater Middle East but not a policy." The notion that US policy towards Iran, inasmuch as it exists, has failed is of course not new, see for example, S Chubin & J D Green Engaging Iran: A US Strategy *Survival* Vol 40, no 3 Autumn (1998): 153–169.

3 Contrast Rice's comments with those of Richard Armitage after the State of the Union address in 2002, "The axis of evil speech was a valid comment [but] I would note there is one dramatic difference between Iran and the other two axes of evil, and that would be its democracy. [And] you approach a democracy differently ... I wouldn't think they were next at all." Richard Armitage quoted in the *Los Angeles Times* 15th February 2003.

4 In this paper, 'realism', and the 'rationality' that it implies are culturally defined and determined, and therefore reflect particular interpretation as opposed to general laws. 'Myth' is here is used as a concept in the social sciences. See for example, P Ricouer *Science and Ideology in Hermeneutics and the Human Sciences*, (Cambridge 1981): 222–246. My reading of myth draws extensively on R Barthes, *Mythologies* (London, 1970).

5 See for example, Leon Harder, 'Operation Iranian Freedom?' *The American Conservative* 25th April, 2005: 3–4; "... the neocons are more entrenched in the power centres while the realists have been cleansed from the CIA and other government agencies.".

6 As Philippe Sands notes in *Lawless World: America and the Making and Breaking of Global Rules* (London 2005): xi, "The rules which were intended to constrain others became constraining of their creators.".

7 See for example, W Beeman 'Double Demons: Cultural Impedance in US-Iranian Understanding', *Iranian Journal of International Affairs* Summer-Fall (1990): 319–334.

8 For details of this interpretation see Gary Sick, *October Surprise: America's Hostages in Iran and the Election of Ronald Reagan* (London, 1992).

9 The notion of 'national interest' became more prominent in discourse, see for example Hossein Seifzadeh 'Estrateji-ye Melli va Siyasatgozari-ye khareji' (National Strategy & Foreign Policy-Making), *The Journal of Foreign Policy*, Vol VII, (1994): 705–722.

10 See the editorial in the *Tehran Times*, February 23rd 1993, which boldly proclaimed now to be the time for 'realism'. There was also an attempt to out-intellectualise and out-rationalise the West, which often took some striking turns. For example one of the key proponents of this movement, Mohammad-javad Larijani, could offer the following assessment of the Islamic Republic: "While an Islamic society is not at ease with technical rationality, it finds itself quite in harmony with the authentic one.

Therefore, Islamic modernity goes far beyond historical modernity and is basically a post-modern phenomenon." 'Islamic Society & Modernism', in *The Iranian Journal for International Affairs*, VII, 1, (1995): 58.

11 See M Khatami 'Observations on the Information World' in *Hope and Challenge: The Iranian President Speaks*, trans. A Mainezam, (Binghamton 1997): 61–71.

12 'Hegemony' is here used in the Gramscian sense.

13 SWB ME/3099 S1/6 dated 11th December 1997, Khatami's speech to the OIC conference dated 9th December 1997. See also BBC SWB ME/3339 MED/2 dated 23rd September 1998, President Khatami addresses Iranian expatriates in the USA, dated 20th September 1998: "the first rule of dialogue … is to know yourself and identity. The second rule is to know the civilisation with which you want to maintain a dialogue …".

14 BBC SWB ME/3120 MED/5 dated 9 January 1998, CNN interview dated 8th January 1998.

15 The importance of the myth of Mosaddeq to contemporary Iranian political culture can hardly be exaggerated. See for example the Persian periodical *Nameh*, 25, Mordad 1382/August 2003, Special Issue on the 50th anniversary of the Coup; or the previous year's issue, Mordad 1381/ August 2002, special issue on 'National Unity', in which the spectre of Mosaddeq looms large.

16 The notion (myth) that 'conservatives' are easier 'to do business with', would in turn be replicated by the Europeans. The standard mantra of this myth is the argument, 'Only Nixon could go to China'.

17 For a traditional conservative critique of the neo-conservative agenda see Pat Buchanan '*No End to War*' in *The American Conservative* 1st March 2004.

18 Abrams was initially appointed National Security Council Staff Chief for 'Democracy, Human Rights, and International Operations, before moving up in 2002, to become Special Assistant to the President and Senior Director on the NSC for SW Asia, Near East and North African Affairs. See David Corn, 'Elliot Abrams. Its Back!' *The Nation* July 2 2001; Terry J Allen, 'Public Serpent: Iran Contra villain Elliot Abrams is back in Action' *In These Times* August 2001; 'The Return of Elliot Abrams' TomPaine.com, www.tompaine.com/feature.cfm/ID/6895 11th December 2002; see also 'Iran-Contra, Amplified' www.tompaine.com/feature2.cfm/ID/8625 18th August 2003.

19 It was noticeable for example that the standard chants of 'death to America' at Fridays prayers were suspended; see the interesting reflection on the attack and Iranian sympathies for Americans in M Hajizadeh 'Aqazadeh-ha' (Their Excellencies' Sons) (Tehran, 1381/2002): 143–146. Popular sympathy for the United States continued, see *Aftab-e Yazd* 5th Esfand 1382/24th February 2004, p 5.

20 Leon Hardar *op cit* 4; see also A Killgore, Neocons 'Concentrate on Promoting US-Iran War' in *Washington Report on Middle East Affairs* March 2005: 32–33.

21 The United States Special Envoy for Afghanistan, Zalmay Khalilzad, publicly made the claims on 18th January 2002, see Iran Press Service 18th January 2002, www.iran-press-scrvice.com/ articles_2002/Jan_2002/afqanestan_iran_qaeda_18102.

22 See www.whitehouse.gov/news/releases/2002/01/print/20020129-11.html; the 'terrorist underworld' highlighted by President Bush was limited to *Hamas, Hizbollah, Islamic Jihad*, and for good measure *Jaish-e-Mohammad*.

23 See commentary in *Nowruz*, 2nd February 2002, BBC SWB Mon MEPol. For an interesting exception to the standard line (albeit written abroad), see G Qoreishi & M Soleimani 'Iran va Amrika: Bazi-ye na-tamam' (Iran & America: The unfinished game), *Aftab*, 2, 15, Ordibehesht 1381/April–May 2002: 14–21, trans J Kheirkhahan.

24 *Khamenei calls Bush 'thirsty for human blood* AFP 31st January 2002. See for example, BBC SWB Mon ME1 MEPol, *Nowruz* website 18th March 2002, on continuing calls by conservatives for a declaration of martial law.

25 See for example, BBC SWB Mon ME1 MEPol, IRIB, 12th July 2002, *Demonstrators support Khamene'i, call for trial of 'fifth columnists'*; also, *Etemad*, 29 Mordad 1381/20th August 2002: 2. There was of course, plenty of public scepticism, see the reader's comment, *Aftab-e Yazd*, 25 Ordibehesht 1381/15th May 2002: 11.

26 See Elahe Koulaee's comments in *Nowruz*, 24 Ordibehesht 1381/14th May 2002, p 2; also *Aftab-e Yazd*, 21 Khordad 1381/11th June 2002: 1.

27 The alternative was of course Israel, despite the best attempts of overseas observers, see A Sheikhzadeh Iran va Emrika: taqabul ya tafahum (Iran and America: confrontation or understanding) *Aftab*, 2, 17, Tir-Mordad 1381/July–August 2002: 16–25.

28 ISNA website, 2nd February 2002, BBC SWB Mon MEPol.

29 Majlis deputies welcomed the possibility of inter-parliamentary talks following comments by Senator Joe Biden, *Hambastegi* website, 16th March 2002, BBC SWB Mon MEPol. Ahmad Zeydabadi quoted in ISNA website 16th March 2002, BBC SWB Mon MEPol; See also Jala'ipour's comments in *Bonyan* 18th March 2002, BBC SWB Mon MEPol. See for example, *Nowruz*, 31 Ordibehesht 1381/21st May 2002: 1.

30 Ahmad Zeydabadi quoted in ISNA website 16th March 2002, BBC SWB Mon MEPol; See also Jala'ipour's comments in *Bonyan* 18th March 2002, BBC SWB Mon MEPol.

31 *Nowruz*, 19 Ordibehesht 1381/9th May 2002: 5.

32 For a later analysis of these developments see Guy Dinmore 'Washington Hardliners wary of engaging with Iran' *Financial Times* March 16th 2004.

33 See the detailed analysis of the various claims in *Nowruz* 26th May 2002, BBC SWB Mon MEPol.

34 See Armin's comments in *Nowruz*, 24 Ordibehesht 1381/14th May 2002:2, and Rafsanjani's reply in *Nowruz*, 25 Ordibehesht 1381/15th May 2002: 2; see also, Guy Dinmore *op cit* Financial Times, March 16th 2004. See also K Royce & T M Phelps 'Secret Talks with Iranian', *Newsday.com* 8th August 2003.

35 Mirdamadi, the Head of the Majlis National Security Commission, had been at the forefront of the charge that 'conservatives' had initiated un-authorised talks, see for example, *Entekhab* 23rd May 2002, BBC SWB Mon MEPol. He was charged with putting the country's national security at risk by the head of the Tehran Judiciary, Alizadeh! See *Resalat* website, 27th May 2002, BBC SWB Mon MEPol.

36 See Mohajerani's comments in *Bonyan*, 14 Ordibehesht 1381/4th May 2002; 2; for public frustration see, *Aftab-e Yazd*, 25 Ordibehesht 1381/15th May 2002: 11; Comment by Habibollah Asgar-owladi, 15th June 2002, BBC SWB Mon MEPol.

37 *Nowruz*, 5 Khordad 1381/26th May 2002: 1.

38 *Nowruz*, 6 Khordad 1381/27th May 2002, pp 1–2; Editorial in *Hadis-e Qazvin* 2nd June 2002, BBC SWB Mon MEPol. See also Mehdi Karrubi's press conference, *Nowruz* 12 Khordad 1381/2nd June 2002: 1–2; *Hayat-e No*, 12 Khordad 1381/2nd June 2002: 1.

39 *Hayat-e No* website, 1st June 2002, BBC SWB Mon MEPol. See also *Nowruz*, 19 Khordad 1381/9th June 2002: 7; *Hayat-e No*, 11 Khordad 1381/1st June 2002: 1.

40 For details see, *Mardomsalari*, 18 Dey 1381/8th January 2003: 4/9; there was some evidence of Ministry of Information collusion, see *Entekhab* website, 24th December 2002, BBC SWB Mon ME1 MEPol; *Babar*, 19 Dey 1381/9th January 2003 p 1; it was indeed February 2003, before the Judiciary provided details to President Khatami, ISNA website, 2 February 2003, BBC SWB Mon ME1 MEPol.

41 See Jannati's speech, IRIB, 8th November 2002, BBC SWB Mon ME1 MEPol.

42 See for example the reader comment, *Aftab-e Yazd*, 17 Shahrivar 1381/8th September 2002, p 5, "In my opinion America has provided the greatest help to Muslims and Iran..."; also reader comment, *Aftab-e Yazd*, 28 Azar 1381/18th December 2002, p 5; see also a critique of the 'myth' of America, see Bana S 'Bar gharari rabeteh bah amrika: faseleh gereftan ba romantism-e siyasi (Establishing links with America: moving away from political romanticism), *Aftab*, Farvardin 1382/April 2003: 84.

43 'Letter of Sholeh-Saadi to Khamene'i December 2002 www.web.peykeiran.com/iran/news/ir_news_92.asp.

44 For details see the editorial in the magazine, *Aftab*, Farvardin 1382/April 2003, along with the interview with Habibollah Peyman. For Elahe Koulaie's criticism of bias of Iranian television against the Americans see Tehran Times website, 7th April 2003, BBC SWB Mon ME1 MEPol. There was of course a certain amount of anxiety in official circles about the rapidity of the fall of Iraq, *Hayat-e No*, 16 Shahrivar 1381/7th September 2002: 1; *Aftab-e Yazd*, 25 Ordibehesht 1381/15th May 2002: 11; see President Khatami's press conference, *Jaam-e Jam* 28th August 2002, BBC SWB Mon ME1 MEPol. Discomfort at US policies gradually emerged after the war, see R Mostaqim *Iranian Reformers Back Hardliners Against War* Inter Press Service News Agency, April 2nd 2003. See also the concerns expressed in the Editorial in 'Jang va Ghodrat menhaye Mardom' (War and power without the people) *Jame'eb No*, 2, 15, Ordibehesht 1382/April 2003: 1–2, these views were reflected in the tone of the rest of the special issue.

45 Among observers of US policy that continued to be translated into Persian were the standard bearers of 'realism', whether as proponents or critiques. See for example, N Chomsky 'Tahlil-e Eqdam Bush dar Araq' (An analysis of Bush's actions in Iraq), *Aftab*, 3, 21, Azar 1381/Nov–Dec 2002): 84–85 trans M Malekan; A Bigdeli 'Amrika: Ostoreh ta Vagheyat' (America: myth to reality) *Jame'eb No*, 2, 13, Esfand 1381/March 2003: 27–28.

46 See for example in this vein, F Fukuyama 'Mohafezeh-kari-ye Emrakayi' (American conservativism) *Aftab*, 3, 22, Dey-Bahman 1381/Jan–Feb 2003: 88–89 trans M Malekan; particularly pertinent to this interpretation is the following article: G Nassri 'Tammoli marafat shenakhti bar falsafe-ye siyasi-ye Habbs va mabna-ye qodrat va amniat dar' an (An Epistemological Meditation on the Political Philosophy of Hobbes) *Etele'at Siyasi-Eqtesadi* Vol 16: 177–178 Khordad-Tir 1381/June–July 2002: 18–31.

47 A view which panders to the *inevitable* 'clash of civilisations'. This perspective was admirably critiqued by Abdolkarim Soroush in *The Three Cultures in Reason, Freedom and Democracy in Islam: essential writings of Abdolkarim Soroush* trans & ed by M Sadri & A Sadri, (Oxford, 2000): 156–170. See also Richard Bulliet *The Case for Islamo-Christian Civilisation* (New York, 2005).

54

CIVILIZATIONAL IDENTITY
AND FOREIGN POLICY

The case of Iran

Ali M. Ansari

Source: B. Shaffer (ed.) *The Limits of Culture: Islam and Foreign Policy*, Cambridge, Mass.: MIT Press, 2006, pp. 241–62.

> This spirit acts as a binding element for all of us despite any ten-
> dency, any ideas or any preference that we might have. If we are
> honest, if we are Iranian, what binding element could be better for
> all of us, despite all the differences that we have in our views and
> preferences, than to seek to create a distinguished Iran and a proud
> nation? Concern for our homeland is the binding element for all of
> us. And what is this homeland? In a material sense, homeland is
> manifested in a piece of land. But one piece of land is no more valu-
> able than any other. What makes a homeland valuable is the fact that
> this piece of land is where people with a common historical memory
> have shared a common experience. In other words, motherland is in
> our hearts and minds, it is in our views and perspectives.[1]

Few would argue with the fact that Iran and the United States have shared a
problematic relationship in the last quarter-century since the advent of Iran's
Islamic Revolution in 1979. These problems have been accentuated and exaggerated by the perception of intimacy which colored the relationship prior to 1979
and, while forged through experience, have been emphatically institutionalized
through a vigorous process of intellectual rationalization which has emphasized
a sense of alienation and distinction.[2] Arguably, the reason few had been able to
foresee the revolution which had transformed the position of the United States
in the Middle East and removed an "island of stability"[3] from an otherwise troubled region was because it was so obviously the product of irrational forces (in
this case, "fundamentalist" Islam).[4] In intellectual terms, the predictive quality
of Western social scientific analysis could be excused because a rational and
reasonable approach to foreign policy analysis had failed to accommodate the

possibility of irrationality on the part of the other. In sum, this was an entirely "reasonable" mistake to have made. Henceforth, the dominant realist paradigm in international relations would come under increasing scrutiny, modification, and even transformation, so that the errors of the past could be avoided and culture would be examined as an important factor. The accommodation of new realities, however, has been a limited affair. While "irrationality" may have been redefined as "culture," many would hold that it remains, by and large, something which afflicts the other. Even, for example, where culture and civilizational factors are accepted as partially determining one's own foreign policy, an implicit assumption of superiority also exists; a rational culture in binary conflict with a culture of irrationality, emphasizing perhaps, the cultural (and ideological) foundations of the method.[5]

This essay will argue that such a dichotomous approach is misleading insofar as it tends to posit distinct and self-contained "cultures." On the contrary, "cultures" are neither indigenously homogenous nor quarantined within local environments. In short, cultural boundaries may be regarded as porous, and the tendency toward analytical categorization should not ignore the reality of continuous—dialectical—interaction.[6] At the same time, while the cultural determinants of foreign policymaking may be accepted, one should be careful not to assign rationality to one and irrationality to the other. All cultures and ideological paradigms contain within themselves the germs of both tendencies and, crucially, affect and influence each other. This is not to argue for cultural relativism, simply for an acceptance of the importance and pervasiveness of cultural (ideological) determinants in conjunction with material interests.[7] Indeed, there can be little doubt that culture informs and in many ways determines the priorities that a given state affords itself when defining its foreign policy objectives, but culture does not exist in a vacuum and is itself shaped by material experience. Interests may be shaped by cultural norms, but an ideological worldview is itself defined (and in many ways propelled) by the harsh realities of experience. At the same time, it will be argued that each foreign policy is determined and informed by competing cultures representing differing (though not necessarily exclusive) values, resulting often in a contradictory mix of policy applications. Iran provides a useful case study for analyzing the limits of culture because of the multiplicity of its constituent cultures and the porous, often ambiguous relationship between these cultural determinants and its material interests.

Iran and the limits of culture

Iran, especially after the revolution of 1979, offers an exceptional case study of the limits of culture in determining foreign policy directions. This is so because, in the eyes of many Western analysts, revolutionary Iran occupies a particular political space which places it beyond the rational pale of foreign policy actors and into the realm of "irrational fanaticism," which cannot be understood but must either be contained or confronted. In this way, Iran is the quintessential

Other; a situation for which, arguably, the Iranians—or to use the more classical designation, the Persians—are well suited. For many analysts, bewildered by the dynamic of revolution, Iran fit the mold of what has been defined by the apposite term, a "martyr state." Indeed, the overthrow of Mohammad Reza Shah Pahlavi and the replacement of the ostensibly pro-Western authentically national Pahlavi state, with a distinctly Shi'a Islamic Republic, in which the virtues of martyrdom were being proclaimed, only seemed to confirm this assessment. Iranians, far from being the rational Persians of the Shah's era, had suddenly revealed themselves to be fanatical Muslims possessed of a martyr complex and devoid of rational judgement. As one former Pahlavi technocrat argued, "Almost willfully, they suppressed their better judgment, refused to involve themselves in meaningful analysis, insisted on total denigration of the prevailing system, fabricated evidence of the nation's socio-economic destruction, exaggerated the reality of political tyranny, and clung to a utopian panacea that simply was not contained in the premises of the revolution."[8] Reports of human wave attacks during the brutal 1980–1988 Iran-Iraq War only served to compound this image and effectively institutionalize it.[9]

As this apparent transition indicates, another important factor for this essay's purposes is the cultural plurality of Iranian society. The notion of "culture" is an integral aspect of Iranian identity; this is particularly true following the revolution, when identity was defined in cultural terms to contrast it more explicitly with what was seen as the ethno-chauvinism of the Pahlavis, which many considered to border on Persian racism. On the contrary, argued the intellectual heirs of the revolution, the exclusivity of Persianism was to be supplanted by an inclusive Iranian-ness, which, through the incorporation of the variety of ethnic groups that constituted the Iranian state, would be defined in cultural terms.[10] Their model for this was the *kultur-nation* of the German Romanticists. Culture, of course, is a difficult concept to define. In the Persian language, the word—*farhang*—encompasses a number of different meanings and associations, denoting not only culture, but education, and the arts. In other words, in Persian—as in English—the term for culture frequently denotes what in the West may be understood as "high culture," and as such its associations with the concept of civilization should be clear. Iranian culture is a vital ingredient in the composition of Iranian civilization, that totality of views and ideas which as Toynbee argued, "comprehend without being comprehended by others." In this way, the concept of a civilization may be usefully related to that of hegemony, as defined by the Italian Marxist Antonio Gramsci.[11] Such an association would certainly permit a more rigorous political analysis and recognize the ideological (and hence political) dimension of culture and civilization.

While Huntington allocates Iranian (or Persian) civilization to a subset of a broader Islamic civilization, many Iranians would disagree and concur instead with Toynbee, who argued the case for an "Iranic" civilization, whose distinctive cultural contributions place it on a par, or in some cases beyond, the Islamic categorization.[12] In distinguishing an "Iranian Islamic" civilization, Iranians are not only appropriating the religion to the nation (the development in essence of a religious nationalism), they are highlighting the belief that Iran enjoys a privileged position among the world's cultures in possessing the characteristics of civilization.[13] It may be argued that this is simply a matter of preference and emphasis, but it does serve to highlight the existence of competing cultures within the modern polity of Iran. While Mohammad Reza Shah Pahlavi sought to drive his people toward the Great Civilization by emphasizing the splendors of Iran's ancient pre-Islamic Aryan past, many of his subjects disagreed and argued that Iranian civilization was in fact being denigrated by a willful ignorance of Islam and subservience to the West. This sin of omission had to be addressed, and in the aftermath of the Islamic Revolution, Islamic Iran was emphasized at the expense of pre-Islamic Iran. Yet, as will be seen, this was not the replacement of one cultural paradigm by another, but a recognition that modern Iranian civilization was the fortunate heir of three particular and distinctive cultures. As the influential lay religious philosopher, Abdolkarim Soroush succinctly argued: "We Iranian Muslims are the inheritors and carriers of three cultures at once. As long as we ignore our links with the elements in our triple cultural heritage and our cultural geography, constructive social and cultural action will elude us.... The three cultures that form our common heritage are of national, religious, and Western origins."[14]

Religious culture

As Soroush argues further in the same article, "Islamic culture ... is qualitatively and quantitatively the dominant culture of Iran."[15] While it is certainly true that religion has played a formative role in the defining of Iranian foreign policy objectives, it is important not to exaggerate its significance, not only because of the impact of experience (especially the Iran-Iraq War between two Muslim-populated states), but because the precise meaning of "Islam" (and specifically *Iranian* Shi'a Islam) was in a constant state of flux. Moreover, the interpretation of Islam as a factor of foreign policy varies, especially since Iran emphasizes Shi'a Islam, which can be more inimical with other Muslim sects than with non-Muslims. Also, Shi'a Islamic identity is often emphasized in Iran as a uniquely Iranian form of Islam and as a way of severing ties to the Arab-centric mainstream Islam. Perhaps the best way to observe this is to assess the process of Islamization which occurred as a reaction to the Pahlavi regime in the revolution's aftermath. Just as the Pahlavi regime was perceived as overtly secular, even laical in its approach to both domestic and foreign policy, so the revolutionary elite sought to emphasize in their policies everything that they perceived as having been rejected by the Shah. Principally, this entailed an intense injection of Islamic rhetoric into all policy discussions, non-alignment in the international arena, and, as with previous revolutions, a commitment to the oppressed and generally unenlightened of the world. This apparent transformation of Iranian policy from a secular to a religious worldview was confirmed both by Western policy analysts—anxious, as noted above, to inject a sense of irrationality into Iranian behavior—and traumatized emigres whose tales of chaos and fanaticism added fuel to the burgeoning fire.[16] The image of the Islamic Republic of Iran as a fundamentalist state—erratic, anarchic, and possessed of a dangerous tendency toward martyrdom that had been forged in the intense heat of revolution—has embedded itself within the Western mind-set and has become a staple of Western popular discourse.

For all its relevance—especially to the early period of the revolution—this revolutionary myth provides only part of the picture, and indeed, as one noted commentator has argued, "For all its apparent exceptionalism, the Iranian Revolution of 1979 followed, in many respects, the pattern of other modern revolutions."[17] Indeed, as Fred Halliday argues, for all the vaunted expressions of Islamic solidarity, there was much in the rhetoric (and actions) of the revolution which drew on anti-imperialism and left-wing ideologies.[18] The behavior of the Iranian state should have been recognized as revolutionary rather than as conveniently irrational and could arguably be better understood as having been drawn from different traditions of logic than from those of the West. Put simply, their interests were defined by different priorities, although even these priorities revealed more continuity with the last decade of Pahlavi rule than would at first appear. The notion of "neither east nor west" first entered official government discourse during the premiership of Iranian Prime Minister Amir Abbas Hoveyda in 1970 when he was attempting to explain the unique nature of the White Revolution (subsequently renamed the Shah-People Revolution).[19] Similarly, the official designation of casualties as martyrs, was not a novelty introduced at the time of the Islamic Revolution.[20]

Nevertheless, one should not underestimate the role of religious conviction in driving the actions of the early revolutionaries. Having successfully overthrown what many considered to be an omnipotent Shah and humiliated his powerful patrons, an empowered generation of idealized Iranian youth felt that there was very little that they could not achieve. But a recognition of this righteous revolutionary fervor should not preclude an appreciation of the internal logic of many of their actions or indeed that other rationalizations had an input in the decision-making process. The seizure of the U.S. embassy on November 4, 1979, is regarded with some justification by observers as a supreme act of political folly rather than one of immediate political expediency that was supported by the embattled authorities, not only because of the perception that a foreign victory was essential if domestic anarchy was to be avoided, but also by the widespread (and cultivated) fear that the United States, after having admitted the ailing Shah for medical treatment (a reality viewed with suspicion), was preparing for a rerun of the 1953 coup orchestrated against Iranian Premier Dr. Mohammad Mosaddeq.

In other words, an act of illegality was justified and rationalized on the basis of a collective historical memory. Indeed, while many Iranians, soon to be preoccupied by other problems, considered the hostage crisis a detail of history justified by U.S. support for the Shah, it was for the American collective memory to be the definitive moment which was to define U.S. attitudes toward Iran and belie the neorealist fiction that U.S. material interests devoid of cultural (historical) determinants drove

U.S. foreign policy toward Iran. Hawks on both sides, for instance, found it convenient to forget that diplomatic ties between the United States and Iran had not been severed with the overthrow of the Shah; that many thought the transition, while tense and undoubtedly antagonistic, could be managed; and that indeed the first occupation of the U.S. embassy in February 1979 had ended on the express authority of the Ayatollah Rouhollah Khomeini, who clearly did not interpret such an action as either legal or expedient.[21]

Similarly, the war against Iraq could not have been fought without a high level of religious fervor, and veterans testify that religious conviction played an important role in rationalizing the suffering that many undoubtedly endured. Yet the harsh experience of war is arguably the ultimate test of any ideological drive, and it was soon apparent that faith alone could not win the war against Iraq. The war clearly tempered the ideology, but it could not eliminate all its excesses; strategy was arguably sacrificed to the needs of mobilization, which dictated the continuation of grandiose rhetoric over the realities of military possibility. Thus, in order to excite the masses to war, the government portrayed it as a new Islamic conquest, although significantly with Iranians rather than Arabs in the lead role.[22] Still, the government was forced to use both religious and overtly national slogans (such as the call to defend the Holy Fatherland[23]), recognizing the need to draw on the other constituent cultures, while the necessities of war forced a review of a number of religious injunctions and their consequent modernization.

Two significant events in particular reveal the limits of culture in this period, although their consequences indicate the complexity of the reciprocal relationship between the notion of material interests and cultural interests in determining foreign policy. The first was the Iran-Contra Affair, the revelations of which probably caused more shock in the United States than in Iran, but an event which revealed a good deal more ruthless calculation in the pursuit of foreign policy. Suffering under the constraints of an arms embargo, Islamic Iran saw no contradiction in placing its immediate material interests over the dictates of revolutionary principle and purchasing arms from the United States via Israel. While the precise mechanics of the negotiations remain shrouded in secrecy, it seems highly unlikely that such an operation would have been initiated without the tacit approval of Ayatollah Khomeini. Similarly, for all of U.S. President Ronald Reagan's subsequent amnesia, his claim of being unaware of the generalities (if not the details) of this covert operation lacks credibility. That it proved disturbing to many Americans highlighted the gulf between the continuing *Realpolitik* of senior policymakers (who saw clear material gains in reaching out to Iran), and the attitudes of the U.S. public weaned on the memory of the hostage crisis. The lessons that each state derived from the experience were, however, diametrically opposed. Iranian politicians, epitomized by then Speaker of Parliament, Ali Akbar Hashemi Rafsanjani, became convinced that a ruthless realism dictated U.S. policy, and that culture was a secondary issue. U.S. policymakers, on the other hand, burnt by the public humiliation of failure, reasoned that culture could no longer be ignored.

Indeed, the realities of war resulted in one of Ayatollah Khomeini's more remarkable speeches, which, as with the Iran-Contra Affair, was both enormously significant and divergently interpreted. In January 1988, in a response to a somewhat verbose and meandering speech by then President Ali Khamene'i concerning the legal powers and prerogatives and Islamic Government, Ayatollah Khomein'i outlined the following striking injunction:

> I should state that the government which is part of the absolute vice-regency of the Prophet of God ... is one of the primary injunctions of Islam and has priority over all other secondary injunctions, even prayers, fasting, and hajj ... the ruler is authorised to demolish a mosque or a house which is the path of a road and to compensate the owner for his house. The ruler can close down mosques if need be, or can even demolish a mosque which is the source of harm if its harm cannot be remedied without demolition. The government is empowered to unilaterally revoke any Shariah agreements which it has concluded with the people when those agreements are contrary to the *interests* of the country or of Islam. It can also prevent any devotional or non-devotional affair if it is opposed to the *interests* of Islam and for so long as it is so."[24]

Khomeini seemed to be signalling in no uncertain terms that the interests of the state should have priority over Islamic law, and though controversial, the Muslim ruler could either overturn or suspend Islamic injunctions (or both), if the interests of the state were threatened. This was certainly the way the interpretation was understood by Ali Akbar Hashemi Rafsanjani, who, with an eye on the presidency, regarded Khomeini's comments as official religious sanction for the politics of pragmatism that he had hoped to emphasize.[25] Indeed, for Rafsanjani and his supporters, the decree was a blow to those reactionary conservatives whose stubborn adherence to dogmatism was adversely affecting the functioning of the Islamic Republic. The conservatives, however, interpreted Khomeini's comments in a radically different direction, noting the primacy of the Islamic State and the use of the term absolute vice-regent. Khomeini, they argued, was not enjoining the people to place the state above religion. On the contrary, he was forcefully arguing for the suspension of all restrictions if the interests of the *Islamic* state were threatened. The definition of interest was therefore very much beholden to one's understanding of the state, and each side adhered to a different logic. Not surprisingly, Khomeini practiced the ambiguity that he preached, showing characteristic pragmatism in making the decision to reverse years of official government policy and accept in 1988 the UN-sponsored cease-fire in the war against Iraq; he followed this with a dramatic *fatwa* condemning the British writer Salman Rushdie to death for allegedly insulting the Prophet Mohammad and, by extension, committing apostasy. If religion had its limits, so, quite clearly, had pragmatism.

National culture

If the first decade of the revolution can be characterized as the era of confrontation and counter-hegemony, in terms of identifying and reaffirming a cultural space between the West and Islamic Iran, the period of Rafsanjani's presidency—the era of reconstruction beginning in 1989—as the new president was to define it, sought to replace confrontation with mutually beneficial interest. Put another way, if the emphasis had been on the religious aspects of nationalism, Rafsanjani now sought to redress the imbalance by appealing to overtly national sentiment and justifying policies on the grounds of national interest. Indeed, the new president sought to present himself as nothing if not pragmatic with a keen eye on specifically national matters, although his interests were driven not only by a desire to leave a legacy of reconstruction, but, more importantly, by the search for commercial advantage. Rafsanjani was the merchant president with a strong populist streak, and he sought to drive reconstruction by cultivating the interests and expanding the opportunities for the mercantile bourgeoisie (as epitomized in his own person), whom he regarded as his quintessential constituency and the driving force behind reconstruction. Economic reconstruction, of course, required better relations with the outside world, and Rafsanjani seemed certain that mutual material interest would prevail over any cultural differences. Even disagreements with the United States would be overcome by the overwhelming temptations offered by economic advantage. After all, it was noted, the United States enjoyed buoyant economic relations with a host of countries with whom it shared little cultural affinity or indeed, which held completely contrary values. In fact, Rafsanjani's administration arguably heralded a return to high *Realpolitik* in its understanding of international relations (although his administration singularly refused to recognize the reality of Iran's modest position within the international system), and a number of international relations institutes were inaugurated and staffed with eager academics, most of whom had been educated in the United States and were devotees of the school of pragmatism.[26]

One of the ways in which this renewed affectation for pragmatism made itself felt was through a gradual reassertion of national interest.[27] Of course, the nation had never really gone away. The revolution, for all its Islamic rhetoric and pretensions about the unity of the *umma*,[28] had at its core a nationalist imperative that was reflected in the composition of the new constitution. Thus, for example, Khomeini himself instructed that all elected officials had to have been born in Iran.[29] Furthermore, in broad cultural terms, while there was every attempt to wipe away the excesses of the last Shah, the revolutionary administration did not attempt to substitute the Islamic calendar that is in common use in most Muslim-populated states in the world for the calendar introduced in 1924 under Reza Khan (who became Reza Shah Pahlavi in 1925), complete with months named after Persian mythological figures.[30] The onset of war, of course, simply confirmed this trend,[31] and after the war, the importance of the nation to Iranian identity could not be easily ignored. Rafsanjani actively played the patriotic card[32] in order to mobilize an exhausted population toward reconstruction and, above all, to attract investment—not only from the business elites within the country, but especially from the many thousands who had left the country. Regional changes were also forcing a reconception of policy, especially when the collapse of the Soviet Union reignited the "Great Game" in Central Asia and the Caucasus. The Islamic Republic suddenly found itself handicapped by its overt Shiism, while in contrast, Persian culture was very much in demand. Indeed, as some Central Asian states rediscovered their Persian cultural heritage with some enthusiasm,[33] as well as with a healthy dose of diplomatic tact,[34] Iran's national reticence seemed curiously out of place; some commentators argued for a vigorously nationalistic agenda in Central Asia, demanding that the two treaties of Gulestan (1813) and Turkmenchai (1829), through which Tsarist Russia had annexed Iran's Caucasian territories, be discarded as irrelevant. Such language was calculated to appeal to national emotions, since most Iranians were taught that Iran's great power status had been ended by these treaties. Even traditionally conservative newspapers were hard-pressed to disguise their nationalist indignation, with *Keyhan International* arguing that these states had suffered a mere "seventy years of artificial separation."[35] Consequently, it was not long before the national economic and cultural interests were being pursued.[36] At the same time, national zealotry was tempered by the new pragmatism that had been reinforced by the dramatic crushing of Iraq in the 1991 Gulf War. Iran's military vulnerability was apparent to all but the most ideologically committed.[37] A more consensual, cooperative, and constructive foreign policy was encouraged, with priorities firmly fixed on economic reconstruction.

Unfortunately, the enthusiasm which greeted the Rafsanjani administration, by both a domestic constituency exhausted by revolution and war and an international business community intrigued by the apparent opening up of Iran, was to be misplaced. Fundamental to the failure was the inability of the two business communities to connect. Rafsanjani, with his crude understanding of interest had believed that capital and commercial advantage would be sufficient to bridge the cultural gap. Quite apart from the fact that the Iranian mercantile community could not relate to the industrial capitalists of the West, the Iranian administration had clearly misunderstood the cultural dimensions of Western foreign policymaking. It was not enough to be counter-hegemonic and nonconfrontational; the West could not be enticed by economic interest alone. The double humiliation of the hostage crisis and the Iran-Contra Affair had hardened U.S. attitudes, while the Rushdie affair, increasingly regarded by Iranian officials as a trivial irrelevancy, had developed into a point of principle among Western elites. The cultural context was simply against the Islamic Republic, such that no major Western politician was prepared to take the domestic political risks.

In the aftermath of the Iran-Contra scandal and with threats of an investigation into the October Surprise, President George H. W. Bush simply was not going to risk his election prospects by responding positively to Rafsanjani's measures to encourage Hizbollah to free the Western hostages in Beirut. For the Iranians, this lack of response was taken as a sign of continuing bad faith. Other problems, however, compounded this situation. While Rafsanjani attempted to signal a more moderate Iranian position toward the Arab-Israeli conflict, continued hardline rhetoric, especially from Supreme Leader Ayatollah Khamene'i, continued support for Palestinian and Lebanese militants, in particular Hizbollah,[38] and an explicit policy of opposition to the Middle East peace process (which of course played well among ordinary Arabs, although increasingly less so with the Iranian population itself)[39], all served to make the bridge unsustainable. Any hopes Iran had for cooperation with Europe were rudely dashed when it became apparent that even economically pragmatic Europe could not ignore the fact that Iranian dissidents were being murdered by the Iranian regime on European territory.[40] Again, the differences in attitudes were striking; some Iranian officials simply could not understand why an internal matter (the elimination of dissidents) should affect inter-state relations. The final nail in the coffin of this brief foray into pragmatism came in 1995, when the Iranian government authorized the awarding of an oil contract to Conoco, a U.S. company. As far as post-revolutionary Iran was concerned, this was an unprecedented and bold move that would provide the ultimate test for the realist theory of international relations. It proved to be a dramatic failure, and rather than help forge a consensus through interest, the dramatic declaration of extensive formal sanctions, along with secondary sanctions targeted against those companies seeking to invest in Iran's oil industry,[41] reversed any progress that might have been made and thrust U.S.-Iranian relations into their worst crisis since the seizure of the U.S. Embassy sixteen years earlier.

Western culture

The Conoco affair and its consequences marked the definitive end to a policy which was already coming under intense criticism within Iran, for the simple reason that many people considered the inherent, ideological antagonism to the West not only to be counterproductive and against Iran's interests, but in contradiction to Iran's own complex identity. Just as Rafsanjani had sought to build his foreign policy on a network of vested economic interests, so too had he sought to construct such a network domestically—and arguably with considerably more success. Those outside this loop—the vast majority of the population—were not impressed with Rafsanjani's economic policy, and the gross disparities in wealth that it seemed to encourage. They were even less impressed with the apparent alliance of convenience Rafsanjani had developed with hardline conservatives, which had not only hampered Iran's foreign relations but seemed to belie Rafsanjani's nationalist credentials. The hardliners, as noted above, drew a much more authoritarian interpretation from Khomeini's remarks about the interests of the state, and in the face of the apparent failure of pragmatism, saw the salvation of the Islamic state in the vigorous pursuit of such policies. Yet for many people, such policies seemed to contradict nationalist pretensions, since to be a genuine Iranian nationalist, it was argued, one had to appreciate and respect the will of the Iranian people; in sum you had to be a democrat (at least by inclination). Hard-line conservatives dismissed this notion as nothing less than the pollution of authentic Islam by Western ideas. What mattered was the Islamic State, in which sovereignty belonged to Allah and his divinely appointed and absolute vice-regent, in this case the Supreme Leader Ali Khamene'i. There was no place for a republic in the Islamic world view.[42]

Herein lies the most intriguing and much misunderstood aspect of Iran's civilizational identity: its relationship with the West. For Iran's foreign policy over the last quarter-century, in the very least, can be said to have been shaped and defined by the way in which its politicians have sought to navigate this relationship, in particular its relationship with the United States. As has been noted, for all the anti-imperialist rhetoric, Iran's relations with the West remained curiously ambivalent for most of the first year of the revolution. While governments may have been roundly criticized, individual Westerners visiting Iran discovered very little personal animosity.[43] On the contrary, there seemed to be an element of confusion insofar as many Iranians coveted (and continue to covet) visas for Western countries. The seizure of the U.S. embassy, however, changed the entire dynamic, and as one revolutionary leader noted with some irony, the United States was not only back at the top of the agenda, but became *the* priority for the revolution. Indeed, for all the success of the practical eviction, the Islamic Republic now found itself defined against the very foe it had sought to remove.[44] Arguably, it was the beginning of a mutual obsession.[45] The point to be made, and regularly overlooked, is that whether as friend or foe, Iran enjoyed an intimate relationship with the West and its epitome, the United States. The counter-hegemony that it had sought to construct was defined and hence related to the hegemonic challenge posed by the West.

The practical lessons of the war and the era of reconstruction encouraged Iranian intellectuals to rethink their understanding of the philosophy of international relations which would also help resolve some of the many contradictions which continued in the Iranian worldview.[46] For a civilization that aimed to contrast itself with that of the West, it was striking how much it had borrowed from the West; starting with the concept of a republic. Since Ayatollah Khomeini had been insistent on the use of the term, the desire to dismiss it on the part of conservatives proved to be problematic.[47] Furthermore, it was quite clear that many of the revolution's highest officials had been educated in the West and felt none the worse for it, while more interestingly, the *narrative* of revolution which was being constructed (by mullah and layman alike), sought to situate Iran's Islamic Revolution within a historical pedigree of revolutionary movements that were sourced to the French Revolution and essentially European. No event better encapsulated this moment than President Khatami's visit to the Pantheon in Paris and his evocation of French Enlightenment philosopher Montesquieu. The intellectual consequence of all this was that hegemonies could neither be considered distinctive and inherently confrontational nor could they necessarily be conceived of as distinct but collaborative where mutual interest dictated; rather, the relationship was far more integrated and intimate than either party would like to admit. History provided ample evidence: Islam (Persia) and the West (Christendom) were after all sister civilizations, and the Islamic Republic was (in theory at least) the living embodiment of this ideal. Such were the ideas encapsulated by Soroush's argument and implicit in the introduction of the policy of "dialogue of civilizations."

The concept of a dialogue of civilizations, formally introduced by President Khatami during a speech to the Islamic Conference Organization, then being held in Tehran in December 1997, was more than a diplomatic response to Samuel Huntington's *Clash of Civilizations* thesis.[48] It reflected more than a decade of intellectual inquiry within Iran on the nature of politics, its extension into the international arena, and represented a serious and genuine attempt to bridge the cultural gap.[49] Simultaneously in the domestic sphere, intellectuals were moving away from the absolutism of religious dogma toward a more interpretative framework in which diverse ideas were shown to be part of a related, integrated whole, rather than distinctive antagonisms: so too did this reflect Iran's more nuanced approach to its international relations. It was no longer simply a conjunction of interests, one now had to understand and relate to the Other, and this was to be achieved through dialogue, understood as a means of intellectual communication. In other words, "we must understand the peculiarities of our era and treat Western civilization as our era's ultimate manifestation and symbol. This means understanding the values and tenets of Western civilization."[50] In arguing for knowledge as a social construction, Khatami was shifting the emphasis from structure to meaning, and since the "West" was part of Iran's cultural heritage, there was no philosophical reason why Iranians could not come to know and relate to it. Indeed, Khatami's appreciation of the concept of dialogue was itself a product of his understanding of the Western, especially German, philosophical tradition, in particular Jurgen Habermas.[51] For a dialogue to be productive, it had to take place between intellectual equals, and it seemed as if Khatami felt that by 1998, Iranian intellectual life had developed enough to make this a realistic possibility.[52] The most intriguing aspect of this intellectual dialogue was the search for cultural common ground between the United States and Iran, and it was found in the most unlikely of places: the relationship between religion and democracy. Some twenty years after the Islamic Revolution, a cultural synthesis that could bridge the apparent antagonisms of a generation appeared to be at hand. President Khatami stated:

> This civilization ... is best described by the renowned French sociologist Alexis de Tocqueville who spent 18 months in the USA in the 19th century and wrote the valuable book entitled "Democracy in America." I hope most Americans have read this book, which reflects the virtuous and human side of this civilization. In his view, the significance of this civilization is in the fact that liberty found religion as a cradle for its growth and religion found the protection of liberty as its divine calling. Therefore in America, liberty and faith never clashed, and as we see, even today

most Americans are religious peoples. There is less war against religion in America. Therefore the approach to religion, which was the foundation of Anglo-American civilization, relies on the principle that religion and liberty are consistent and compatible. I believe that if humanity is looking for happiness, it should combine religious spirituality with the virtues of liberty."[53]

Conclusion: a monologue of civilizations?

This paper has argued for the centrality of culture and civilizational identity to the formation of foreign policy, while at the same time indicating the limitations of these cultural factors and the importance of material experience in defining cultural parameters. The concept of culture must clearly be understood as heterogenous and multi-faceted, and while three distinct characteristics have been the focus of this paper, they should not be considered as exclusive. Policy is defined through the interaction of competing cultures and their interpretations of experience, providing the logic through which interests are rationalized and prioritized. In a multicultural polity such as Iran, this can often result in a contradictory experience at different levels of policymaking, a reality which can make any constructive international response problematic. This is not a circumstance unique to Iran, but given its geopolitical situation and the plurality of its revolutionary politics, the mechanics of policymaking are both relatively more visible and immensely consequential.

At the same time, Iran shows quite well the difficulties in demarcating between material interest and culture and the ways in which different arguments may be brought to bear to justify a single policy. In accordance with Iran's diverse inheritance, it is not, for instance, unusual to see policies legitimized in diverse, apparently contradictory ways. For example, Iran's support of Hizbollah in Lebanon is frequently raised as an example of Islamic fraternity, while its seeming disinterest in the plight of the Chechens or, more interestingly, the Tajiks, is assumed to show the primacy of national interest. Yet, it can be shown, and is indeed argued, that support for Hizbollah has less to do with cultural loyalties and more with the realities of a grand strategy of bolstering Iran's role as an important regional power in the Middle East. At the same time, neither justification is proving satisfactory in convincing an increasingly skeptical and anti-Arab leaning population.[54] A similar logic has been expressed by some officials with respect to the 2003 war in Iraq. Here, the complexity of Iran's three cultures comes into its own, while also indicating the dynamic relationship between interest and cultural determinants. On the one hand, its Western sympathies have been expressed by the unprecedented popular support for the war against Saddam Hussein among the Iranian population, mirrored by the sympathetic approach to the U.S.-led coalition afforded by the Iranian government. While there was a clear affinity among some Iranians with Iraq's Shi'a, there was little sympathy as a whole for the Baathist state (defined broadly), and some Iranians went so far as to ascribe their own difficulties with the interference of "Iraqis" in Iranian politics (the key figure here was the Head of the Judiciary, Ayatollah Shahrudi, who many Iranians called 'al-Shahrudi' to emphasise his Arabness). On the other hand, some hard-liners sought to justify broad Muslim sympathies on the basis of national interest, in that as a part of the "axis of evil," Iran had an interest in preventing the United States from achieving stability in Iraq. This view would certainly not have carried any weight had U.S. policy since September 11, 2001, not turned definitively antagonistic and confrontational toward Iran. Indeed, the absence of an avenue for engagement of any sort has reduced the room for maneuvering among Iranian politicians, who are finding the logic of adopting a hard-line posture difficult to resist on grounds of religious, national, or, indeed, material interest.

Here, the importance of symmetry and reciprocity in international relations should be apparent. It has been argued that cultures are not limited by national boundaries producing distinct hegemonies, but on the contrary, enjoy an international dimension which is both reciprocal and dialectical. The distinction between the "rational" Self and the "irrational" Other is unsustainable. While the balance of reciprocity remains to be defined and would clearly depend on the relationship being addressed, it would be fair to assume that the West will remain the dominant partner.[55] It is the principle of reciprocity which needs to be acknowledged. At the beginning of the Islamic Revolution, Iran's idealistic revolutionaries sought to construct a counter-hegemony which would ostensibly protect them from being "corrupted" by the West. Any form of dialogue was regarded as dangerous and the emphasis lay with confrontation. The onset of the war with Iraq provided practical fuel to this conception; while it remains a powerful influence in some quarters of Iranian political life, it was superseded in the aftermath of war by the pragmatism of cooperation defined through mutual interest. The cult of religious martyrdom gave way to the culture of national self-sacrifice, but this soon descended into the dogma of personal interest. Foreign policy was in many ways an extension of these domestic developments. Yet it was quite clear that these in turn were being influenced by the international arena (specifically the West), and Khatami's success on the international stage can largely be put down to his recognition of this reciprocity and his willingness to work within it. Khatami's logic and his understanding of regional politics dictated that, in redefining the cultural parameters of an international relationship, the particularities of an antagonism could in time be overcome.[56] The danger was that, in failing to tackle the details, these details would paradoxically undermine the grand strategy of cultural integration which was being pursued, especially if the proposed international partner has chosen a decidedly different path. Cultural dialogue obviously requires an interlocutor and must suffer as a credible option in its absence, providing succor for those who would seek to reinstate the culture of confrontation.[57]

It remains a supreme and distinctly cruel irony that 2001, the year designated by the United Nations at the suggestion of the Iranian President to be that of "Dialogue of Civilizations," should have been marked by one of the most dramatic acts of terrorism to be committed against the West. Official messages of support and commiseration, along with widespread public sympathy for the United States among ordinary Iranians, showed how far the environment had changed from 1979—and to what extent the Islamic Republic was willing to work with (and in some cases within) U.S. hegemony. For the United States, however, dialogue was no longer a politically acceptable option domestically. A generation after the Islamic Revolution, the United States had rediscovered Iran's revolutionary credentials. Comprehending without being comprehended by others, a new political culture was rationalizing a new worldview with different priorities and a radical interpretation of U.S. interests. Indeed, as the war on terrorism extended toward the war on Iraq, justified through a doctrine of pre-emptive idealism, and the United States castigated its critics for placing material interest over principle, it appeared as if culture, which never really had gone away, had returned with a vengeance.

Notes

1 President Mohammad Khatami's speech to Iranian expatriates in New York, September 20, 1998, in BBC SWB ME/3339 MED/1–2, dated September 23, 1998.

2 See for example, Nikki R. Keddie, "Can Revolutions be predicted?" in Nikki R. Keddie, ed., *Iran and the Muslim World: Resistance and Revolution* (London: Macmillan, 1995), pp. 13–33.

3 The phrase "island of stability" had been a staple of Iranian foreign policy rhetoric for some years. However, it is most memorably associated with President Jimmy Carter's speech on the occasion of his New Year's Eve visit to Iran on December 31, 1977; For highlights of the speech, see James A. Bill, *The Eagle and the Lion: the Tragedy of American-Iranian Relations* (New Haven, Conn.: Yale University Press, 1988), p. 233.

4 Such reactions to revolution were not without precedent; see Alexis de Tocqueville, *The Old Regime and the Revolution*, Vol. 1, François Furet and Françoise Melonio, eds., Alan S. Kahan, trans. (Chicago: University of Chicago Press, 1998), p. 95.

5 Since September 11, 2001, numerous texts have emerged to try and explain the curious cultural inheritance of "Muslims," building on and arguably misreading Samuel Huntington's *The Clash of Civilizations and the Remaking of the World Order* (London: Simon and Schuster, 1996). At one end of the spectrum are the contributions of Bernard Lewis in *What Went Wrong?* (London: Phoenix, 2002), pp. 200, while at the other are offerings such as Oriana Fallaci's *Rage and the Pride* (New York: Rizzoli, 2002), p. 187, a work which discards any pretense to scholarly analysis. For an extremely useful antidote to such arguments, see Dale F. Eickelman and James P. Piscatori, *Muslim Politics* (Princeton, N.J.: Princeton University Press, 1996).

6 See, for example, Huntington, *Clash of Civilizations*, p. 43.

7 See Max Weber, *The Protestant Ethic and the Spirit of Capitalism* (London: Routledge, 1992), p. 183.

8 Gholam R. Afkhami, *The Iranian Revolution: Thanatos on a National Scale* (Washington, D.C.: The Middle East Institute, 1985), p. 4. One should never forget that initial interpretations of the Islamic Revolution among Western observers derived much of its information from the "victims" rather than the "victors."

9 The Iranians, however, with a surfeit of manpower over technology, were doing no different than the Soviets during the "Great Patriotic War" (1941–1945).

10 The Iranian population is composed of a variety of different ethnic groups, including Persians, Azerbaijanis, Turkmen, Arabs, and Kurds, and while their integration has been facilitated through education and the modern mass media, differences undoubtedly persist. For details, see John W. Limbert, *Iran: At War with History;* (London: Croom Helm, 1987), pp. 19–28; and Brenda Shaffer, *Borders and Brethren: Iran and the*

Challenge of Azerbaijani Identity (Cambridge, Mass.: MIT Press, 2002). It should be stressed that this paper relates to *ethnie* as fluid constructs; see Max Weber, *Economy & Society*, Vol. I, (London: University of California Press, 1978), pp. 387–393.

11 For further details see Chantal Mouffe, "Hegemony and Ideology in Gramsci", in Chantal Mouffe, ed., *Gramsci & Marxist Theory* (London: Routledge and Kegan Paul, 1979), pp. 168–204.

12 Arnold J. Toynbee, *A Study of History*, Vol. I (Oxford: Oxford University Press, 1934), p. 72, note 2. Toynbee explains his categorization thus: "'Iranic' is less cumbrous than 'Perso-Turkish,' and it is not really less accurate. 'Perso-Turkish' expresses the fact that most of the peoples in the original home of this society spoke either Persian or Turkish vernaculars (as one might coin the name 'Latino-Teutonic' to express a corresponding fact about Western Christendom). 'Iranic,' however, expresses the more significant fact that the vehicle of the new culture which was emerging in this region was the classical language and literature of Iran."

13 This view, which includes its own "myth of origin," was probably best expressed by President Khatami in his speech to Iranian expatriates in the United States in September 1998, when he referred to the mythology and "spirit" of Iran (see note 1 above); BBC SWB ME/3339 MED/1–2, dated September 23, 1998. For the localization of religion, see Anthony D. Smith, *The Ethnic Origins of Nations* (London: Blackwell, 1986), pp. 105–125. For an extreme example of this trend, see Houshang Tale, *Tarikhcheh-ye Maktab-e Pan-Iranism* (The history of the doctrine of Pan-Iranism), (Tehran: Samarkand, 1381/2002)

14 Abdolkarim Soroush, "The Three Cultures," in Mahmoud Sadri and Ahmad Sadri, trans., *Reason, Freedom, and Democracy in Islam* (Oxford: Oxford University Press), p. 156.

15 Ibid, p. 162.

16 It is worth noting that de Tocqueville considered the universalist pretensions of the French Revolution to qualify it as a "religious" revolution; Alexis de Tocqueville, *The Ancien Regime and The French Revolution* (Manchester: Fontana, 1966), p. 41.

17 Fred Halliday, *Revolution and World Politics* (London: Macmillan, 1999), p. 124.

18 See also Ervand Abrahamian, "Fundamentalism or Populism?" in Ervand Abrahamian, ed., *Khomeinism* (London: I. B. Tauris, 1993), pp. 13–38.

19 BBC SWB ME/3562/D/1, dated December 27, 1970—Hoveida's speech to the Central Committee of the Iran Novin Party, dated December 15, 1970. See also BBC SWB ME/3568/D/1, dated December 28, 1970—Hoveida's statement to Iran Novin Party meeting, dated December 22, 1970. The *Islamic* revolution was in many ways following a well-trodden tradition in modern Iranian politics.

20 See, for example, FO 248 1494, file 101/5, Summary of *Mardum*, File No. 1015/87/50, dated August 19, 1950; FO 371 180804 EP 1942/6, dated April 12, 1965; *Rastakhiz*, 6th Bahman 2535/1355 / January 22, 1977, p. 1.

21 BBC SWB ME/6043/A/14, February 15, 1979—"Developments in Iran," Tehran Home Service, February 14, 1979. Also, BBC SWB ME/6044/A/4—"Developments in Iran," Tehran Home Service, February 14, 1979. The U.S. embassy was not the only embassy to be occupied during the year; both the Moroccan and British embassies had suffered the same fate, and the fact that all occupations had been ended arguably led to a sense of complacency on November 4.

22 The belief in some circles that the Iranians were the heirs of true Islam (i.e., Iranian Shi'a Islam) could of course be supported by selected *hadith* of the Prophet.

23 The parallels with Soviet policy in World War II are striking.

24 BBC SWB ME/0043 A/7, January 8, 1988; Tehran Home Service, January 7, 1988. Emphasis added.

25 See BBC SWB ME/0043 A/8, January 8, 1988; Tehran Home Service, dated January 7, 1988.

26 This attempt to out-intellectualize and out-rationalize the West often took some striking turns. For example, one of the key proponents of this movement, Mohammad Javad Larijani, could offer the following assessment of the Islamic Republic: "While an Islamic society is not at ease with technical rationality, it finds itself quite in harmony with the authentic one. Therefore, Islamic modernity goes far beyond historical modernity and is basically a post-modern phenomenon." "Islamic Society & Modernism," in *The Iranian Journal for International Affairs*, Vol. 7, No. 1 (Spring 1995), p. 58. See also the editorial in the *Tehran Times*, February 23, 1993, which boldly proclaimed now to be the time for "realism."

27 See, for example, Hossein Seifzadeh, *Estrateji-ye Melli va Siyasatgozari-ye khareji* (National Strategy and Foreign Policy-Making), *The Journal of Foreign Policy*, Vol. 7, (Winter 1994), pp. 705–722.

28 The *umma* is the greater nation of all believing Muslims.

29 Vanessa Martin, *Creating an Islamic State: Khomeini and the Making of a New Iran* (London: I. B. Tauris, 2000) p. 166; see also David Menashri, *Iran: A Decade of Revolution and War* (London: Holmes and Meier, 1990) p. 120.

30 See Marvin Zonis, *Majestic Failure: The Fall of the Shah* (London: The University of Chicago Press, 1991), pp. 81–83.

31 Significantly, "Persian" names were already dominating over "Islamic" names among newborn babies as early as 1982; see Nader Habibi, "Popularity of Islamic and Persian Names in Iran before and after the Islamic Revolution," *International Journal of Middle East Studies*, Vol. 24 (1992), pp. 253–260.

32 For example, he was the first post-revolutionary leader to pay a visit to Persepolis in April 1991. For further details of this process, see Shireen T. Hunter, *Iran after Khomeini* (New York: Center for Strategic and International Studies, 1992), pp. 92–100.

33 President Rafsanjani, for example, made a point of noting in his New Year speech of March 1992 that Novruz was now being celebrated throughout Central Asia; see BBC SWB ME/1336 A/3–6, March 23, 1992, Vision of the Islamic Republic of Iran, March 20, 1992. For broader discussions see Farhard Kazemi and Zohreh Ajdari, "Ethnicity, Identity and Politics: Central Asia and Azerbaijan between Iran and Turkey," and Shireen T. Hunter, "Iran and Transcaucasia in the Post-Soviet Era," both in David Menashri, ed., *Central Asia Meets the Middle East* (London: Frank Cass, 1998), pp. 52–73, 98–128.

34 Initially, even Azerbaijani officials would proclaim their affection for Iran when diplomatic necessity required it; see Tamelan Karayev's comments on his visit to Iran in BBC SWB ME/1302 A/9, February 12, 1992, Voice of the Islamic Republic of Iran, February 9, 1992.

35 See BBC SWB ME 1334 A/10–11, dated May 26, 1993, IRNA, May 24, 1993.

36 See, for example, Edmund Herzig, *The New Caucasus: Armenia, Azerbaijan and Georgia* (London: RIIA, 1999), p. 111. Also Eric Hooglund, "Iran and Central Asia," in Anoushiravan Ehteshami, ed., *From the Gulf to Central Asia* (Exeter: University of Exeter Press, 1994), pp. 114–128.

37 It is difficult of course to distinguish between the religious and nationalist dimensions of commitment, and certainly in Iran's case, a combination of the two is better suited with any distinction resulting from emphasis.

38 These groups were referred to as resistance fighters in Iran, and, of course, as terrorists by the United States. While support for Hizbollah, in large part because of the Shii affiliation, has remained consistent and popular, support for extreme Palestinian groups has enjoyed less popularity among ordinary Iranians and is occasionally justified on the purely *Realpolitik* grounds of antagonizing and ensuring the preoccupation of Israel. Interestingly, this is a view increasingly used to justify support for Hizbollah—that it has less to do with religious affiliation and more with a need to maintain a "deterrence" against Israel.

39 The Iranian government was in the habit of holding alternative Palestinian conferences at times calculated to irritate the United States, for example in October 1991; BBC SWB ME/1193 A6–7, dated October 3, 1991, IRNA report October 1, 1991.

40 Relations were especially soured by the Mykonos trial, in which Iranian officials were convicted in Germany for the murder of dissidents at the Mykonos restaurant in Berlin. See David Menashri, *Post-Revolutionary Politics in Iran* (London: Frank Cass, 2001), pp. 103, 201–202.

41 For extensive detail of the sanctions policy, see Hossein Alikhani, *Sanctioning Iran: Anatomy of a Failed Policy* (London: I. B. Tauris, 2000).

42 For an excellent critique of this authoritarian tendency, see Abdollah Nuri, *Shokoran-e Eslah* (Hemlock of Reform), (Tehran: Tar-e No, 1378/1999–2000), pp. 117–121; see also Mohsen Kadivar, *Baha-ye Azadi: defaat Mohsen Kadivar* (The Price of Freedom: the Defence of Mohsen Kadivar), (Tehran: Ghazal, 1378/1999–2000).

43 See, for example, John Simpson, *Strange Places, Questionable People* (London: Pan, 1999), pp. 219–220.

44 Discussions about the merits of relations with the United States were a staple of Iranian political life. See, for example, *Iran Focus*, June 1990, p. 1, which notes that factional fighting over the issue of direct talks with the United States were (yet again) gaining momentum. Note that this is before the Iraqi invasion of Kuwait. See also BBC SWB ME/1698 A/4, May 26, 1993, IRNA, May 24, 1993, during the presidential elections of that year.

45 On the Iranian side, this obsession was reflected in the print media and books; see for example, *Rabeteh?! (Relations?!) Salam*, Teheran, 1378/1999; *Nowruz*, 19 Ordibehesht 1381 / May 9, 2002, p. 5; many articles of course dealt with the coup against Mosaddeq; *Khordad* 28 Mordad 1378 / August 19, 1999 p. 6; *Neshat*, 28 Mordad 1378 / August 19, 1999, pp. 8–9; *Jameeh*, 28 Mordad 1377 / August 19, 1998, p. 6.

46 See, for example, the interesting article by Mohammad Reza Dehshiri "*Charkhe-ye Armangerayi va Vaghegerayi dar siyasat-e khareji-e Jomhuri-ye Islami-ye Iran*" (Idealism and Realism Cycle in the Foreign Policy of the Islamic Republic of Iran), *The Journal of Foreign Policy*, Vol. 15 (Summer 2001), pp. 369–397.

47 See Mehdi Karrubi's comments in *Salam*, 24 Aban 1376 / November 15, 1997, p. 1–2.

48 Such misreading was not limited to foreign observers. Many Iranian international relations specialists also viewed this move as simple pragmatic policy; see for example, the special issue of the Foreign Ministry's "Foreign Policy" journal, *Siyasat-e Khareji*, Vol. 12 (Summer 1998). The articles tend to focus on rebutting Huntington, discussing the notion of "civilization," or both.

49 It also reflected Iran's sense of its own identity; while President Khatami may talk of *Islamic* civilization, the evidence suggested a tendency toward *Iranian Islamic* civilization, in which "Islam," if referred to at all, was very much a junior partner.

50 Mohammad Khatami, "Observations on an Information World," in Mohammad Khatami, ed., *Islam, Liberty and Development*, Hossein Kamaly, trans., (Binghamton, N.Y.: Institute of Global Cultural Studies, Binghamton University, 1998), pp. 130–131. The speech was originally delivered in 1995.

51 Habermas visited Iran in May 2002, delivering a series of lectures and receiving a rapturous welcome from students as well as, significantly, a visit from a delegation of mullahs; *Nowruz*, 19 Ordibehesht 1381 / May 9, 2002, p. 9; *Nowruz*, 25 Ordibehesht 1381 / May 15, 2002, p. 1.

52 This sense of intellectual inadequacy in the face of Western civilization was well expressed by Mojtahed Shabestari, quoted in Mehrzad Boroujerdi, *Iranian Intellectuals and the West: the Tormented Triumph of Nativism* (New York: Syracuse University Press, 1996), p. 168

53 President Khatami, interviewed on CNN, BBC SWB ME/3210 MED/2, January 9, 1998, Iranian TV, January 8, 1998.

54 When Special Police were placed on the streets of many Iranian cities in the summer of 2002, they were widely interpreted as "Arab mercenaries," a nice twist on the "Israeli mercenaries," which the Shah was meant to have imported into Iran to quell the revolution.

55 Reciprocity, however, is altering our conception of the "West," such that some philosophers now talk of the "decline of the West."

56 Iranian officials never tire of repeating, for example, that Iran's nuclear program had been initiated under the Shah with considerable support from the West, while it must be conceded that some U.S. allies in the region are certainly more active in the pursuit of weapons of mass destruction support for "Islamic terror," and consequent interference in the "Peace Process."

57 See, for example, Knut Royce and Timothy M. Phelps, "Secret Talks with Iranians," *Newsday*, August 8, 2003.

55

CULTURAL TRANSMUTATIONS

The dialectics of globalization in contemporary Iran

Ali M. Ansari

Source: T. Dodge and R. Higgott (eds) *Globalization and the Middle East: Islam, Economy, Society and Politics*, London: RIIA, 2002, pp. 132–48.

> ... if you speak to a student of theology about your concerns over the ideal society, he might say "I have heard about globalization from one of my friends. It is a prelude to the reappearance of Imam Mahdi (May God hasten his reappearance). Therefore we must welcome this development."[1]

Introduction

Globalization is a term that may be fairly characterized as 'essentially contested'. It is a term that has gained wide currency not only in social science literature but also in the media, through which it has embedded itself in popular discourse. This popularity, of course, almost ensures a wide variety of interpretations and an ambiguity that tends to hinder rather than help its productive application. Thus, there are many who dismiss the concept as a convenient cloak intended to disguise and in some cases justify the continuous expansion of Western values and economic modes of production throughout the globe. Others reject the concept altogether, pointing to the realities of localization and particularization, and argue that the world is less unified today within a global political or economic system than it was in the nineteenth century, at the height of European imperialism. Yet arguably, it is the very fractures in the post-colonial global order that have assisted the development of the complex dynamic now defined as 'globalization'. Indeed, drawing on the transformationalist thesis I shall argue that what distinguishes the process of globalization from that of imperialism, which preceded it, is the reciprocal and dialectical nature of this process at work. Where advances in military technology once assisted the formation of European empires which imposed a particular cultural vision on the world, contemporary advances in media technologies are providing the 'weak' with a means to gain access to the developed world and to appropriate and in a very real sense reciprocate cultural transmissions.

Although there can be little doubt that in economic terms the global initiative lies with the West, the impact of cultural globalization is much more nuanced and complex, and it is on this aspect of globalization that this chapter will focus. This is not to argue that the West does not dominate the transmission of cultural norms throughout the globe but simply to point out that the reception and appreciation of these norms varies enormously and that in some cases a process of reciprocation is beginning.[2] One place where this process may be witnessed is the Islamic Republic of Iran. At first sight Iran seems an unlikely subject in which to explore the appropriation and reciprocation of cultural globalization, given the widespread assumption that it has somehow managed to isolate itself from the world. Yet observers have already noted the apparent impact of globalization not just in the field of economics – Iran has already applied to join the World Trade Organization – but also, and most interestingly, in the cultural sphere. Travellers to Iran are often shocked at the level of Western cultural penetration, especially among the country's youth, and hold this up as a prime example of the inexorable march of globalization. Yet in their haste to characterize and justify a process, they fail to appreciate the complex dynamic at work.

Islamic revolution and globalization

For many in Iran, the Islamic revolution of 1979 was essentially an act of national resistance to a particular type of globalization, in this case Americanization.[3] That the shah had to be overthrown was almost incidental to this process of cultural retrenchment and assertion. He was widely seen as the prime vehicle for the process of Americanization, and therefore he had to be removed.[4] The Islamic revolution can therefore be characterized as ideological and cultural in determination and counter-hegemonic in construction. All aspects of Americanization had to be rooted out, however brutal the consequences of this policy might be, and replaced with an authentic culture that was both Islamic and Iranian.

Two factors made this policy of cultural retrenchment difficult to accomplish. First, there was the reality of Iran's international situation and technological changes that had increasingly penetrated its cultural defences. For all the genuine, if misplaced, efforts to 'purify' the country, it was clear to the new government that international relations had to continue and that trade commitments had to be honoured. Thus although the war with Iraq (1980–88) fostered a sense of isolation and self-reliance, military needs necessitated contacts with the outside world. If anything, the Western arms embargo ensured that Iran had to pursue links to countries it had hitherto had negligible contact with in order to broaden its supply base. In this sense, therefore, Iran was far from isolated in the 1980s. These contacts were developed and expanded in the aftermath of the war. An example of this was Iran's trading links with Europe. They developed to such an extent that it soon became apparent that the protestations of European countries anxious to internationalize the human rights agenda could not be ignored. Iran's response, which in many ways foreshadowed its reaction to globalization, was to appropriate and reinterpret the agenda in terms of *Islamic* human rights.

The attempted universalization of these ideas was, of course, not new. The pursuit of a human rights agenda had, after all, done much to undermine the authority of the last shah and had given encouragement to his opponents. Yet the intensity of cultural transmission – the mode of global interaction – had now changed. This was in large part because of the advent of new technology, which made the control of information much more difficult. But, in addition, one must not neglect the consequences of massive emigration in the aftermath of revolution and war, which ensured that most Iranian families had a relative in an at least one major international city. It is estimated that at least two million Iranians have emigrated, mainly to the West, since 1979, although the figure could be considerably higher if second-generation Iranians are included in these statistics. These migrants have not only justified and, to some extent, excused the vastly increased use of international networks of communication but also facilitated the transmission of cultural ideas. Moreover, their presence abroad has often encouraged further travel by relatives in Iran, which again increases cultural interaction. This trend more than compensates for the comparative lack of Iranian students studying abroad since 1979. At its peak the number reached 75,000, of whom 50,000 studied in the United States.[5] Students remain an important source of cultural transmission, but the proportion going overseas is now much smaller, and their destinations are much more diverse.

Technology is the key determinant that has allowed these geographically diverse but culturally affiliated communities to maintain contact with one other. Although the Islamic Republic has sought to prevent 'cultural pollution' through its rhetorical battle against the 'onslaught', its practical means of control have been less than effective. The needs of trade and international interaction rapidly predominated over the desire to maintain cultural isolation, and it also became increasingly impractical to monitor the use of electronic media of cultural exchange. Initially, one had to hold a licence in order to operate a fax machine. This injunction was swiftly ignored, found to be impossible to monitor and subsequently abandoned. Next came the video machine, whose use was rapidly endorsed when what was widely known became officially apparent: that many members of the *ulama* (the Shia clergy in Iran) were in possession of the machines, ostensibly to watch reruns of Ayatollah Khomeini's speeches! After fax machines and videos came the debate over the use of satellite dishes, regarded by many in authority as the most powerful tool of cultural imperialism. Having failed so dramatically to prevent the use of faxes and videos, the government took an initial attitude to satellite dishes that was ambivalent and non-committal, with the result that many people acquired the dishes. There were even instances of poorer communities clubbing together to purchase the equipment, and it was widely believed that some government agencies were actively involved in their procurement and distribution. Nevertheless, conservative elements within the clerical hierarchy ensured that eventually the

Majlis ratified a formal ban. This did not have the desired effect: several years on, satellite dishes still exist in abundance throughout the country.[6]

This failure has been well reflected by the determination to promote and encourage the use of the Internet. All political factions use the Internet, to acquire and also to disseminate information. Attempts have occasionally been made to shut down undesirable sites, but there has been no concerted effort, as, for example, in China, to control what appears on the servers. On the contrary, Internet cafés have mushroomed, especially in Tehran, and provide the country's youth with immediate access to a world of information. The Internet has provided a means of access to dissident ayatollahs under house arrest, and also a tool for a press corps under severe pressure. Iranian students established their own news-wire service in response to the mass closure of the country's newspapers in April 2000.[7]

The second significant factor working against cultural isolation was (and is) the determination and, arguably, the inexorable logic of the revolution to export its ideas. Those promoting both 'Iran' and 'Islam' have been universalist in their pretensions. Although this fact is often ignored or dismissed by Western analysts,[8] it is a historical reality that begs reassessment. Iran or 'Persia', to use the culturally more palatable term, has always sought to disseminate its ideas regionally and internationally. Commentators are often struck by how Iranian communities abroad, while eager to adapt, have at the same time stubbornly retained a high level of cultural homogeneity that they have sought in turn to impart (if not impose) on others. A major aspect of this 'cultural imperialism' has been in the field of religious ideas, with Islam forming the second universalizing element. In fact Islam shares with Christianity an evangelizing and total vision of the world that is absent from other major religions. It is this tendency that has made it the fastest-growing religion in the world. Combine both Iran and Islam and one has a highly intense and determined motor for the globalization of an ideal. In the early days of the revolution this was appreciated, if wilfully misinterpreted in the West, to suit political needs, in the fear of a 'fundamentalist wave' overturning regimes in the Middle East. When the impact of Iranian ideas seemed to be wholly negative, they appeared to be a very real threat to the stability of the region. Latterly, as the revolution has matured and its ideas have become more nuanced and complex, it is curious how this transmission of ideas has suddenly become irrelevant and unrealistic.

For Iran, however, the dissemination of its ideas continues to be a central aspect of its cultural and revolutionary heritage. Thus it has appropriated the means of dissemination and transmission with considerable enthusiasm, including the development of a satellite television network and, most of all, the use of the Internet. Iran's appreciation of the technological revolution and its response to it was well expressed by President Khatami in 1995, when he was the head of the National Library:

> In its contemporary, complex forms, information technology represents
> one of the highest achievements of modern culture which uses its control

over information to solidify its domination of the world. Thus, inquiry into the nature of the information world is inseparable from uncovering the nature of modern civilisation itself. And until we address this important question we will not be able to muster the confidence and wisdom to understand our relationship to modem civilisation. Otherwise, we will live in a world whose rules have been set by others, at the mercy of circumstance, not as masters of our fate ...

... This does not mean that we must isolate ourselves from the Western-dominated information world. Such a thing is undesirable and practically impossible as the global reach of information constantly expands. Awareness of today's world events is an imperative for understanding our place in the world and planning our future in it. Being isolated from the world's information networks can only turn us into pawns of others because it is they who control the flow of this vital and strategic resource.[9]

The reformist world-view

When Khatami was elected president in 1997, his chief of staff Hojjat-ol-Islam Abtahi pointed out that Iran now had a chief executive who knew Iran and, importantly, understood Iran's place in the world. Khatami, while symbolic of the reformist tendency in Iran, also reflected it, and in many ways he was the political manifestation of an intellectual renaissance that had captivated the Iranian intelligentsia and youth over the previous decade. This renaissance was itself a product of the fractures in authoritarian rule that had emerged after the revolution and the experience of war. They encouraged people to be more critical of their relationship with the state, and also to re-evaluate Iran's relationship with the global order. Indeed the war with Iraq and the devastation it caused, both materially and psychologically, was a major factor in forcing intellectual reflection. The somewhat simplistic (if reassuring) notions of revolutionary fervour were increasingly questioned and challenged. Although some continued to cling tenaciously to notions of cultural purity and glorious isolation, others, including some senior ayatollahs, were acutely aware that Iran was not an island which could be easily quarantined and that some form of engagement was needed.[10] It was argued that Iran could not resist globalizing trends, even if they were characterized as a 'cultural onslaught'. Instead, the country had to accommodate, appropriate and respond. Interestingly, it was understood that for this to occur, there first had to be a fuller appreciation of 'Western culture'. This movement took its cue from Khomeini himself, who had taught aspects of Western philosophy, if only to show their inadequacy. Of even greater influence was the chief ideologue of the Islamic revolution, Ayatollah Motahhari, who had explicitly referred to Marx and Engels in unusually sympathetic terms as thinkers who, although clearly incorrect in their conclusions, had at least tried to *do* something about the nature of the world.

Many Iranian intellectuals, including clerics, decided to immerse themselves in the Western intellectual tradition. Some seminaries even took the decision to send their students abroad.[11] Cultural globalization was, in this respect, not so much imposed on Iran as fully endorsed but then transformed by it.

This was not, of course, an uncritical immersion. It was, on the contrary, a strategy for inclusion. Rather than be the object of globalization, as many would have argued was the case during the time of the shah, the new Islamic Republic wanted to *participate*. In order to participate, it had to learn and to integrate itself in the international intellectual community. This view was well expressed by the noted clerical intellectual Mojtahed Shabestari as far back as 1988:

> The fact that our seminaries have separated their path from that of the social sciences and are minding their own business without any awareness of the developments in these disciplines has brought us to the present condition in which we have no philosophy of civil rights or philosophy of ethics. [Furthermore] we have neither a political nor an economic philosophy. Without having a set of solid and defendable theories in these fields, how can we talk of universal or permanent laws and values? How can we [even] gain admission to the international scientific communities?[12]

By gaining 'admission', Iranian intellectuals hoped to understand and appropriate Western ideas and to refashion them in a manner suitable to Iranian culture. By internalizing global cultural norms, these ideas could then be re-exported, both regionally and internationally. An interesting case study of this process in operation is that of the appropriation of democratic values. Not only have Iranian intellectuals sought to reinterpret 'democracy' within the context of Islam, they have also offered a challenge to the normative ideas of democratic development, which rely heavily on a particular conception of secularism. This is, to be sure, the beginning of a challenge, but there is little indication that ideas of 'religious democracy' have as yet impacted on the global (Western-defined) consciousness. It remains an interesting challenge nonetheless, and given the religious roots of the Western intellectual tradition, it may yet fall on fertile ground.

In the same manner, although for different reasons, Iranian culture has proved to be remarkably receptive to the ideology if not the practice of democracy. For the better part of a century, and largely through the infusion of ideas from the West, Iranian intellectuals have sought to limit the powers of the shahs and to implement some form of elective constitutional government. Although these ideas have in the main been the province of a limited circle of intellectuals, the advent of mass media communication has allowed their dissemination to a much wider section of society. Several historical periods have witnessed a particularly vibrant press culture, and the low level of literacy did not prevent the transmission of ideas through group readings.[13] But far more influential in the preparation of the popular consciousness was the development and use of the radio, which did not depend on literacy. Mass political movements such as the National Front during the oil nationalization crisis (1951–3) lent further popular credence to the idea of an accountable elected government. That this did not materialize did not extinguish the idea. Nor did it prevent Mohammad Reza Shah from paying lip service to expressions of democracy, such as in the retention of a parliament and senate. The Islamic revolution itself was in part the heir of a growing democratic tradition, and it was expected to fulfil its promise in this respect. Certainly the constitution, which was ratified in 1979, contained enough assertions of democratic intent to lead some justifiably to believe that this would indeed be the case.

This belief was sustained through the early years of the revolution and war, when to all intents and purposes it appeared that anarchy had facilitated the reestablishment of authoritarian government. Certainly there were those who were anxious to rid the revolution of any democratic tendency and impose a particularly harsh interpretation of authoritarian Islam. Unsurprisingly, these groups were the most enthusiastic about maintaining the purity of the revolution and defending against any sort of cultural penetration. They were unable, however, to silence fully their critics, who continued to maintain that the state was an Islamic *republic* and therefore had to fulfil its popular as well as its Islamic character. Indeed, the republican element of the constitution and the title of the post-revolutionary Iranian state proved to be extremely difficult for conservative authoritarians to deal with; they complained that despite Ayatollah Khomeini's clear sanction of the term, it was wholly imported and possessed no Islamic pedigree.[14] Such were the difficulties that some of the more extreme elements sought to dispense with the term 'republic' altogether and argued for an 'Islamic State' over an 'Islamic Republic'.

In terms of cultural authenticity, if not political justice, there was much to commend their argument. It was indeed curious that this term should have entered the Iranian political lexicon at a time when cultural retrenchment and isolation seemed to predominate, and it should have served notice that even at this time, Iran was not immune to cultural penetration. Nevertheless, by the late 1980s and the early 1990s an intellectual debate began to emerge over the direction of the Islamic Republic and, in particular, over the precise nature of its republican content. In order to authenticate and legitimize this consequence of cultural globalization, some Iranian thinkers decided to redefine the boundaries of East and West in such a way as to make the latter a part of the inheritance of the former. Thus the first step in cultural appropriation and reinterpretation was the 'Iranianization' and, to some extent, the 'Islamization' of Western discourse, removing the exclusive subject–object dichotomy and replacing it with an inclusive tradition applicable and belonging to all. Arguably, by localizing the idea of 'republic' they accelerated its internationalization and global penetration. Central to this process was the Iranian lay religious philosopher Abdolkarim Soroush.

Soroush: the forging of an intellectual synthesis

Soroush, like many Iranian intellectuals, had absorbed many ideas from the Western intellectual tradition and had sought to reconcile them with those he had inherited. A student of the philosophy of science at London University, Soroush was influenced by the writings of such diverse thinkers as Karl Popper and Thomas Kuhn.[15] On his return to Iran, his first important task after the Islamic Revolution was the deconstruction and de-legitimization of what may be termed 'vulgar' Marxist doctrine as espoused by the various left-wing secular political groups that were then active in Iran, in particular the Communist Tudeh Party. This intellectual encounter was to have a lasting influence on Soroush's political views, and left him with a suspicion and dislike of what he considered 'monopolistic', insular and exclusive ideologies, which to all intents and purposes seemed to stifle the progress of knowledge. He recognized that these closed ideologies were predicated on assumptions that had achieved the status of doctrine and that such doctrine could be undermined only if one challenged and deconstructed those root beliefs.

After the successful intellectual deconstruction of the secular left in Iran, Soroush turned his sights on the increasingly authoritarian and dogmatic religious right, which in his view harboured similar monopolistic and exclusive tendencies. He was struck by the extent to which this group relied on constant antagonism with an apparently monopolistic and exclusive Western 'cultural onslaught'. The parallels between the intellectual construction of the religious right and secular left were striking. Each sought to impose a world vision on the other and each resolutely rejected, effectively in absolute terms, the admonitions of the other. This was a 'clash' in a very real sense, and even if one succeeded in imposing its will on the other, it had already forfeited its social and cultural legitimacy. The solution, according to Soroush and his supporters, was to integrate existing traditions in a new inclusive intellectual discourse that would not only facilitate the legitimate penetration of Iranian culture by Western ideas (a reality his critics were quick to point out) but also allow a degree of counter-penetration. His first task was to challenge the notion of a unified, impenetrable 'West': 'Where do you draw the boundaries of the West? Is this moral decline present where-ever there is the West, or where-ever there is the West is there moral decline? Should we know the "Western spirit" based on the West or should we distinguish the "West" from the "Western spirit"?'[16]

Developing this argument further, Soroush added that far from being positioned in contradiction to Western culture, Iranian (and Islamic) civilization had in fact contributed to it, and therefore was a legitimate heir. 'We Iranian Muslims are the inheritors and carriers of three cultures at once. As long as we ignore our links with the elements in our triple cultural heritage and our cultural geography, constructive social and cultural action will elude us ... The three cultures that form our common heritage are of national, religious, and Western origins.'[17] This view was echoed by President Khatami in his speech to the Islamic Conference Organization in December 1997 on the issue of an 'Islamic civil society':

> The civil society which we seek to establish in our country – and would also like to recommend to other Muslim countries – is fundamentally different to the civil society born out of Greek classical philosophy and the Roman Empire's political heritage; that is to say a civil society which has passed through the Middle Ages and has now gained its special identity in the modern world. However, the two concepts of civil society should not necessarily contradict each other as far as their manifestations and outcomes are concerned. For this reason, we should never downplay the importance of learning – without imitating and copying – from the positive achievements of Western civil society.[18]

In short, the very ambiguity of cultural boundaries made globalization and its political scion democratization a legitimate process. This legitimation was enhanced by a process of deconstruction and synthesis by which Soroush also sought to challenge and undermine Western assumptions about development as generally summarized within the 'modernization thesis'.[19] This thesis argued in robust terms that development was predicated on the secularization of society and the elimination of religion as a social and political force. Soroush understood that this thesis was unlikely to endear its conception of modernity to its critics in the Muslim world in general and Iran in particular. Inclusivity could be achieved and globalization encouraged only if the relationship between East and West were redefined, and this could be achieved only if the 'West' were understood in terms familiar to the East. This process had already begun with the study of Western philosophy and a greater appreciation of those philosophers who were considered 'religious' in their orientation. In a dialectical response to globalization, Soroush, among others, sought to remind the West of its religious roots and the spiritual foundations of its social and political structures. 'Secularism' was redefined in much more ambiguous terms. For Soroush, exclusivist definitions were incorrect. He endorsed 'secularism' insofar as the rigorous scientific questioning it fostered reinvigorated religious thought. Thus:

> The notion that the new world gradually rids itself of religion is only half true. It is true insofar as the modern world condemns ignorant and vulgar religiosity to extinction. However, it also shows a different kind of religiosity, a learned and examined religion, to prosper on a higher level. Scientific treatment of political and economic affairs does in no sense preclude a well-defined role for God and religion in political, social and natural affairs. Determining the limits of that role and the exact form of that relationship remains to be worked out by scholars. The least we can say in this respect is that religiosity, or the lack thereof, do[es] not enter

the essence of government. However, as an external reality, government is subordinate to society and constitutes one of its forms of realisation. If a society is religious, its government too will take on a religious hue.[20]

Religious democracy was therefore not absent from the West, contrary to popular assertions; its existence depended on the will of society. Echoing views held by Muslim scholars over the past two centuries, Iranian intellectuals pointed to the continuous use of religious imagery, symbolism and justifications by 'secular' Western democracies and asked why the use of Islamic justifications within political discourse should, in contrast, be interpreted as backward. Was not (in theory at least) the United Kingdom, with its established Church and its monarch as 'Defender of the Faith', a Christian democracy?

Far more telling, and with no little irony, was the model of religious democracy used by Iranian intellectuals to show how a religious society would be reflected in government – the United States. It was in the United States that Iranian intellectuals found evidence of the compatibility between religion and democracy, a point stated quite categorically by President Khatami in his interview with CNN in January 1998, when he drew attention to the writings of Alexis de Tocqueville.[21] In legitimizing the use of Western ideas in Iran, Soroush and other like-minded thinkers were of course involved in a far more reciprocal process insofar as they drew attention to the ambiguities in Western thought. While this reciprocation might have been slight, President Khatami's use of the international media to highlight his views reflected globalization in action. In its possession of a large portion of the world's means of mass communication, the West is not only the largest producer of knowledge but arguably also its greatest consumer. President Khatami, in appearing on CNN, was able to gain access to a far greater proportion of the American population than any of his predecessors, and although it is difficult to ascertain the precise reception of his views, there were reports that sales of de Tocqueville's *Democracy in America* had indeed received a boost following his comment that he hoped all Americans had read the book.

The impact of this aspect of cultural globalization on Iranian political life has been much easier to evaluate. There is little doubt that in legitimizing the argument for greater democratization, Soroush and other thinkers have encouraged its indigenous development. As what is essentially a product of Western political thought has been localized, the pursuit of democratization becomes culturally valid, and Iranian thinkers and political activists have pursued it with some determination. Although the visual, and arguably superficial, aspects of global culture have caught the imagination of foreign observers, it is in the field of intellectual appropriation and political mobilization that the profundity of cultural globalization becomes truly apparent. A popular appreciation of 'Madonna & McDonald's' may indeed have penetrated youth culture in Iran, although significantly, for all its imitators, an 'authentic' McDonald's restaurant has yet to be granted permission to open; and 'Madonna & McDonald's' may reflect the palpable weakness of central government to contain the influx of cultural icons from abroad. But these icons are a symptom rather than a cause of the real impact of Western political philosophies and activism. The impact is, again, one of degree. It is generally recognized that student activism against the Vietnam war in the 1960s and 1970s and the student activism that galvanized France in 1968 had a profound influence on a generation of Iranian students, who later sought to emulate their predecessors by seizing the American embassy in Tehran in 1979.

The political activism which accompanied the rise of President Khatami has been similarly influential, and on a hitherto unprecedented scale.[22] Student numbers had increased dramatically, nearly tenfold, in the two decades since the Islamic revolution. And the means by which students could communicate with one another and the outside world had also improved exponentially. Besides the fax machine, students could now use both the Internet and the mobile phone, and it is significant that during the widespread student demonstrations which gripped the country in July 1999, one of the first moves of the authorities was to switch off the mobile phone network, through which student 'cells' had been communicating and coordinating. The Internet and other computing facilities such as desktop publishing allowed students to produce their own literature much more easily and to disseminate it more widely and with much greater rapidity. Technology was facilitating the growth of civil society and undermining the pillars of the authoritarian state.

It is also increasingly clear that technology is facilitating the absorption and appropriation of ideas from abroad. Iran's resistance to intellectual property rights, a major aspect of legal globalization, has allowed the speedy reproduction of knowledge. Books and articles are read avidly, translated and reprinted in the Persian language, providing a broader reading public access to the great philosophical and political discourses of the West. It is true, of course, that the writings of Nietzche, Marx and Weber are unlikely to have been read or indeed understood by the wider public. But it is remarkable how well-embedded the ideas of these writers (among others) have become among the literate and intellectual public and how these people in turn have sought to disseminate them in an accessible manner through the organs of the mass media.[23] That some Western commentators have criticized the interpretation of these thinkers in Iran misses the point entirely. There can be no single reading of these large and complex texts. In order to make them relevant to Iran's historical experience, they must be interpreted in the light of relevant events. In order to be truly globalized, they must first be localized and particularized; and this, as noted above, was well understood by Iranian intellectuals. Encouraged by thinkers such as Soroush, Iranian students and activists saw no contradiction in adapting the democratic theories, along with the symbolic values, of the West for their own purposes. It has become commonplace, for instance, for the authoritarian right to be described as 'fascists', a term that has no intellectual pedigree in the Iranian political tradition. More particularly, the investigative journalist Akbar Ganji has drawn from Arendt's *Banality of Evil* in order to try to explain the actions of right-wing vigilantes.[24]

105

On a more practical level, Iranians also avidly watched and learned from the experiences of other countries, which were relayed with relative immediacy via the new tools of media technology. Not only were vast events such as the collapse of the Soviet Union and the 'velvet revolutions' of eastern Europe digested with increasing curiosity by Iranians of all political shades, but issues of finer detail were also studied for the lessons they may yield. Students watched the unfolding of political movements in other countries with great interest. The fall of Milosovic was studied carefully, and the differences and similarities with the incumbent regime in Tehran identified, so that lessons could be learned. Both sides of the political divide in Iran drew their own lessons. The Palestinian intifada is an interesting case in point. Iranian state television relentlessly showed pictures of unarmed Palestinians in combat with the might of the Israeli Defence Force, in an effort to show 'Muslim' resistance. However, the message received by Iranians depended very much on their political position. There is little doubt that while activists drew comparisons between themselves and the hapless if heroic Palestinians, the authoritarian establishment drew succour from the apparent reality that 'might' seemed very much to equal 'right'. A similar analogy was drawn from the anti-apartheid struggle. Again the Iranian authorities sought to draw a favourable comparison between their own battle against 'global arrogance' (i.e. the United States) and the anti-apartheid movement. Of course, the manner in which the establishment sought to draw international comparisons and social interpretation often varied dramatically. For conservatives, Iran's struggle with the United States was universalized as part of a wider international contest. For reformists, on the other hand, international struggles were internalized in order to show how the domestic struggle for reform was part of the grand narrative of the unfolding of freedom and consciousness.[25] Both reflected a particular conception and perspective on the process of globalization.

The reformist interest in de Tocqueville's *Democracy in America* has already been noted, but far more specific interest is shown in developments in the United Kingdom, which is regularly held up as a model of political stability. Iranians of all political hues have long enjoyed an essentially schizophrenic relationship with Britain, at once fearful of political manipulation while unashamedly admiring what they perceive to be the astute management of the state by its political establishment. For reformists Britain represents a successful example of a state that has managed a peaceful transition from an authoritarian monarchy to a democracy. For the authoritarians, much more emphasis is placed upon the establishment's ability to maintain its power and traditions, reflected in both the monarchy and the distribution of wealth and, by extension, power. The former concentrate on Britain's ability to manage change while the latter emphasize the continuity. The election victory of New Labour in 1997 and the apparent attack on tradition, symbolized by the reform of the House of Lords, that ensued were therefore viewed with great interest by the reformists and with some dismay by the authoritarian right, which discovered that its source of political reference had begun to shift. These are of course idealized impressions mediated through time and space, and there is clearly an argument for New Labour's avowed support of tradition from which the right in Iran can draw some reassurance. Yet the palpable changes are having an impact. People viewed with great interest the developments in both the David Shayler case and the extradition proceedings against former Chilean president Pinochet. In the former, analogies were drawn with Iran's own intelligence ministry. In the latter, there is little doubt that the Iranian leadership viewed Pinochet's predicament with some consternation. Rafsanjani ceased to be a modern Cardinal Richelieu (see footnote 24) and now became Iran's Pinochet.

Conclusions

The fact that there is a debate on the nature and limits of globalization in contemporary Iran is itself an indication of the reality of the process at work. In intellectual terms at least, it is a development whose recognition and comprehension are central to the Islamic Republic's identification of itself within the global order. Indeed, the political debates that have galvanized Iran over the past two decades can be defined, and understood, from the perspective of the wider emerging debate on the nature of globalization. Thus the Islamic revolution can be understood as a rejection of the 'hyper-globalists', those who believe in a global culture, largely defined by the Western experience, which had to be imitated and adopted wholesale. The subsequent debate between reformists and conservatives similarly can be defined as a struggle between 'transformationalists' and 'sceptics', those who see the development of cultural interaction between Iran and the West and those who reject this process as simply an extension of imperialist subjugation that must be resisted at all costs.[26] While one side seeks to engage and the other to disengage, both want to be active in shaping the future direction of globalization.

Their key battleground is over culture, for in economic and migratory terms the contest would appear to be singularly unequal. Even the 'sceptics' are anxious to utilize fully the growing facility to travel, relocate and, crucially, export capital. (The ease with which money flows out of the Islamic Republic is one of the most significant and most serious problems facing any Iranian government determined to retain as much of the national wealth as possible within its borders and to encourage investment.) In cultural terms the relationship is more nuanced and subtle. Among many in Iran, there is a growing realization that the best way to deal with the process of cultural globalization is to engage with it and seek to reshape it in a manner that is acceptable to the local environment and to some extent beyond. Thus Iranian intellectuals have sought to deconstruct the cultural icons and myths of global culture through a process of absorption, appropriation and synthesis, which arguably facilitates the internalization of global culture while changing it. In this sense, Iran seeks to reiterate its historical role not only as a consumer but also as a producer of cultural norms, and it is this conviction that underpins the development of the concept of the 'dialogue of civilizations'. This reciprocation is in its infancy, but as we move increasingly towards the 'mediasation of modern culture',[27] its potential may yet be realized.

Notes

1 Hojjatoleslam Nabavi, quoted in a roundtable discussion, 'The Effects of Globalization on the Islamic Republic of Iran', *Discourse*, Vol. 2, No. 2, fall 2000, p. 13. See also page 46 above.
2 See J. B. Thompson, *Ideology and Modern Culture* (Cambridge: Polity Press, 1990).
3 Hence the use of the term 'global arrogance' by Iranians lo define the United States.
4 See, for example, M. Reza Behnam, *Cultural Foundations of Iranian Politics* (Salt Lake City: University of Utah Press, 1986).
5 See James A. Bill, *The Eagle and the Lion* (New Haven: Yale University Press, 1988) p. 211.
6 For a detailed analysis, see S. Barraclough, 'Satellite Television in Iran: Prohibition, Imitation and Reform', *Middle Eastern Studies*, Vol. 37, No. 3, July 2001, pp. 25–48.
7 See, for instance, the 'Iranian Students News Association' (ISNA) or the discussion forum of Amir Kabir University: *clubs.yahoo.com\club\akunews*.
8 Consult, for example, D. Held, A. McGrew, D. Goldblatt and J. Perraton, *Global Transformations: Politics, Economics and Culture* (Cambridge: Polity Press, 1999), p. 332. The authors make the curious assertion that while Christianity and Judaism 'have spread their adherents to most corners of the world' and 'Hinduism, Buddhism and Confucianism are all more tightly concentrated in their regional strongholds … Islam occupies a middling position.' Islam's universalizing tendencies are probably more accurately reflected in Huntington's essay on 'The Clash of Civilizations', although his emphasis is somewhat mischievously laid on the antagonistic and conflictual aspects of this process.
9 M. Khatami, 'Observations on the information world', in *Hope and Challenge: The Iranian President Speaks*, trans A. Mafinezam (New York: Binghampton University Press, 1997), pp. 61 and 65.
10 Interview carried out by the author, Tehran, Iran, September 1999.
11 Interview carried out by the author, Shahr-Rey, Iran, July 1997.
12 Quoted in M. Borujerdi, *Iranian Intellectuals and the West* (New York: Syracuse University Press, 1996), p. 168.
13 Note the comments of the British ambassador in Tehran in FO 248 1427, 24 April 1943.
14 See, for example, Mehdi Karrubi's comments in *Salaam*, 24 Aban 1376/15 November 1997, pp. 1–2.
15 For a more detailed exposition and interpretation of Soroush's ideas, see A. M. Ansari, *Iran, Islam and Democracy: The Politics of Managing Change* (London; Royal Institute of International Affairs, 2000), pp. 71–9.
16 Quoted in Borujerdi, *Iranian Intellectuals and the West*, p. 161.
17 A. Soroush, 'The Three Cultures', in A. Sadri and M. Sadri (trans and ed.), *Reason, Freedom and Democracy in Islam* (Oxford: Oxford University Press, 2000) p. 156.
18 BBC Summary of World Broadcasts (SWB), ME/3099 S1/4–9, 11 December 1997 and Iranian Television, 9 December 1997.
19 See N. Keddie, 'Secularism and the State: Towards Clarity and Global Comparison', *New Left Review*, No. 226, 1997, pp. 21–40.
20 A. Soroush, 'The Sense and Essence of Secularism', in Sadri and Sadri (trans and ed.), *Reason, Freedom and Democracy in Islam*, p. 61.
21 See A. Soroush, 'Tolerance and Governance', in Sadri and Sadri (trans, and ed.), *Reason, Freedom and Democracy in Islam*, p. 153; and also President Khatami's interview on CNN, 8 January 1998, BBC SWB ME/3210 MED/2, 9 January 1998. For the relevant passage in de Tocqueville, see his *Democracy in America* [first published in 1835] (London: Everyman Library, 1994), Part I, ch. 17, pp. 300–14 and Part II, ch. 5, p. 22.
22 For the importance of the student movement in Iran, see Ansari, *Iran, Islam and Democracy*, in particular pp. 116–18.

23 See, for example, A. Ganji, *Tarik-khaneh-ye Ashbah* (The Cellar of Phantoms) (Tehran: Tar-e No, 1378/1999), p. 68. The book is a collection of his articles that have appeared in the mainstream press. In this particular article Ganji explicitly discusses Weber's concept of 'charisma' and its possible trajectories into 'patrimonialism' or 'rational/legal' structures.

24 Ibid., pp. 26–8. More metaphorically, and with much more popular success, Ganji has managed to apply the phrase 'His Red Eminence' (an allusion to the 'Machiavellian' Cardinal Richelieu) to Hashemi Rafsanjani. This identification has done Rafsanjani an enormous amount of political damage.

25 See, for example, ibid., pp. 291–301, in which parallels with transitions in apartheid South Africa, eastern Europe and Chile were increasingly drawn.

26 See Held, McGrew, Goldblatt and Perraton, *Global Transformations*, p. 7.

27 Thompson, *Ideology and Modern Culture*, pp. 12–20.

56

UNIVERSALIST
COUNTER-PROJECTIONS

Iranian post-revolutionary foreign policy
and globalization

Henner Fürtig

Source: K. Fullberg-Stolberg, P. Heidrich and E. Schone (eds) *Dissociation and Appropriation: Responses to Globalization in Asia and Africa*, Berlin: Das Arabische Buch, 1999, pp. 53–74.

World-wide fascination with the Iranian Islamic revolution is still alive. Since 1978/79, dozens of academic and journalistic publications have been printed about its course, and its various political, strategic, economic, cultural and religious impacts. The revolution in itself might have attracted many politicians and scholars but – in addition to this – it occurred in one of the most politically sensitive areas of the world.

As is commonly known, the Middle East is one of the cradles of mankind. It has been a source of many civilizational impulses throughout history and is the home of three monotheistic world-religions. As the border area of the three continents of Europe, Asia and Africa it is a traditional cultural bridge, too.

However, it was the establishment of a new global political order after the Second World War and the simultaneously emerging dominance of liquid and gaseous hydrocarbon as the most important source of energy and raw material for the industries of the developed countries, that enabled the Middle East, which possesses more than 60 per cent of this vital raw product, to start playing a key role in global politics. In the emerging East-West conflict, political, economic and military control of the Middle East as well as securing the grip on its most important raw products promised decisive advantages for either the East or the West. External factors such as the massive interference of both global camps coupled with attempts to recruit respective clients among the local elite had thus acquired great significance for the evolution and nature of the sovereignty of the regional states after 1945. In general, their development was decisively impaired and degenerated by this foreign interference.

In this regard, the Persian Gulf region gains special importance since the lion's share of Middle East oil is to be found in that area. Iran is not only one of the biggest countries of the region but also one of its main oil producers. Therefore, to influence the production and marketing of the region's oil, or at least to secure free access to it, the main global competitors concentrated their efforts to control and to lobby that country. These efforts coincided with Iran's own endeavours to gain a dominant position in the Persian Gulf, particularly under the Pahlavi dynasty rule. The hegemonial ambitions of Mohammad Reza Pahlavi were symbolically connected to an American strategy to build up Iran as a corner-stone for securing its own interests in the Gulf area. As a result of this symbiosis, the Islamic revolution of 1978/79 not only liquidated the monarchy in Iran but had a strong anti-Western, namely anti-American approach, too.

It is of little importance whether or not the Iranian revolutionaries knew the word "globalization" when they toppled the Shah. What is important is that they considered the West to be the dominant power in the world and therefore responsible for all the existing injustices, inequalities and misfortunes in international relations. By trying to impose norms of political, economic, military and even cultural behaviour on mankind, the West was suppressing – according to their view – any development in the world that went against its interests.

In his last will and testament, the revolution's leader, Ayatollah Khomeini, wrote in 1983:

> Among the gravest conspiracies ... has been the plot to alienate colonialized countries and make them look to the West ... as their model. So much so that those nations eventually lost their self-esteem and their trust in their own cultures ... (concluding) that their countries could not but become dependent ... More saddening, however, is that the (West has) checked the progress of the nations whom (it) attempt(s) to make consumption-orientated, and install a fear in us of (its) technological advancements and of (its) Satanic power and destroy our self-confidence. This sense of self-nothingness and this feeling of dullness is inculcated in us by the big powers served to make us distrust our own knowledge and expertise and capacity in all areas and let us simply try to imitate the West ... blindfoldedly ... even though (this) might be totally absurd and ridiculous ...[1]

In an interview with the journal of the Revolutionary Guard, Khomeini added:

> (The West) claims that civilisation, science and development are peculiar to (it) and they – especially Western and more recently American – are the 'superior race' while others are of lower races; therefore, their progress is the result of their 'noble race' and these other people's backwardness stems from their being an imperfect race. (They) ... are still on the way to perfection which, after millions of years, will gain proportional

111

perfection; therefore, the effort for our own progress is useless ... In other words, we don't have anything and must beg everything from either East or West, be it science, civilisation, law or development.[2]

The revolution's attempt to interrupt the one-sided dependency on the West meant a tremendous strategic defeat for the United States. For the next ten years at least, American Middle East policy was designed to compensate for the losses inflicted on it by the Iranian revolution. Not only did Iran, with its enormous geographic area, its large population, its material resources and its military strength have to be written off by Washington and the West in a more general sense, but the emerging Islamic Republic of Iran took another – even more surprising – step by evading the East-West formula, i.e. it did not lean towards the Soviet Union and the Warsaw Pact.

On the contrary, it began a specific foreign policy of its own, fighting "Western imperialism" as well as "Eastern communism" while simultaneously propagating an independent "Islamic" foreign policy. At this point at the latest, it becomes clear that the Iranian revolution of 1979/80 was not merely an upheaval against a hated dictator but one of the "great" revolutions of modern times. All fundamental social and political change, be it 1789 in France or 1917 in Russia, has been characterised by universalist efforts and the claim to have set new norms of social, political and cultural behaviour with global validity.[3] It was Crane Brinton, in his classic "The Anatomy of Revolution", who made the pattern that these "great" revolutions "as gospels, as forms of religion ... are all universalist in aspiration" common wisdom.[4]

The lack of change in the regions surrounding Iran was considered a challenge by the revolutionaries. They wanted to bring about the same conditions there as in their own country. Victory over former rulers, seen to be invincible before, seemed to be a "miracle" which was sufficient legitimisation and an incentive to presuppose success not only in the region but in the whole world. Since this "miracle" became reality only after disregarding formerly valid rules and laws, the revolutionaries were convinced that they were legitimised to act beyond the recognised norms of diplomacy and international law when pursuing their political aims. Depending on the type of the respective revolution, it became one of the most important tasks to fight for the international standing of civil liberties, socialism or – in this case – Islam.[5]

Khomeini's universalist aspirations

The Iranian revolutionaries saw themselves duty-bound to explain to every single Muslim that nationalism, socialism, communism and capitalism, all Western imports, had been tried and found wanting. Instead of these Western ideologies, Islam, indigenous and comprehensible to the Muslim masses, literate and illiterate, was shown by Khomeini and his disciples to be a viable belief system, even when opposed by a military formidable monarch supported by a superpower.[6]

According to Iran's revolutionary leader, there was, therefore, only one way left for mankind to escape the negative impacts of Western and Eastern ideological imports, and that was to rely on Islam as the only indigenous worldview not affected and thus not degenerated by Western ideas and thoughts. Only Islam could stop the vicious circle of the formerly oppressed becoming the new oppressors because the eternal laws of Islam are valid for all people.[7] In this sense, Khomeini never changed his credo: "Rely on the culture of Islam, resist Western imitation, and stand on your own feet."[8]

Without doubt, Khomeini felt himself and the Iranian revolution obliged to reintroduce Islam in the sense of Prophet Muhammad, that is as a revelation for the whole world. His universalist approach was at least as total as he thought the West's universalist schemes were. He firmly declared:

The Iranian revolution is not exclusively that of Iran, because Islam does not belong to any particular people. Islam is revealed for mankind and the Muslims, not for Iran … An Islamic movement, therefore, cannot limit itself to any particular country, not even to the Islamic countries; it is the continuation of the revolution by the prophets.[9]

Time and again he emphasised the responsibility of the Iranian Islamic revolution to spread Islam's message.

The Islamic Republic intends to implement the ordinances of the Quran and those of the messenger of God in all countries. Iran is the starting point. It intends to demonstrate to all countries that Islam is based on equality, brotherhood and unity.[10]

Islamic unity

In Khomeini's view, the source of the Muslim world's problems is the estrangement from the divine path of Islam, its adoption of corrupt ways of either the East or the West and its disunity, which is partly due to the intrigues of the Oppressors. Their salvation would be a return to Islam, the establishment of a truly Islamic government and the overcoming of division to achieve unity.

There is no difference between Muslims who speak different languages, for instance the Arabs and the Persians. It is very probable that such problems have been created by those who do not wish the Muslim countries to be united … They create the issues of nationalism, of pan-Iranism, pan-Turkism, and such isms, which are contrary to Islamic doctrines. Their plan is to destroy Islam and Islamic philosophy.[11]

Khomeini, on his part, tried to enforce the unity of all Muslims, making the *umma* the only legitimate concept of Islamic politics. He strongly denied any particular nationalism among Muslims or even Muslim nation states based on language, ethnicity or geography.[12] Thus, in the end, national boundaries would become obsolete in an Islamic society, since Islam would demand the creation of a single state (*yek kešvar-e hamegāni*), uniting all people under one flag and one law.[13] Consequently, the initial years of Iran's post-revolutionary foreign policy were dominated – apart from of Khomeini – by a group of clerical leaders and laymen who considered national borders simply a heritage of colonialism.

In their opinion, the Islamic world used to be united but was later disintegrated by the two aggressive elements of Western culture, i.e. nationalism and colonialism. This led to racial and national hatred between different Muslim nations and overshadowed Islamic cultural values. By espousing the powerful "Islam does not know any borders" concept, they could well justify themselves and legitimise their actions.

The struggle for the unity of the *umma* was therefore laid down in the constitution of the Islamic Republic, too.

> Based on the ordinances of the Quran, that 'Lo! that your community is a united one and I am your Lord, so worship me' (XX:92) the Islamic Republic of Iran is to base its overall policy on the coalition and unity of the Islamic nation. Furthermore it should exert continuous effort until political, economic and cultural unity is realised in the Islamic world.[14]

Article 10 reads:

> All Moslems form a single nation, and the government of the Islamic Republic of Iran has the duty of formulating its general policies with a view to the merging and union of all Moslem peoples, and it must constantly strive to bring about the political, economic and cultural unity of the Islamic world.[15]

The revolution's leader often said that "nobody could defeat one billion Muslims if they were united". Thus, the Muslims and other oppressed groups and nations should cooperate in order to change the global balance of power and to put an end to their subjugation and exploitation.[16]

As mentioned before, in the early days of the revolution the entire Iranian leadership spoke with one voice in this regard. The then Speaker of Parliament, Hojjat ol-Eslam Ali Akbar Hashemi Rafsanjani, declared in a Friday prayer in 1982:

> If the Islamic world would have acted on the basis of Islam and the words of the Prophet, it would be the most powerful force in the world. I don't exaggerate when I say 'the most powerful force' ... Some of you may ask: 'Bigger than America? More powerful than the Soviet Union? Stronger than China?' I say 'Yes!' Right now, we would have been stronger than

China, stronger than the Soviet Union, stronger than America and all their satellites if we only would have been able to establish a global and united Islamic government.[17]

In the early 1980s, it was seen as a betrayal of the revolution to act merely for the benefit of Iran. To work for the domestic development of the country alone would lead to the destruction of revolutionary values and the existing model of the Islamic revolution.

Therefore, continuous aggression against values dominating the existing international system and efforts to overthrow neighbouring regimes were the main objectives of the Iranian leadership. For this purpose it was ready to use military force, guerrilla attacks and intelligence, and to arm the national liberation movements in order to jeopardise "non-Islamic" regimes. It would agree with national development only in the context of creating a series of revolutionary movements in Islamic nations and of threatening the international interests of the Western system.[18]

Export of the revolution

These efforts were summarized in the conception of *sodūr-e enqelāb*, the export of the revolution, which became the overall credo of early post-revolutionary Iranian foreign policy.[19]

> For its part, postrevolutionary Iran saw its neighbours not as independent nation states but as parts of the Islamic world for which the 'Islamic republic' and 'Islamic revolution' had duties in mind which included what others would call 'intervention'.[20]

It was Ayatollah Khomeini once again who was most outspoken in this regard.

> We should try hard to export our revolution to the world. We should set aside the thought that we do not export our revolution, because Islam does not regard various Islamic countries differently and is the supporter of all the oppressed people of the world. On the other hand, all the superpowers and all the powers have risen to destroy us. If we remain in an enclosed environment we shall definitely face defeat.[21]

Khomeini felt the Islamic revolution was obliged to spread its ideas all over the world, to pave the way for the ultimate establishment of an Islamic world order when the Mahdi, the Twelfth Imam, appears.

> We will export our revolution to the four corners of the world because our revolution is Islamic. The struggle will be continued until there is everywhere the call: 'There is no God but God, and Muhammad is his prophet'.

As long as people are being oppressed all over the world our struggle will be continued.[22]

Khomeini repeated these ideas several times, directing them to different audiences, to allow for no misunderstanding. For example, he told a group of Iranian youth before travelling abroad:

> Today we need to strengthen and export Islam everywhere. You need to export Islam to other places, and the same version of Islam which is currently in power in our country, Our way of exporting Islam is through the youth, who go to other countries where a large number of people come to see you and your achievements.[23]

The leader of the Iranian revolution, however, did not assign this task only to the youth but considered it the duty of every Muslim citizen in his country and of all its institutions. Also, according to him, it was not exclusively the responsibility of the Ministry of Foreign Affairs to pursue these political aims. In the early days of the revolution a so-called Liberation Movements Bureau was even assigned to the Ministry to co-ordinate the efforts of exporting the revolution. To increase its importance, the Bureau was soon put under the authority of the Supreme Command of the Revolutionary Guard Corps (*Pāsdārān*). For the Pasdaran, created as a kind of praetorian guard for the clerical regime to counterbalance the uncertain attitude of the regular forces, it became – according to the constitution – one of their most important tasks to fight for the expansion of the rule of the *šarī'a* in the world.[24] Nevertheless, other individuals and organisations also continued their independent efforts to export the revolution by creating their own networks and structures.

In 1984, the Intelligence Ministry established yet another bureau from which to orchestrate Iran's Islamic activity abroad.[25] Because Khomeini's version of the Islamic revolution did not recognise international laws and frontiers, i.e. Islamic peoples were all one, he felt free to use the already existing links between different religious communities across the Muslim world, and to create new ones, to establish a world-wide Islamic network with Iran at its centre. Therefore, these efforts were not only directed at the region around Iran itself but at communities as far away as the Maghreb or even South East Asia, including Indonesia and the Philippines. The policy included all the means of enforcing revolutionary political and ideological ideas – arms, financial support, training, international congresses, propaganda, radio programmes.[26]

Nevertheless, it should also be mentioned that Iran indeed saw itself duty-bound to export the revolution and to support all peoples struggling for independence and freedom but Khomeini also reminded them that "a right is something you have to fight for. The people must rise for themselves and destroy the rule of the superpowers in the world"[27].

But not only revolutionary Islamic idealism drove the Iranian leadership to export the revolution. Pragmatic considerations also led to the conclusion that an utmost level of admiration and influence within the Islamic world might safeguard the young revolutionary state which felt exposed to a variety of internal and external challenges.

For example, the Iranian leadership soon became aware of the economic, political and military weaknesses of its Islamic Republic and had to conclude that the export of the revolution would not be accomplished in one step or within a very short period of time. Furthermore, the response from the Muslim addressees of the export idea was not at all encouraging. This situation added to the further differentiation of the Iranian leadership; a more moderate and pragmatic policy began to take shape. The export of the revolution was to be well balanced between peaceful coexistence and opportunism. In other words, the Islamic Republic was to inflict blows to "puppet and dictatorial states" if national interests required and the situation permitted; if not, it was to continue peaceful relations.

Of course, Ayatollah Khomeini and his followers could not propagate this shift in their politics officially. But they tried to downplay the apparent threat contained in their declamatory policy to export the revolution without, however, disavowing it altogether. In late September 1982, Khomeini for example declared, "by exportation of Islam we mean that Islam be spread everywhere. We have no intention of interfering militarily in any part of the world"[28].

Setting an example

As a modified approach, the Iranian leadership began to propagate that the Islamic Republic of Iran was to set an example for the Muslims of the world to follow instead of actively exporting its revolution. Its mere existence should convince Muslims of their revolutionary responsibility. It should encourage them to follow suit and topple their respective dictatorial, pro-Western and non-Islamic regimes.

At first the revolution should succeed internally, laying the ground for propagating its values and objectives internationally. The success and stabilisation of the Islamic revolution in Iran would inevitably influence other suffering Muslims living in a world of advanced systems of telecommunication. "When we say we want to export our revolution we mean we would like to export this spirituality and enthusiasm we see in Iran ... we have no intention to attack anyone with swords or other arms ..."[29], Khomeini, elaborated.

The attempt to be recognised as a model by the Muslims was not new in itself but it gained momentum as the vision of an immediate export of the Islamic revolution gradually vanished. Right from the early days of the Islamic revolution, Iran had presented itself as the centre of that aspired world-wide drive for Islamic unity, as a model all Muslims should follow, as an alternative to the existing Arab/Islamic regimes.

Mohammad Javad Larijani, Deputy Chairman of the parliament's foreign policy committee, went so far as to even advocate the acceptance of the *velāyat-e faqīh* (rule of the jurisconsult) principle by other Muslims.

> ... we have and have had the velayat, both during the Imam's (Khomeini's) time and during Ayatollah Khamenei's. This velayat is a righteous jurist ruling the entire Islamic nation. Muslims may not even realise that we have such a jurist ruling here, but this does not undermine the reality of this guardianship. Of course, it affects the ruling, jurist's effectiveness, but not the principle. As long as this guardianship exists, the vejayat is responsible for the Islamic world, and it is the duty of the Islamic world to protect the ruling jurist ... As long as our country is the seat of the true ruling jurist, we are responsible for the whole Islamic nation, and the Islamic nation is duty-bound to safeguard the Umm ol-Qura.[30]

In a more general sense, A.N. Memon wrote enthusiastically:

> ... Iran, as an Islamic republic, has inspired numerous Muslims to advocate changes in their own governments. The Iranian Revolution has become a symbol of defiance against the West. Iran has superseded Saudi Arabia as the leading voice among many Muslims seeking an alternative to Western culture.[31]

The former Foreign Minister Velayati even used the word "Mecca" in connection with Iran's revolution to show that the centre of gravity in the Islamic world had shifted to Iran.

> Iran's friends and foes alike perceive Iran as the country that is the centre and Mecca of the aspirations of all Muslims ... Iran is a model for the fifty Islamic countries. This is because the domineering powers have not have very pleasant experiences regarding Iran.[32]

Becoming a source of inspiration and emulation for all Muslims, which was not unattainable in the Middle East and in the Persian Gulf region where Muslims are dominant and politically active, would result in increased political strength and diplomatic manoeuvrability for Iran. The revolutionary Iranian leadership could refer to the many miseries in the Islamic world to gain respect and sympathy. The absolute majority of Muslims around the world, including those in the oil-rich Middle East, live under conditions of economic hardship and/or political oppression. Regardless of the real Iranian influence among Muslims, the revolution had a great impact on them because it supported the anti-status quo posture of the suppressed Muslim majority. Thus its popularity was also a result of the acutely inept economic policies of the existing governments in the region.[33]

However, apart from this and from Iran's assertion that it is the only country in the world where Islam has officially become the foundation of society and government, thus implying that it is the duty of all Muslims to support it, there were other reasons for Muslims to admire the Iranian revolution. Among them were Iran's uncompromising stand with regard to the Palestinian issue and the question of Jerusalem and its strict adherence to an independent and non-aligned foreign policy, both of which have great appeal for many Muslims.

The long shadows of Khomeini's heritage

Once convinced of the much greater usefulness of this more sophisticated policy, Khomeini dropped the more aggressive overtones from the propaganda of the Islamic Republic for the time being. In 1981, he told a group of Iranian ambassadors and chargés d'affaires who had been recalled to Tehran for consultations:

> It does not take swords to export this ideology. The export of ideas by force is no export. We shall have exported Islam only when we have helped Islam and Islamic ethics grow in those countries. This is your responsibility and it is a task which you must fulfil. You should promote this idea by adopting a conduct conducive to the propagation of Islam and by publishing the necessary publications in your countries of assignment. This is a must. You must have publications. You must publish journals. Such journals should be promotive and their contents and pictures should be consistent with the Islamic Republic, so that by proper publicity campaigns you may pave the way for the spread of Islam in those areas.[34]

Thus, other Islamic countries were to get the impression that living under the threat of exporting the Iranian revolution meant books, journals, leaflets, radio and TV commentaries, conferences, mass rallies but not tanks and missiles, not even guerrilla warfare.[35]

After Khomeini's change in propaganda tactics, it was not surprising that other leading functionaries of the Islamic Republic followed this directive, too. The then President of the Republic, Hojjat ol-Eslam Ali Khamenei, while pointing out that "the foundation and the idea of this revolution is not limited to our country and this nation,"[36] stated that

> Foreign Ministry officials are the apostles of the revolution. The nature of an official despatched abroad by a government demonstrates the nature of his government. If our diplomatic representative in all his dealings, including with people and government officials of the country to which he is despatched, adopts an Islamic approach, then he will be utilising the best method to demonstrate the role of the Islamic Republic of Iran.[37]

119

Later, when he was already the ruling Faqih, Khamenei declared on the occasion of the beginning of the Iranian year 1372 (21 March 1993):

> The Islamic Revolution of Iran has taken place and was simultaneously exported throughout the world. The revolution was exported once, and that is the end of the story.[38]

The Iranian Prime Minister of the eighties, Mir-Hossain Mussavi, added:

> We have declared time and again that we have no intention of interfering in other countries' internal affairs, but what is shaking the Islamic world is a movement springing from this revolution among the Moslem masses of the world and, naturally, each people will shape their movement according to their own peculiar circumstances. They will force their governments to tread this path and, if not, naturally they will be confronted by the people's moves.[39]

The influential Hojjat ol-Eslam Rafsanjani, President of the Republic from 1989 to 1997, became active in this regard, too. While agreeing with Khamenei when declaring that "from early on when the revolution succeeded we realised that a revolution is not a phenomenon which would stay limited within one border,"[40] he later specified:

> The phrase 'exporting the revolution', if it is mentioned here, means that we introduce our revolution and (that) anyone who wishes to use our experience can do so. But interference and physically exporting (revolution) has never been our policy.[41]

Voices that legitimised the Iranian concept of exporting the revolution by pointing at the "permanent Western approaches to export its value-system throughout the world," and thus declaring the Iranian efforts a simple counter-measure became a minority.[42]

But it might not have been mere pragmatism which led to this remarkable change in the Iranian policy of exporting the revolution.

> The "reluctance to export the revolution by force of arms has deep roots in the Shia theory of war and peace, which holds that wars to spread Islam can only be waged by the Imams. And since the Shia world has been without an Imam since the Twelfth Imam was occluded, no expansionist wars can be waged."[43]

Trial and error

After the death of Khomeini in June 1989, power was – more or less – shared between President Rafsanjani and the new ruling Faqih, Ali Khamenei. Both had the approval of the late Ayatollah and tried to continue the foreign policy course set by him in the late 1980s. They encouraged further changes in the revolutionary rhetoric. Even more moderate considerations crept in. Khamenei, for instance, repeatedly stated that other nations need not adopt Iran's structures but they should imitate its attitude: steadfast, unyielding, uncompromising, an inflexible spirit in the face of global power and world domination. The new ruling Faqih nevertheless made clear that Iran regarded the defence of all Muslims throughout the world and Islamic sanctities everywhere as among the great tasks of its great mission.[44]

Simultaneously he hastened to declare that he would not deviate from the lines set by Khomeini, insisting that divisions in the Islamic world, as well as deviation from true Islam by some states, were the root cause of failure. Every state that was subservient to the United States and abetted its designs to weaken Islam was a traitor to be eliminated. Khamenei compared the Islamic revolution to "a permanent volcano" and said that the revolution was still alive.

Today's Iranian President, Mohammad Khatami, was cited in 1990 in support of Khamenei: "Today, Islam in the world is primarily defended by the Islamic Republic of Iran under the leadership of Ayatollah Khamenei."[45]

In general, however, after a decade of revolutionary zeal without adequate success, the post-Khomeini leadership started to look for new answers to the burning question of how foreign policy objectives could be achieved. The already mentioned Mohammad Javad Larijani asked:

> Should Iran pursue what it wants through the promotion of national liberation movements in the manner done by the communists or should it engage in plotting coups d'état as was practised by the U.S. or other Western powers? The answer to both options is clearly and forthrightly negative ... our understanding of the Islamic renaissance values its generative potential *within* various countries.[46]

Compared with Khomeini's approach, which envisioned a complete merger of all Muslims within an organic *umma*, this new approach suggested that the Iranian government handle the issue flexibly and be more sensitive to the adverse impacts of this objective. The post-Khomeini foreign policymakers – at least within the government – no longer subscribed to the utopia of a Muslim world without national frontiers. Instead, they advocated more and more Muslim solidarity.

> Theoretically, this reflects a shift from a monist concept of Umma to a more complex and pluralistic concept in which the principle of ethnic and national difference ... is respected.[47]

But one should not conclude from these changes that the post-Khomeini government's commitment to sustain and spread Islam was less firm than that of the previous leadership.[48] It revised and refined the methods employed to fulfil the mission. At least six factors, three of them internal and the other three external ones, should be summarised for this tactical adjustment.

Three main internal aspects limited Iran's foreign policy ambitions: First of all, the country's Persian character. Despite the government's attempt to minimise Iranian nationalism, the Persianness of Iran has limited its ability to reach the Arab masses. On the contrary, ethnicity and nationalism have proved to be much stronger than the appeal of Islamic universalism.

Secondly, Iran's Shia nature. This has also hindered Iran's ability to appeal to larger groups of Muslims beyond the Shii minorities. Indeed, in some cases, Iranian activities have brought Sunni fundamentalist groups closer to their governments. Iran has been forced to focus most of its attention and efforts on these areas where the existence of Shii majorities or sizeable minorities creates a relatively more receptive environment for its visions and influence.

Thirdly, the financial and economic limitations of the country.[49]

Among the external factors, it should be mentioned first and foremost that continued attempts to subvert governments in the name of "true Islam", particularly when applied to the Gulf region, were incompatible with efforts to forge economic ties with those same governments, which was much more important for the survival of the Islamic Republic. Secondly, emphasis on spreading Iran's brand of Islam can be too easily exploited by Iran's detractors who tend to accentuate the differences between Shiism and Sunnism.

And thirdly, experience has shown – especially in the Gulf region – that Iran's revolutionary call to topple existing governments has had limited appeal. Nevertheless, the post-Khomeini leadership continued to insist that Iran's "Islamic responsibility" transcended national borders. Yet, it appears to have accepted – tactically, pragmatically and perhaps temporarily – international boundaries. However, this has neither implied nor required Iran's abrogation of responsibility to assist Islamic societies within other states in their struggle for "true Islam". Iran's 1990 budget reportedly allocated $120 million in support of Islamic groups and movements. This amount was increased by 20 per cent the following year.[50]

Resistance of reality

The remarkable influence of the Islamic Republic of Iran among Muslims and Islamic movements cannot be denied. It enabled Tehran to use the latter as power boosters and barraging tools, as identifying and legitimising tools and as sources of strategic purpose and direction.[51] But contrary to many allegations and/or expectations as well as the Iranian assumption of being the centre of the Islamic world there was never an institution such as "Islamic Comintern", headquartered in the holy city of Qom to instruct Muslims and direct their activities according to a grand strategy worked out by the Iranian leadership to spread the revolution.

Iran's record of influencing Muslims has rather been characterised – like many other aspects of its post-revolutionary life – "by a great deal of parallel, and often contradictory, actions by a host of official and semi-official organisations and groups. Similarly, Iranian activities in regard to the export of revolution rather than following a strategic blueprint have been marked by what could be called tactical opportunism. Thus, Iran seems to have concentrated its efforts in areas where local conditions have created opportunities for it to expand its influence."[52]

Nevertheless, even ten years after his death, Khomeini's legacy of the overall universalist nature of Iran's foreign policy is still valid. As one of the basic marks of its identity, the Islamic Republic cannot afford to conceal it. If Islamic foreign policy is a reflection of Islamic belief, having a global mission with a message for the people of the whole world and thus unable to accept limits or remain bound within the framework of national, regional, ethnical or geographical structures, how can the responsibility of an Islamic state then be limited to its borders? But, as already mentioned, Iran's leadership had to learn its lesson, and was forced to adapt its foreign policy objectives to the real world.

In the decade between 1979 and 1989, when the majority of the Iranian revolutionaries felt themselves a part of the mighty revolutionary wave, no one really noticed the overall declamatory character of Khomeini's foreign policy statements or dared to ask questions about commonly recognised Islamic propositions concerning international relations. But as soon as the situation in Iran began to normalise, both politicians and clerics painfully felt the widening gap between the pursuit of Islamic foreign policy and the pressure to secure the interests of Iran as a nation state in a world becoming more and more complex. In particular, diplomats and members of the Foreign Ministry were asking questions as to how Islamic foreign policy could be handled in detail.

With increasing frankness they accused the religious jurists of Iran of not providing sufficient and satisfactory answers despite the importance and sensitivity of the issue.[53] Contemporary *foqahā'* and Islamic scholars would either deal with foreign policy matters in a very cursory manner or would pursue extremely idealised principles impossible to implement in the present world such as collecting tribute (*ğezye*) from those who refuse to convert to Islam, rejecting present borders between countries, insisting on the religious duty of directing others to do good or enjoining others not to commit anti-religious deeds.

According to Iranian foreign policy specialists, also "befriending God's friends" (*tawalli*) and "avoiding God's enemies" (*tabarri*) is not possible in the foreign policy arena due to conflict with existing international law and the interests of certain powers.

On the other hand, those directly involved in Iran's day to day foreign policy do not feel themselves legitimised to call their pragmatism Islamic foreign policy. Be that as it may, in contemporary Iran both its clerics and diplomats seem to have reached at least one common denominator in the seven basic principles that should not be left out in a foreign policy claiming to be Islamic. These are:

Protection of dār al-islām.   Both clerics and laymen within the Iranian leadership have agreed upon the protection of the Islamic system as the most important and fundamental principle in the foreign policy of Islam. Thus, the Foreign Ministry and the diplomats are obliged to keep this vital principle in mind throughout their activities and should not move towards a practical path that undermines it.

Glory, Protection of Independence and Rejection of Dominance. The second important and basic principle in the foreign policy of an Islamic government should be the glory and the authority of Islam and its government. The experts among the Iranian politicians know that the relevant texts on this principle were compiled and arranged when the Muslims were at the height of their power, when their domain was spreading, and other states were conquered by them. Thus, the principle reflects the honour and glory of the Islamic state at a time of powerful presence in the global arena. Under present circumstances, the Iranians are therefore concentrating their foreign policy efforts on the second part of the principle, i.e. the rejection of dominance by non-Muslims (*nafī-ye sabīl*). It forbids any relations that lead to the dominance of foreigners over the destinies of Muslims such as giving concessions, specific powers or exclusive economic and commercial rights that promote foreign dominance. Articles 152 and 153 of the Islamic Republic's Constitution refer especially to this principle. According to most clerical leaders of Iran the principle of *nafī-ye sabīl* is one of the fundamental commands and rules of Islamic jurisprudence and has priority over other rules.[54] But despite the importance of this principle, there is an ongoing dispute among the Iranian leadership over the feasibility of implementing *nafī-ye sabīl* under the conditions of an accelerating globalization, leading to "mutual dependence among countries" and making "concepts such as independence and absolute (national) sovereignty obsolete … in the not too distant future"[55].

Interest (maṣlaḥat). The third principle is grouped around the rules of ability (*vosˁ*), no harm (*lā żarar*) and avoidance (*taqiyye*). The *vosˁ* rule connotes the fulfilment of one's duty according to one's ability. The *lā żarar* rule means choosing the easier way if the more difficult one implies the possibility of losses.[56] The *taqiyye* rule suggests going along with an opponent in order to ward off harm and injury.[57] There is a deep rift within the Iranian leadership on the question of whether *maṣlaḥat* primarily refers to the Islamic Republic of Iran or the whole Muslim *umma*, on the extent of *vosˁ*, the amount of noticeable *żarar* and the necessity of *taqiyye* in the contemporary era. In general, Iran's acceptance of UNSCR # 598, which led to a cease-fire with Iraq in 1988, is seen as a convincing example of applying the *maṣlaḥat* principle by the Iranian government.

Establishment of relations, coexistence and cooperation with other countries. According to the present Iranian leadership, there is no other way to implement the above mentioned major principles than to establish cooperative relations with other countries, in order to avoid isolation, strengthen the Islamic state, and relay its message to the people of the world. The IRI should have an active and authoritative presence in the global arena.

Support for the rights of the Muslims and the oppressed throughout the world. According to Article 154 of the Iranian constitution, every citizen of the country and all its institutions are obliged to "support the righteous struggle of the downtrodden in face of tyranny all over the world"[58]. The Iranian leadership is sure that all its relations with Muslim and non-Muslim opposition movements throughout the world are legitimised by this principle, including material and ideological support. Although the Iranian leaders dealing with the country's foreign policy are well aware that their uncompromising attitude towards the rights of the *umma* and the world's oppressed has fostered their prestige among Muslims, they also know that such a policy has many harmful effects for Iran, too. Because their support for political movements in other countries is often answered by the governments of those countries with extensive pressure and boycotts, Iran has to consider the pros and cons of the various foreign policy principles, especially that of *maslahat.*

Invitation and propagation (daʿvat). In Islamic jurisprudence, there is no major disagreement among the *ʿulamā* on the obligatory nature of *daʿvat.* But the Iranian clergy has not reached a final conclusion as to whether this obligation should be imposed on each and every individual in society.[59] Some of them definitely believe that *daʿvat* has priority over other principles in foreign policy, both in terms of timing and value.[60] In that sense, it would be impossible to direct the responsibility for the propagation of and invitation to the Islamic faith exclusively to specialised organs such as propaganda, cultural and media organisations. Therefore, given the sensitivity and importance of propagation and the Koran's emphasis on it, most of Iran's *foqahāʾ* consider it one of the foreign policy principles of the Islamic Republic and thus one of the main duties of the country's diplomacy. Seyyed Ali Qaderi, for example, stated:

> The first social duty of any prophet after mission is invitation – this principle constitutes the essence of Islam's foreign policy … Avoidance of invitation not only confronts Dar al-Islam with the danger of extinction, but also carries punishment in the next world.[61]

Gaining the endearment of others. The principle of giving financial or non-financial assistance to other countries should not be confused with the fifth principle, i.e. the support of Muslims or oppressed people. This seventh and last approved principle intends rather to gain the affinities of other countries or to moderate their views in relation to the Islamic Republic of Iran and its policies (*taʾlīf qolūb*). Donations or interest-free loans to countries like Syria, North-Korea, Sudan or the former PDRY can be seen in the light of this principle.[62]

Although these principles of the Islamic Republic's foreign policy have been agreed upon by the majority of the country's leading personalities, there is still no common opinion about the rank of each principle in relation to the other ones.

Especially diplomats know that the realisation of Islamic ideals and sacred objectives, such as support for the rights of the Muslims and the deprived, and invitation and propagation, is a large and dangerous responsibility, with its own particular effects, for instance the threat of becoming isolated. Thus, none of them is really sure whether the efforts to realise one or more of the above mentioned principles might harm others. Iran's foreign policy is therefore caught in a trap between pretension and reality.

But, taking into consideration what little is really known about the nature of the Islamic Republic of Iran and its leadership, one can predict – at least for the time being – that it will not try to resolve the conflict by relying completely on either idealism or pragmatism. By accepting reality, Iran's leaders will proceed more cautiously, they will opt for a step by step strategy, permanently testing to what extent their foreign policy principles are tolerated by the international system.

The ordinary observer may mistake this shift for normalisation, in the sense of a pragmatic, nation-focused foreign policy. But we should know better. As long as the system of the *velāyat-e faqīh* remains the foundation of the Islamic Republic of Iran, the country' will have a universalist message for us all.

Conclusions

Not only the outcome of the Arab-Israeli conflict but also regional develop-ments along Iran's northern and eastern borders as well as in the Persian Gulf will decisively influence Iranian behaviour. In addition, much will depend on the development of Islamic radical movements elsewhere. Although Iranian diplomats such as Kamal Kharrazi, previously ambassador to the United Nations and now the new Foreign Minister, constantly emphasise that Islamic revivalism is bound to the respective countries and situations, and thus perhaps inspired but not con-trolled by Iran[63], the remarkable success of these movements might encourage the Iranian leadership to repeat its demand for hegemony in the Islamic world more frequently.

Iran's future behaviour will definitely be influenced by the reaction of the West, particularly the United States, as well.[64] Western capitals might be on the right track to criticise, for instance, Iran's human rights record or to fight terrorism organised by some Iranian radicals, but it will only strengthen these very ele-ments within the Iranian establishment by continuing an undifferentiating policy of containment in the long run.

Resulting from the heterogeneity of its system of power and the continuing existence of parallel power centres, Iran will, as in the past, seek to normalise ties with its most important neighbours while cultivating and maintaining its options for subversion and agitation. Mohammad Khatami will probably try to start his presidency with a foreign policy that keeps Iran from deepening the rift with its neighbours and intensifying its isolation.

The question still remains as to what degree the Islamic revolution in Iran really has influenced the Islamic world and to what degree it will probably continue to do so. Will there be repetitions of what happened in Iran?

In the first flush of victory after the overthrow of the Shah, Iran was giddy with its own success and utterly confident that it could reshape the world in its own image. As mentioned before, it rejected traditional diplomacy, traditional economics and even traditional ideology in the pursuit of its own version of universal Islamic rule. The Islamic state supported terrorist groups, seized American hostages, rejected any dependency on either East or West, turned up its nose at the United Nations and earned a reputation as a maverick state in the Western hemisphere.

But – just to repeat it – this is a common experience for revolutionary societies. The toppling of the old regime, which had seemed impossibly powerful and well entrenched, is typically regarded as a miraculous event. It is no wonder that the revolutionaries expected a spreading of their doctrines and ideas everywhere. Most genuine revolutions carry the seed of new ideas that transcend the locality and the parochial circumstances that first permitted it to take root and flourish.[65]

But coming back to the question raised at the beginning, the answer is relatively easy: the Iranian revolution has not spread and fundamentalism has been contained. But at best this is only half the answer, because it adopts too small a timescale. Revolutions and revolutionaries, whether Islamic or otherwise, are impatient, and expect other peoples to imitate them immediately: in this regard they become disappointed just as quickly as their opponents become relieved.[66] When a transformation of the international system proves to be exclusively difficult, dangerous or expensive, the proselytising impulse usually wanes and is progressively subordinated to more traditional objectives. Thus, the activities of the revolutionary state gradually come to resemble those of a conventional country.[67]

In that sense, the Iran of 1999 is less of a threat to its neighbours and to the international system than the Iran of 1979/80 was. Ideologically, much of the early boisterousness of the revolution was eroded by the relentless pressure of economic realities and the unforgiving demands of governing a large country with severe problems. At present, Iran is much less likely to undertake adventurous and costly intervention in the affairs of its neighbours than it was in the early eighties.[68] At least this is the situation at present. Nobody can exclude the possibility of radical and adventurous foreign policy steps by Iran in the event of a substantial economic crisis.

And there is the timescale to be remembered. The international impact of a revolution is not evaluated in a few years but in several decades. It was Chou En-lai who suggested that the effects of the French Revolution continue to be felt two centuries after the event.[69] Thus, the impact of the Iranian revolution can only be analysed completely by future generations. Even now the impact has been substantial, though no other state – except perhaps Sudan – has become an Islamic Republic such as Iran. It is only necessary to look at the rise in Islamist political consciousness in a range of countries, or to recognise the increased interest in Islamic clothing, Islamic literature, mosque attendance, etc., to see how far Iran has influenced the political behaviour of Muslims.

> Whether or not Islamist forces of the Iranian variety do come to power in the following years or decades, the impact of the revolution and of the broader trend with which it is associated is undeniable.[70]

Summarizing these aspects, it has to be stated that despite the more pragmatic – or rather, national – Iranian foreign policy since the beginning of the nineties, religiously motivated universalism will retain its importance as long as the Iranian Republic and its leadership identify Islam as the precondition and the essence of its statehood.

Notes

1 Imam's Final Discourse. The text of the political and religious testament of the Leader of the Islamic Revolution and the Founder of the Islamic Republic of Iran, Imam Khomeini. In: The Iranian Journal of International Affairs, Tehran 1 (1989) 2&3, pp. 328–329.

2 Message of Revolution (Islamic Revolution Guard Corps), Tehran (1983) 21, p. 6.

3 See E. Baktiari, Revolutionary Iran's Persian Gulf Policy: The Quest for Regional Supremacy. In: H. Amirahmadi/N. Entessar (eds.), Iran and the Arab World, London 1993, p. 72.

4 C. Brinton, The Anatomy of Revolution, New York 1965, p. 196.

5 G. Sick, Iran: The Adolescent Revolution. In: Journal of International Affairs, New York 49 (1995) 1, p. 146/147.

6 See G. Linabury, Ayatollah Khomeini's Islamic Legacy. In: H. Amirahmadi/N. Entessar (eds.), Reconstruction and Regional Diplomacy in the Persian Gulf, London-New York 1992, p. 33.

7 See Farhang Rajaee, Islamic Values and World View: Khomeyni on Man, the State, and International Politics, Lanham et al. 1983, pp. 80–81.

8 Message to the Pilgrims. In: Hamid Algar (ed.), Islam and Revolution. Writings and Declarations of Imam Khomeini, Berkeley 1981, p. 304.

9 Eṭṭlāʿāt, Tehran, 3 November 1979.

10 Quoted in: Rajaee, Islamic Values …, loc. cit., p. 83.

11 Quoted in: H. Amirahmadi/N. Entessar, Iranian-Arab Relations in Transition. In: Amirahmadi/Entessar (eds.), Iran …, loc. cit., p. 3.

12 See S.K. Anderson, The Impact of Islamic Fundamentalist Politics within the Islamic Republic of Iran on Iranian State Sponsorship of Transnational Terrorism, Ann Arbor 1994, p. 152.

13 R. Khomeini, Kašf-e asrār, Tehran 1980, p. 337.

14 Constitution of the Islamic Republic of Iran, Tehran 1979, Principle 11.

15 Quoted in: J. Calabrese, Revolutionary Horizons, Regional Foreign Policy in Post-Revolutionary Iran, London 1994, p. 27.

16 See S.T. Hunter, Iran and the World. Continuity in a Revolutionary Decade. Bloomington 1990, p. 40.

17 Hoṭbe-ye namāz-c ǧomʿe-ye Tehrān. Vol. 4, Tehran 1989, p. 185.

18 Echo of Islam, Tehran, (1996) 142/143, p. 42.

19 See also W.G. Millward, The Principles of Foreign Policy and the Vision of World Order expounded by Imam Khomeini and the Islamic Republic of Iran. In: N. Keddie/R. Hooglund/E. Hooglund (eds.), The Iranian Revolution and the Islamic Republic, Washington DC 1982, pp. 189–204.

20 S. Chubin, Iran and the Persian Gulf Stales. In: D. Menashri (ed.), The Iranian Revolution and the Muslim World, Boulder 1990, p. 74.

21 FBIS, Daily Report, Middle East and Africa, 24 March 1980, Vol. V, No. 058, Supplement 070.

22 Rāhnemūnhā-ye emām, Tehran 1979, p. 28.

23 FBIS, Daily Report, South Asia, 9 March 1982, Vol. VIII, No. 046.

24 G. Sick, Iran …, loc. cit., p. 148.

25 J. Calabrese, Revolutionary …, loc. cit., p. 144.

26 F. Halliday, The Politics of Islamic Fundamentalism: Iran, Tunisia and the Challenge to the Secular State. In: A.S. Ahmed/H. Donnan (eds.), Islam, Globalization and Postmodernity, London-New York 1994, p. 101.

27 Bayānāt-e Emām Homeinī be monāsabat-e yekom sālgerd-e enqelāb, Tehran 1982, p. 5.

28 Tehran Times, 30 September 1982.

29 Quoted in: F. Rajaee, Iranian Ideology and Worldview: The Cultural Export of Revolution. In: J.L. Esposito (ed.), The Iranian Revolution. Its Global Impact, Miami 1990, p. 68.

30 Quoted in: M. Mohadessin, Islamic Fundamentalism. The New Global Threat, Washington D.C. 1993, p. 38.

31 A.N. Memon, The Islamic Nation. Status & Future of Muslims in the New World Order, Beltsville, MD, 1995, p. 150.

32 Resālat, Tehran, 15 February 1993.

33 See H. Amirahmadi, Iran and the Persian Gulf: Strategic Issues and Outlook. In: H. Zanganeh (ed.), Islam, Iran, & World Stability, New York 1994, pp. 116–118.

34 Sorūš, Tehran, March 1981, pp. 4–5.

35 See also M. Muhajeri, Islamic Revolution. Future Path of the Nations. Jihad Sazandegih, Tehran 1983, p. 175.

36 A. Hāmeneʾī, Čahār sāl bā mardom, Tehran 1985, p. 354.

37 FBIS, Daily Report, South Asia, 11 March 1982, Vol. VIII, No. 048.

38 Kayhān Hawaʾī, Tehran, 4 April 1993.

39 Tehran Journal, 10 October 1981.

40 Peyām-e šāhedān, Mashhad n.d., p. 8.

41 BBC SWB, 3–4 February 1993.

42 See I. Sangar, Nofūd-e Amrīkā dar Īrān; Bar-rasī-ye sīyāsat-e hāreǧī-ye Amrīkā va ravābet-e bā Īrān, Tehran 1989, pp. 33–35, 59.

43 Hunter, Iran …, loc. cit., p. 41.

44 See S. Chubin, Iran's National Security Policy. Capabilities, Intentions & Impact, Washington DC 1994, p. 12.

45 Ettelāʿāt, Tehran, 28 June 1990.

46 M.J. Larijani, Iran's Foreign Policy: Principles and Objectives. In: The Iranian Journal of International Affairs, Tehran 7 (1996) 4, p. 756.

47 K.L. Afrasiabi, After Khomeini. New Directions in Iran's Foreign Policy, Boulder et.al. 1994, p. 203.

48 See also M.H. Fayyāzī, Bar-rāsī-ye ʿavāmel movātīr dar dast-yābī va ʿadam dast-yābī be ahdāf enqwlāb-e eslāmī. In: Faslnāmeh huqūq va ʿolūm-e sīyāsī, Tehran 2 (1992) 2, pp. 47–60.

49 See Hunter, Iran …, loc. cit., p. 180.

50 See Calabrese, Revolutionary…, loc. cit., p. 145.

51 Amirahmadi, Iran …, loc. cit., pp. 117–118.

52 S.T. Hunter, Iran and the Spread of Revolutionary Islam, In: Third World Quarterly, Washington DC 10 (1988) 2, p. 740.
53 See A. Ghazvini, On the Foreign Policy of Islam: A Search into the Juridical Dimension of Iranian Foreign Policy. In: The Iranian Journal of International Affairs, Tehran 7 (1996) 4, pp. 780–796.
54 See A. Šakūrī, Oṣūl-e sīyāsat-e ḥāreǧī-ye eslām. In: Feqh-e sīyāsā-ye eslām. Vol. 2, Tehran 1982, p. 387.
55 Ghazvini, On the Foreign..., loc. cit., p. 786.
56 See A. al-ʿAlawī, Al-Taqīya fī riḥāb al-ʿālamayn al-šayḫ al-aʿẓam al-Anṣārī wa-l-sayyid al-imām al-Ḥumaynī, Qom 1994, p. 4.
57 See M. al-Anṣārī, Al-Taqīye, Qom 1994, p. 11.
58 E. Amīnī (Āyātollah), Sīyāsat-e ḥāreǧī-ye ḥokūmat-e eslāmī, Tehran 1985, p. 7.
59 See Šakūrī, Oṣūl-e ..., loc. cit., p. 360.
60 See ʿA. Qāderī, Ṭarḥ-e tahqīq-e mabānī-ye sīyāsat-e ḥāreǧī-ye eslām. In: Maǧallāt-e sīyāsat-e ḥāreǧī, Tehran (1989) 1, p. 226.
61 Ibid., p. 228.
62 See Šakūrī, Oṣūl-e ..., loc. cit., pp. 501–514.
63 See U.S.-Iran Review, Washington DC 1 (1993) 2, p. 1.
64 See F. al-Mazidi, The Future of the Gulf. The Legacy of the War and the Challenge of the 1990s, London—New York 1993, p. 3.
65 See Sick, Iran ..., loc. cit., p. 147.
66 See Halliday, The Politics ..., loc. cit., p 90.
67 See Sick, Iran ..., loc. cit., p. 141.
68 Ibid., p. 165.
69 Ibid., p. 147.
70 Halliday, The Politics ..., loc. cit., p. 97.

57

IRAN'S FOREIGN POLICY

A revolution in transition

Gary Sick

Source: N.R. Keddie and R. Matthee (eds) *Iran and the Surrounding World*, Seattle and London: University of Washington Press, 2002, pp. 355–74.

The Iranian Revolution of 1979 demolished the entire architecture of Iran's foreign relations and left Iran isolated and menacing to its neighbors. The excessive costs of such a policy became evident by the mid-1980s, when Iran began to cultivate better relations with Europe, its neighbors in the Persian Gulf, and even the United States. Although Iran created a new policy environment in the region, it was Saddam Hussein of Iraq who transformed the political and strategic landscape of the Gulf, chastened the Iranian Revolution, and set it on a new, more nationalistic and pragmatic path. The Iranian Revolution was like no other in modern times. Its attention to the popular will through the medium of elections created a new image that challenged U.S. sanctions and struggled to provide a model of a democratizing state in an Islamic context. The ferocious counter-attack on the forces of democracy and openness by revolutionary ideologues and vested interests, however, demonstrated just how perilous and uncertain such an experiment would be.

The foreign policy of any country is a function of its domestic politics. That truism was never more applicable than in the case of the Islamic Republic of Iran. The Iranian Revolution of 1979 demolished at a stroke the entire architecture of Iran's foreign relations, sweeping away an edifice of relationships that had been carefully constructed over more than a generation and replacing them with wild and unpredictable actions that threw its region into turmoil and inspired fear and undisguised hostility from its neighbors.

The extreme rhetoric of the revolutionaries was compounded by an organizational void. As the new leadership struggled to define itself, small groups of militants seized the opportunity to pursue their own vision of a global

Islamic politics. As in any revolution, there were ancient grudges to be settled, and these enmities rippled out from Iranian territory, like Islam itself, acknowledging no borders and contemptuous of "Western" notions of temporal sovereignty. The earliest targets of attention by the revolutionaries were their brethren among the disadvantaged Shi'i populations of Iraq, Bahrain, Saudi Arabia, and Lebanon, but their zeal and revolutionary triumphalism were boundless.

This is the common experience of revolutions, which initially try to redefine the world in their own image, only to discover by bitter experience that the world does not so easily yield to their ministrations. Twenty years later, the radicals who confidently set forth to introduce Islamic rule to their neighbors would scarcely recognize the foreign policy practices of the Islamic Republic. When a senior Iranian official can remark casually that, in his view, "The revolution was not a renaissance. It was more a riot,"[1] without himself prompting a riot, it is clear that something important has happened.

Iran's learning curve

In the exuberant atmosphere following the overthrow of the shah, Iranian leaders displayed no interest in diplomatic niceties, much less support for any legacies of the shah's rule. Revolutionary leaders almost casually let it be known that they did not consider themselves bound by any of the shah's agreements. Instead, spokesmen for the Islamic Republic pointedly noted that in traditional Islam there were no borders dividing the faithful. Those remarks, when coupled with fiery rhetoric calling for export of the revolution to all of the Islamic world, gave Iraq and other neighbors of Iran justifiable grounds for concern. The basic principle was written into Iran's constitution.[2]

Even the crucial 1975 border agreement with Iraq, which favored Iran, was allowed to languish in a kind of diplomatic limbo until a full month after Iraq launched its invasion in 1980. The war, however, had a sobering effect. By mid-1983, Iran's repeated failures to breach Iraqi defenses, combined with the growing effectiveness of Iraqi air strikes, compelled Iran to undertake a thorough reappraisal of its diplomatic and military policies. In October 1984, Khomeini summoned Iran's diplomatic representatives from abroad and instructed them to take a new approach.

> We should act as it was done in early Islam when the Prophet … sent ambassadors to all parts of the world to establish proper relations. We cannot sit idly by saying we have nothing to do with governments. This is contrary to intellect and religious law. We should have relations with all governments with the exception of a few with which we have no relations at present.[3]

Iranian Prime Minister Mir Hosain Musavi expanded on these comments, offering assurances to the nations of the region who had feared the export of Iran's revolution. "We do not want to export armed revolution to any country. That is a big lie. Our aim is to promote the Islamic Revolution through persuasion and by means of truth and courage. These are Islamic values."[4] These words of reassurance, repeated regularly by all senior Iranian leaders, appeared to be more than rhetoric, as Iranian subversion gradually subsided.

After the death of Ayatollah Khomeini in 1989, the new government of Ali Akbar Hashemi Rafsanjani initiated a major effort to repair relations with Europe, Iran's neighbors in the Persian Gulf and surrounding area, and even with the United States. Rafsanjani, who was a businessman as well as a cleric, made reconstruction of Iran's shattered economy his top priority, and he understood that this would require foreign investment and cooperation.

His plans, however, were repeatedly disrupted. The fatwa against Salman Rushdie that was issued by Ayatollah Khomeini before his death caused a major crisis with the British government and other members of the European Union, greatly complicating Rafsanjani's efforts to repair relations. In August 1991, just before Rafsanjani was scheduled to make the first Iranian state visit to France since the revolution, former prime minister Shahpour Bakhtiar was stabbed to death at his home while under the protection of French security services, and the visit was canceled. In Germany, the leader of a Kurdish opposition group was assassinated in 1992, eventually leading to the formal indictment of Iranian Minister of Information [Intelligence] Ali Fallahian. This was compounded in October 1993 when the Norwegian translator of Rushdie's novel, *The Satanic Verses*, was shot outside his home, eventually leading Norway to withdraw its ambassador.

These and other incidents gave the impression that there were several centers of power in Iran that were working at cross-purposes. Specifically, it appeared that the hard-liners in the Iranian intelligence services were pursuing an independent vendetta against enemies of the revolution and that they were not entirely displeased to embarrass the more moderate president and the foreign ministry. The killings in Europe stopped in about 1993, suggesting that Rafsanjani was finally able to exert some control. But the aftermath of those events continued to poison relations with Europe and other countries for years after.

A new beginning

In March 1997, Rafsanjani met with Crown Prince Abdullah of Saudi Arabia during an Islamic summit in Islamabad. This was the beginning of a diplomatic rapprochement between these two major powers in the Persian Gulf region. This was particularly auspicious for three reasons. First, Ayatollah Khomeini had denounced the Saudi royal family in scathing terms in his will, so this opening represented a move away from the revolutionary orthodoxy of the past. Second, Saudi Arabia was the leading power in the Gulf Cooperation Council, which meant that a restoration of businesslike relations would speed the process of reconciliation with the other five members of the GCC, healing rifts that had been created by Arab support for Iraq during the Iran-Iraq war. Finally, since Saudi Arabia was a close political and military ally of the United States, the improved relations provided Iran with some independent maneuvering room at a time when the United States was maintaining severe economic sanctions against Iran.

The full effect of these policies was not felt, however, until the presidential election in May 1997 of Seyyed Mohammed Khatami, a reformist who campaigned on a platform of civil society, rule of law, and expanded personal liberty. In that election, 90 percent of the eligible voters went to the polls, and Khatami received 70 percent of the vote. His surprise landslide election was decided almost entirely on the basis of domestic issues. From the beginning, however, the new president indicated that his electoral themes could and would be extended to Iran's foreign policy. Contrary to expectations, some of the most striking early accomplishments of the Khatami government were in the realm of foreign policy. The former Minister of information, Fallahian, was removed. The previous foreign minister, Ali Akbar Velayati, who had been in office for nearly the entire postrevolutionary period and who symbolized the confrontational policies of the past, was replaced by a respected diplomat who had represented Iran for nearly nine years at the UN.

Before the end of Khatami's first year, Iran had mended its fences with many of its Arab neighbors in the Persian Gulf, invigorated its role in the United Nations, hosted a very successful Islamic summit, and restored relations with the European community, Turkey, and Bahrain. Most striking was the continued rapprochement with Saudi Arabia. Saudi Crown Prince Abdullah attended the Tehran summit of the Organization of Islamic Countries (OIC), met twice with President Khatami, and openly praised the new president.

During Khatami's first few years he consistently broke new ground. He visited Italy, France, Germany, China, Syria, Saudi Arabia, and Qatar. He restored full diplomatic relations with Great Britain, Norway, and Bahrain. He attended the United Nations and launched an international movement for "dialogue among civilizations." And he dramatically changed the international image of Iran. Khomeini had once remarked that "There is no joy in Islam." The smiling visage of President Khatami, his emphasis on tolerance and rule of law, and the unmistakable love of much of the Iranian populace for him personally went very far to remove the dour and forbidding visage of the Iranian Revolution and to inspire a degree of respect and even trust among Iran's neighbors that would have been unimaginable only a decade earlier.

The role of Saddam Hussein

The Iranian Revolution terminated Iran's close relationship with the United States and demolished the U.S. "twin pillar" policy of relying on regional states to protect its interests. Although this transformed the foreign policy environment in the Persian Gulf, actual changes in the political and strategic landscape were due almost entirely to the actions of President Saddam Hussein of Iraq, who reacted forcefully to the new circumstances and fundamentally altered the regional balance of power. Iraq's invasion of Iran in September 1980, its invasion of Kuwait in August 1990, and its decade-long sparring with the United Nations Security Council created an entirely new set of facts on the ground. In effect, the Iranian Revolution was the trigger for a rampage of more than two decades by Saddam Hussein's government that rewrote the strategic situation in the Gulf, perhaps permanently. It is worth reviewing the interaction between Iran and Iraq, these two traditional rivals whose mutual depredations, like those of a pair of hateful Siamese twins, set off a sequence of events whose end is still unknown.

In 1975, the shah of Iran and Saddam Hussein concluded an agreement concerning their mutual border, and, particularly, the boundary line of the Shatt al-Arab River. This major concession by Saddam Hussein, which moved the boundary from the eastern bank of the river to the *thalweg*, the center of the navigable channel, was undertaken while under pressure from a Kurdish rebellion in northern Iraq supported by Israel and the United States via Iran. Five years later, after the Iranian Revolution, the departure of the shah, the near-collapse of the Iranian military, and a series of hostile acts by Iran and its agents in Iraq, including some border skirmishes, Saddam Hussein publicly renounced the 1975 agreement as null and void. On the night of September 21, 1980, Iraq launched a massive air and ground attack against Iran. This military campaign was intended to restore total Iraqi control of the Shatt al-Arab waterway, to conquer Iran's predominantly Arab province of Khuzestan, which had long appeared as a lost province on Iraqi maps, and to restore Arab control over the islands of Abu Musa and the Tunbs. But its broader aims were probably intended to bring down the revolutionary Islamic government in Tehran, to rescue the Gulf Arab states from the menace of revolutionary Shi'i subversion, and to win recognition for Saddam Hussein's Iraq as the savior of the Arabs and the dominant power in the Persian Gulf.

The Iraqi invasion, modeled at least in part on Israel's Six-Day War against Egypt, encountered unexpected levels of Iranian resistance and dragged on for eight full years. It mobilized Arab support for Iraq, but it also persuaded the Gulf Arab states to begin to take their security into their own hands. Under the leadership of Saudi Arabia, the six smaller states banded themselves together as the Gulf Cooperation Council in May 1981, thus completing the third point of the strategic triangle with Iran and Iraq. Although the GCC was slow to develop a common defense policy, it evolved as a convenient—and often influential—forum for the political and diplomatic articulation of mutual interests.

The war also provided the one unequivocal example of Iranian revolutionary expansionism. In 1982, after Iranian forces had pushed Iraqi troops back to approximately the original border, there was a pause in the fighting. Iran had the option of either promoting a diplomatic settlement or else continuing the war and attempting to drive into Iraqi territory. At the time, Iran enjoyed what appeared to be a decisive advantage on the battlefield, and after intense internal debates Iran announced that its forces would march to Jerusalem via Baghdad. This was a catastrophic decision. Iraqi forces stiffened in the defense of their own territory, and Iran's "human wave" tactics proved incapable of overcoming Iraq's lines of defense and superior weaponry. The eventual cease-fire that was negotiated in 1988, which Ayatollah Khomeini likened to drinking poison, was probably not very different from the settlement that Iran could have obtained on its own terms in 1982. The decision to continue the war became a major point of contention for Iran's reform movement nearly twenty years later, when journalists began to raise questions about who was responsible for the enormous economic, political, and military costs it had produced.[5]

The war also brought the United States into the Persian Gulf far more directly than ever before. The key turning point came in March 1987, when the United States accepted a Kuwaiti request to reflag some Kuwaiti tankers and to provide military escort for some of their shipping that had begun to come under attack by Iran. This decision had three main effects: first, it linked U.S. military deployments explicitly to Kuwait and other Arab states of the Gulf, as opposed to the previous "over the horizon" policy; second, the United States began to construct a military support infrastructure in the region that would eventually become permanent; and third, the United States was soon drawn directly into the fighting between Iran and Iraq, including the sinking of an Iranian mine layer and retaliatory attacks on Iranian oil platforms and naval vessels. In July 1988, a U.S. naval ship shot down an Iranian civilian aircraft after mistaking it for a fighter plane, killing 290 people. In all but name, the United States became a party to the conflict and for the first time established a major, continuous, military presence in the region.

The U.S. "tilt" towards Iraq continued after the cease-fire in August 1988 and was maintained until Iraq's invasion of Kuwait in 1990. Unlike the invasion of Iran, which was largely ignored by the international community, the attack on Kuwait prompted an immediate and dramatic response. The UN Security Council immediately demanded an unconditional withdrawal of the invading forces and imposed on Iraq the most severe sanctions in the history of the international community. When Iraq failed to comply, the United States took the lead in organizing a massive military buildup that eventually defeated the Iraqi forces and ejected them from Kuwait. In the process, the United States developed, in close cooperation with the regional Arab states, a military infrastructure that was gradually formalized by a series of defense cooperation agreements, a high level of routine U.S. military deployments, and several huge depots of pre-positioned materiel.

The new strategic landscape

Thus, over a period of less than twenty years, the strategic landscape of the region had been almost totally redrawn. The Iran-Iraq-GCC triangle was expanded to a quadrangle, with the United States as a direct participant in regional affairs. With the signing of the Camp David Accords in September 1978, which removed the likelihood of a new Arab-Israel war, and with the simultaneous explosion of the Iranian Revolution, the center of gravity of Middle East strategy and politics shifted from the eastern Mediterranean to the Persian Gulf.

The Carter Doctrine of 1980 unequivocally asserted U.S. interests in the Gulf and expressed U.S. intentions to act—by military force if necessary—to prevent any attempt "by an outside force to gain control of the Persian Gulf."[6] This largely symbolic statement was given some teeth by the U.S. military buildup during the Reagan administration. Nevertheless, the U.S. presence remained relatively discreet and episodic until the mid-1980s. In fact, the roughly 40,000 U.S. military personnel deployed in the Persian Gulf during World War II to protect the supply lines to the Soviet Union represented the largest U.S. presence in the region until the buildup for Desert Storm in 1990 and early 1991.

Desert Storm also coincided roughly with the collapse of the Soviet Union and the end of the Cold War. For decades, U.S. strategy in the Persian Gulf had been based on two principles: access to the oil supplies of the region and opposition to control of those resources by the Soviet Union. By the 1990s, the threat from the Soviet Union had dissipated and was replaced, without fanfare, by Saddam Hussein's Iraq. Although Iran was officially given equal billing under the rubric of the U.S. "dual containment" policy, in reality Iran cooperated silently with the campaign to eject Iraq from Kuwait, confiscated Iraqi planes that were flown in to Iran without warning at the start of the war, and refused to make common cause with its recent enemy, despite Saddam's unilateral offer to restore the 1975 border agreement and to give Iran "everything you wanted."[7]

By 2000, the routine U.S. presence in the Gulf had become substantial. According to the Department of Defense, at any given time the United States had in the region some 17,000–25,000 personnel, about 30 naval vessels, and some 175 aircraft.[8] The reasons for this considerable level of permanent military presence were all related to Iraq.

A chastened revolution

Iraq's effect on the Iranian Revolution was no less remarkable. In the early 1980s, Iran evinced boundless optimism and unlimited goals. By the end of its war with Iraq, the optimism had faded and the universalist Islamic goals had been replaced by a gritty nationalism. Even the composition of the Iranian government was changed. Immediately after the revolution, the primary qualification for any job was a past record of revolutionary action, preferably augmented by some religious training. Professional background and actual job experience were regarded as secondary or irrelevant. After eight years of conflict, a new generation of technocrats had begun to emerge, responding to the demands of the economy, military organization, and administration. The system was still very far from a meritocracy, but young seminarians who had taken to the streets for Khomeini could no longer count on automatic job preference.

After eight years of combat and austerity, there was a vast appetite for consumer goods and other benefits. The new generation of Iranians, many with little or no memory of the revolution or life under the shah, were now coming on the job market with only limited prospects. There was a shortage of housing, schools

were overwhelmed by the tidal wave of youth produced by the pro-natal policies of the early revolutionary years, social services were limited, and the burst
of consumer spending that accompanied the end of the war created a bubble of
foreign debt that would take a generation to erase. Mismanagement of the economy
and omnipresent corruption blighted the reputation of the revolutionary regime,
dimming even its genuine accomplishments, such as the extension of roads, tele-
phones, and electricity to the villages. The promises of the revolution to serve
the "dispossessed" seemed little more than idle talk. Khomeini was once said to
remark that the revolution was not about the price of melons. Suddenly, it seemed
to be about little else.

Iran and its neighbors

After the dissolution of the Soviet Union and the creation of a series of new states in
Central Asia and the Caucasus, Iran was left in the peculiar position of having land
and direct sea borders with fifteen different states. It had fought an eight-year war
with its neighbor to the west, suffering more than 600,000 casualties, including the
most extensive use of chemical weapons since World War I.[9] Its eastern neighbor,
Afghanistan, had been invaded by the Soviet Union and then collapsed in a civil
war. From these various conflicts, Iran had inherited some two million refugees
within its own borders, together with hundreds of square miles of minefields.

Another neighbor, Pakistan, itself a nuclear power, supported forces in
Afghanistan that were hostile to Iran. Iraq harbored a terrorist organization that
conducted cross-border operations into Iran. Northern Iraq was in an unstable balance of power between rival Kurdish factions, punctuated by periodic forays by
both Turkish and Iraqi forces, while the Shi'i region of southern Iraq was the site
of a prolonged, low-level rebellion. The United Arab Emirates and its Arab allies
in the GCC pressed Iran to resolve the dispute over the islands of Abu Musa and
the two Tunbs that had been occupied by Iran in 1971.

The new states of the former Soviet Union along Iran's northern border were
all in the early stages of nation building, and the former Communist officials who
dominated their governments were instinctively suspicious of Islamic movements.
Many of these states were engaged in ethnic and territorial strife of their own, as
they sorted out the residue of the Soviet empire.

Iran also had a superpower on its doorstep. The ships and planes of the United
States operated in the confined waters of the Persian Gulf and conducted frequent
exercises with the Arab states of the region. The United States also conducted
periodic military reprisal raids against Iraq, and U.S. and British aircraft patrolled
daily over northern and southern Iraq, just across the Iranian border.

Given this perilous situation, the Islamic Republic of Iran opted for a strategy of
accommodation. In the period beginning after the Iran-Iraq war, and accelerating
during Khatami's presidency, Iran muted its Islamic message when dealing with the
new states on its northern border and deliberately tried to avoid a secular-Islamist
rivalry with Turkey. Iran refused to take sides in regional disputes and offered its

good offices on such thorny issues as Nagorno-Karabagh and Chechnya. Instead, it focused primarily on commercial and regional cooperation, taking a lead role in creation of the Economic Cooperation Organization (ECO) and offering technical assistance and even aid on engineering and other projects. While preserving its position in the complex dispute over division of resources in the Caspian, Iran refused to be provoked into an escalation of words, or worse. It vigorously argued in favor of a pipeline route from the Caspian to northern Iran and in opposition to the U.S. plan of a Baku-Ceyhan (Turkey) connection, with some modest success. Iran appeared to be more concerned with stability and good relations than with any short-term political or economic gains which might be achieved by a more aggressive stance.

With regard to Iraq, Iran maintained cool but businesslike relations while keeping its powder dry. Talks proceeded slowly on repatriation of pows and on such mundane issues as pilgrim visits to the Shi'i shrines in Najaf and Karbala. Iran refused, however, to return some 125 aircraft that Iraq had flown to Iran without warning at the beginning of the war over Kuwait, insisting on reparations of up to one trillion dollars from Iraq in compensation for damages sustained as a result of the Iraqi invasion.

Both sides used surrogates to carry out hit-and-run operations against the opposition forces housed on either side of the border: the Mojahedin-e Khalq Organization (MKO), operating against Iran from a complex of bases and installations in Iraq, and the Supreme Assembly of the Islamic Revolution in Iraq (SAIRI), which had its headquarters in Tehran and conducted operations in southern Iraq. However, despite occasional exchanges of mortar fire and missiles, both sides resisted the temptation to push the confrontation to a climax. Iran gave lip service to the international sanctions against Iraq, but often looked the other way at the lucrative smuggling of Iraqi oil through Iranian waters. Neither side provided a level of support that would permit its surrogates to launch a major cross-border offensive.

At the same time, Iran pursued a determined program of missile development, indigenous production of weaponry and combat equipment, and regular military exercises along its border with Iraq. This demonstration of readiness and self-reliance was clearly intended to deter Iraq from any consideration of further military activities against Iran. Iraq, in turn, viewed the warming relations between Tehran and the regional Arab states as a betrayal of the Arab cause and as part of a greater plot by the United States to isolate the Iraqi government, but its blandishments had little effect.

An important element of Iran's deterrent policies was the burgeoning relationship with Russia. Following the collapse of the Soviet Union, Iran chose to cooperate with Russia in pursuit of stability along its northern border, to purchase modern military equipment that was unavailable from the West, to acquire nuclear technology for the power plant that Russia was building for Iran at Bushehr, and to develop some measure of diplomatic support for its positions, particularly in its running confrontation with the United States. The United States imposed some limited sanctions on Russian institutes, and the question of Iran became a perennial staple of U.S.-Russian relations. It was evident, however, that the Iranian-Russian connection was primarily a marriage of convenience and a matter of mutual commercial benefit. Neither side demonstrated desire for any long-term commitment; each seemed suspicious of the other and was willing to take opposing positions (on Caspian demarcation, pipeline strategy, and relations with particular Caspian states, for example) when it suited its immediate interests.

With regard to the GCC states, after about 1990 Iran made a concerted effort to develop a relationship of trust. In 1987, more than four hundred people had died when Saudi security forces confronted Iranian pilgrims during the annual Hajj. The pilgrims were performing a symbolic demonstration against the United States and Israel, contrary to Saudi rules against political demonstrations during the Hajj. This incident led to a three-year break in diplomatic relations between Saudi Arabia and Iran and marked the low point of relations between Iran and the Arab states of the Gulf. In later years, Iran took measures to prevent a recurrence of this tragedy by ordering its pilgrims to carry out their demonstrations on a small scale and within the confines of the Iranian encampment.

Iran also sent a string of goodwill emissaries to the Arab states and actively sought to change its earlier image of hostility and radicalism. Memories of Arab support for Iraq during the Iran-Iraq war were not forgotten on either side, but reconciliation was made easier by mutual acknowledgment of Iraq as the primary military threat in the region, following its invasion of Kuwait in 1990. After the election of Mohammed Khatami in Iran, high-level visits between Iran and the Arab regional states became commonplace, and Iran began to call for military confidence-building measures and for a regional security pact.

The terrorist bombing of the U.S. military barracks at Dhahran, Saudi Arabia, in 1996 killed nineteen American servicemen and raised concerns that Iran was behind the attack. Those charges were never proved, however, and the rapprochement between Saudi Arabia and Iran continued after a pause. Similarly, charges of Iranian complicity in Shi'i riots in Bahrain during the early 1990s were eventually set aside, and the two countries restored full diplomatic relations in January 1998, after a thirty-month lapse.

By far the most persistent of the issues separating Iran and the Arabs of the Gulf was the dispute over Iran's 1971 occupation of the islands of Abu Musa and the two tiny Tunb islands. Both Iran and the United Arab Emirates were passionate in their claims of sovereignty, and scholars in both countries conducted elaborate historical research to support national claims.[10] At the same time, new technology greatly reduced the strategic importance of the islands, while commercial sharing of the undersea resources of the islands was unaffected by political differences. Thus, the dispute became one of competing symbolic claims and national pride, which, ironically, may have rendered it even more difficult to resolve.[11] Although Iran offered talks, neither side showed the least interest in relinquishing its claims or seeking a compromise, suggesting that the islands issue would persist as a long-term irritant in relations. It did not, however, prevent a gradual warming of relations between the GCC states and Iran, including commercial relations with the U.A.E. In fact, during the height of this controversy, Iran became the number-one trade partner of the U.A.E. in the Islamic world.[12]

One of the most significant areas of Iran's new policy of accommodation was its participation in the Organization of Petroleum Exporting Countries (OPEC). In a series of difficult decisions during the late 1990s and early 2000, Iran generally set aside its earlier ideological objections and participated with Saudi Arabia and others to increase oil-production quotas in 1998, and then to reduce them in 1999 when oil prices collapsed in the face of the Asian financial crisis. After the recovery of oil prices above $30 per barrel, Iran argued strenuously against a new increase in production levels. At the Vienna OPEC meeting in March 2000, Iran formally disassociated itself from the consensus, preserving its classic position as a price hawk and protesting U.S. pressure tactics, which was important in terms of its domestic politics. Once the decision had been taken, however, Iran quietly increased its own production in accordance with other producers.[13] The very muted reaction of Saudi Arabia to Iran's rhetorical protest suggested that this bit of posturing had been prearranged. Throughout, Iran's production and exports remained well within the OPEC guidelines, and the relationship with Saudi Arabia was carefully nurtured.

Relations with the United States

The very close political, economic, and strategic relations between the United States and Iran collapsed under the weight of the revolution and the hostage crisis. Those events, and particularly the 444 days of the hostage-taking, created an American image of Iran as a fanatic nation committed to undermining fundamental U.S. interests. That image was not improved in 1985–86, when the Reagan administration attempted a disastrously conceived opening to Iran that exploded in scandal and nearly brought down the government.

In the years after Iraq's invasion of Kuwait, the Clinton administration in effect declared a plague on both Iran and Iraq with the "dual containment" policy, which spelled out broad guidelines for containing and isolating both countries.[14] In the case of Iran, the objective was to persuade the Islamic Republic to change its policies in a number of areas: terrorism, subversion, violent opposition to the Arab-Israel peace process, and the pursuit of weapons of mass destruction. To that end, and despite the opposition of its allies, the United States instituted an array of unilateral measures intended to isolate and punish Iran, including a secondary boycott against foreign companies investing in the Iranian oil and gas sector.

The U.S. position began to change after the election of Mohammad Khatami as president of Iran. In January 1998, President Khatami spoke to the American people via an interview with CNN, in which he addressed the key issues of major concern to the United States.[15]

On terrorism: "Any form of killing of innocent men and women who are not involved in confrontations is terrorism. It must be condemned, and we, in our turn, condemn every form of it in the world."

On the peace process: "We have declared our opposition to the Middle East peace process, because we believe it will not succeed. At the same time, we have clearly said that we don't intend to impose our views on others or to stand in their way."

On weapons of mass destruction: "We are not a nuclear power and do not intend to become one."

In addition, Khatami went as far as any Iranian political figure could go in expressing regret about the 1979–81 hostage crisis, and he pledged that such "unconventional methods" would not and could not be employed in today's Iran.

In response, Secretary of State Madeleine Albright in June 1998 spelled out a new U.S. policy calling for the establishment of "a road map leading to normal relations."[16] Over the following two years, the United States made a series of small but significant gestures to Iran. U.S. officials softened their language and no longer referred to Iran as a "rogue" or "outlaw" state; removed Iran from the narcotics list; designated the Mojahedin-e Khalq (and its multiple front organizations) as a terrorist organization; cooperated with Iran on the "6 + 2" talks on Afghanistan at the UN; waived sanctions against foreign oil companies that invested in Iran; lifted restrictions on the sale of agricultural and medical goods to Iran; authorized the sale of spare parts needed to ensure the safety of civilian passenger aircraft previously sold to Iran; and eased visa regulations for academic exchanges and for travel by Iranian UN diplomats in the United States.

Following the February 2000 elections for the sixth Majles in Iran, which resulted in an overwhelming popular vote for candidates supporting Khatami's reform movement, Secretary Albright again addressed the issue of Iran.[17] She acknowledged the U.S. role in the countercoup that overthrew Prime Minister Mohammad Mosaddeq in 1953 and commented that "the United States must bear its fair share of responsibility for the problems that have arisen in U.S.-Iranian relations."[18] She further acknowledged that "aspects of U.S. policy towards Iraq during its conflict with Iran appear now to have been regrettably short-sighted." While reiterating U.S. grievances toward Iran, she welcomed the prospect of "regional discussions aimed at reducing tensions and building trust." She announced the lifting of U.S. sanctions on the purchase of Iranian carpets and food products such as caviar and pistachios, promised to remove impediments to the travel and operation of exchange programs and nongovernmental organizations, and vowed to increase efforts to conclude a global settlement of all outstanding legal claims (often incorrectly referred to as Iran's "frozen assets"). Reiterating U.S. willingness to enter into direct official discussions without preconditions, she added, "surely the time has come for America and Iran to enter a new season in which mutual trust may grow and a quality of warmth supplant the long cold winter of our mutual discontent."

This was the most far-reaching expression of U.S. interest in a rapprochement with Iran in the twenty-one years since the revolution. It came, however, at a moment of intense political conflict in Iran. Conservative forces were striking back at the reformists, closing many newspapers, throwing key journalists into jail, and attempting to assassinate Sa'id Hajjarian, a member of the Tehran Municipal Council and one of the architects of the reform movement.

Iran's supreme leader, Ayatollah Mohammad Ali Khamenei, was reportedly offended by a phrase in Albright's speech referring to the fact that many of Iran's institutions remained in the hands of "unelected" officials. He made a scathing attack on the U.S. position in a speech in Mashhad on March 25,[19] and Iran's official response to the Albright speech was muted and tended to fall back on the formulas of the past.

Remarkably, however, less than two weeks later an important reformist organization published an alternative analysis of the Albright speech. Without reference to the Khamenei address, the Organization of the Mojahedin of the Islamic Revolution of Iran (OMIR), which was closely associated with Behzad Nabavi, a key supporter of President Khatami in the sixth Majies, praised the candor of Albright's speech and concluded that it was "a kind of victory and an achievement for ... Khatami's government." In a clear reference to the U.S. call for direct talks, the OMIR declaration asked Iranian policy makers "to carry out a logical, calculated and wise analysis of the changes that have come about in American stances and policies. Instead of relying upon a wave of blind emotions, they must act on the basis of national interests."[20]

Thus, although the Albright speech and the Iranian response could not be seen as a breakthrough, it was evidence of substantially changed attitudes in Washington and in some important circles in Tehran. Unlike the "dual containment" policy of the previous six years, after 1998 the United States deliberately began to make an explicit distinction between Iran, where it sought dialogue and eventual normalization of relations, and Iraq, where regime change was the objective.

A revolution like no other

Iran is the exception to the history of modern revolutions. With the French Revolution as the intellectual model, we have come to anticipate certain stages through which any revolutionary society is likely to pass. We anticipate the rise of a radical clique that appropriates the revolution in the name of its own ideological persuasion, leading to a dictatorship, highly centralized authority, and one-party rule by the victors in the ideological combat. We have come to expect massive suppression of dissent and the enforcement of a strict ideological canon, leading almost inevitably to the use of mass terror and purges.

Iran had encounters with all of these symptoms, but it avoided the extremes of the French, Russian, or Chinese revolutions. The difference appeared to lie in a fundamental respect for the popular voice that was quite remarkable under such extreme economic and political circumstances.

The Iranian constitution is an ambiguous document. It leaves unanswered the central question of whether sovereignty and legitimacy arise from the people or from God. Iran is an Islamic Republic, and it is not clear whether the emphasis should be placed on "Islamic" or "Republic." At various times the pendulum has swung in different directions. Even in the earliest days, however, Iran insisted on elections. None of these elections rose to the level of international standards of "free and fair." Candidates were prescreened by a body of revolutionary over-seers and severe limits were placed on the terms of public expression and debate. The Islamic nature of the revolution was not to be questioned, nor would criticism of the supreme leader be tolerated. The media were not equally available to all candidates, and radio and television remained in the hands of the conservative ruling elite, which was not hesitant to use them for its own ideological purposes.

Nevertheless, voting itself was generally unfettered and there appeared to be no effort to rig the vote, even when it was not what the conservative elite wanted or expected. Over time, and especially in the decade after Khomeini's death, candidates and the electorate demonstrated a willingness to challenge official orthodoxy and go their own way. The first major evidence of this was the 1993 presidential election, in which Ali Akbar Rafsanjani was running for his second term. He had won by 94 percent in his first election, when he was seen as a pragmatic reformer who would bring order and good management to the country. Partly due to the vagaries of the oil market and other developments that were not entirely under his control, the government's record in his first term was less than compelling, and the voters responded accordingly. In the election for his second term, 42 percent of the voters stayed home—a huge percentage in a country where voting was routinely described as a religious duty—and of those who voted, he received only 63 percent.

The watershed, however, was the presidential election of 1997. Mohammad Khatami, a virtual unknown, was paired against the well-known speaker of the Majles, Ali Akbar Nateq-Nuri. Khatami ran a Western-style campaign, whistle-stopping throughout the country with his unique message of civil society and rule of law. The youth population immediately embraced his message, and they went to work for him in a huge burst of enthusiasm and grassroots campaigning. Only weeks before the election, most observers in Iran and elsewhere confidently expected Nateq-Nuri to win, but the popular shift was irresistible.

This performance was repeated in the municipal council elections of February 1999 and especially the Majles elections of February 2000, which saw three of every four incumbents go down to defeat, while those associated with the newly organizing reform movement won almost everywhere. In each case, the conservative establishment fought a rear-guard action, disqualifying some elected candidates after the fact, closing reformist newspapers and hauling their publishers and journalists into court on trivial charges, and, most ominously, conducting a series of murders of intellectuals and writers. However, there was no systematic attempt to nullify the elections, and the hardline tactics only reinforced the negative image of the antireform forces and eroded their legitimacy.

The Khatami forces gradually extended their control to an increasingly wide range of governmental institutions in a kind of envelopment strategy, slowly but surely excluding the ultraconservatives from one area after another, all without serious violence or involvement of the military. There was no precedent for such a development in any other major revolutionary society, and there was no real precedent for electoral rejection of an entrenched political elite anywhere in the Middle East, with the exception of Israel.

In some respects, former president Rafsanjani was both the emblem and eventual victim of this process. A cleric close to Khomeini, one of the organizers of the revolt against the shah, a coalition-builder and strategist behind the scenes, the consummate insider with perhaps the most distinguished résumé of all the revolutionaries of his generation, an early proponent of reform, and the sponsor of the first really successful party of largely nonclerical technocrats, Rafsanjani appeared to be the millennium man. In the 2000 elections, however, he was viciously attacked by the new breed of reform journalists, who asked why he had apparently done nothing to curb the past excesses of the intelligence ministry, why he had apparently supported the continuation of the war with Iraq in 1982, and how he could account for his considerable personal wealth.

Although Rafsanjani and his family genuinely—and with some considerable justification—saw themselves as the progenitors of the reform movement, their pained reaction to these highly personal attacks associated them with the conservative faction, and Rafsanjani came in at the very end of the list of thirty Majles candidates in Tehran.[21] The fact that he symbolized the past, which he would have expected to work in his favor, was the reason for his decline.

The new politics of Iran was less respectful, more aggressive and unintimidated in its efforts to get answers to some of the unanswered questions of the past. Rafsanjani was caught up in this maelstrom and was totally at a loss over how to handle it. It was clear, however, that a corner had been turned and the politics of the revolution were unlikely to return to their earlier status.

Conclusion: the new image of Iran

At the start of the new millennium, Iran was one of the most interesting and politically innovative countries in the Middle East. Its freshly minted image of moderation and regional cooperation was still regarded with skepticism by some of its neighbors and by many in the United States who had watched the fanaticism of the earliest days of the revolution and who were unlikely soon to forget the sight. Moreover, doubts persisted about the ability of the reform movement to withstand the relentless counterattack by diehard conservatives who were willing to exploit—even abuse—their access to the courts and other institutions to preserve their own vision of the revolution.

This fierce struggle for the soul of the revolution was kept in check only by the determination of the reformists to operate peacefully within the constitution and by the equal determination of Iran's top leadership, especially the supreme leader and the president, to compromise at critical moments to prevent an outburst of violence. Could the popular demand for change by a youthful and restless electorate be accommodated within the context of a revolutionary Islamic state without collapsing into anarchy and violence? The answer could not be predicted, but the very effort to construct a new politics within an existing constitutional model was a unique experiment for the region.

Europe, Japan, and China, which had placed their bets early on the possibility of a working relationship with Iran, and which staunchly opposed U.S. unilateral sanctions, moved quickly to take advantage of emerging commercial opportunities while U.S. companies were still forbidden to compete. By early 2000, major European companies, particularly in the energy sector but also in other commercial areas, were setting up offices in Tehran. The Japanese, who had acceded for nearly a decade to U.S. demands to withhold development loans, once again began to signal that they would proceed with such loans despite U.S. objections. Even the World Bank disregarded U.S. pressure and approved loans for two long-standing Iranian development projects in May 2000, citing the promising direction of Iran's political reforms.

This new commercial dynamic was directly related to changes in U.S. policy. The partial lifting of U.S. sanctions on the purchase of Iranian non-energy products, and the absence of any U.S. reaction to a spate of European, Canadian, and Australian energy deals, seemed to indicate that the United States was no longer willing—or perhaps able—to resist international commercial pressures for an opening to Iran. It was also understood that the most onerous U.S. third-party sanctions (the Iran-Libya Sanctions Act of 1996) would expire in August 2001 and were unlikely to be renewed by any administration in Washington. The U.S. government certainly was not anxious to engage in another showdown with its allies in a quixotic effort to deprive Iran of revenues that might be used for military or other purposes. In fact, Iran's military budget had been pared back in favor of social programs, and its hard-currency expenditures on defense were smaller than those of any other country in the Gulf.

Close observers of Iran understood the power of the reform movement and the near-impossibility of putting the genie back in the bottle, but they were also aware of the tenuous balance between the forces of change and the resistance by an earlier revolutionary generation that saw its most cherished slogans being challenged or set aside. It was well understood that if the reformists failed to fulfill their early promises, they could share the fate of their predecessors, who also started with high hopes and wide public support.

This drama would not only play itself out domestically, it would be watched with rapt attention by Iran's neighbors. It was one of the great ironies of the Iranian revolution that its most significant "export" to its neighbors in the Middle East might prove to be a model of a democratizing system within an Islamic context.

Some of those in the neighborhood might regard that as a threat at least as great as the export of radical Islamism. The ferocious counterattack by revolutionary ideologues and vested interests, however, demonstrated just how perilous and uncertain such an experiment would be.

Notes

1 Hosein Valeh, political adviser to President Khatami, interview cited in Susan Sachs, "As Ballots Are Counted, Iran's Moderates Fear Backlash," *The New York Times*, 22 Feb. 2000, 1.

2 The Preamble of the Constitution of the Islamic Republic declares that "in the development of international relations, the Constitution will strive with other Islamic and popular movements to prepare the way for the formation of a single world community ... and to assure the continuation of the struggle for the liberation of all deprived and oppressed peoples in the world."

3 Foreign Broadcast Information Service, 30 Oct. 1984.

4 Ibid.

5 Rightly or wrongly, this was one of the charges that reformist journalists attributed to Rafsanjani in the February 2000 Majles election, which contributed to his very poor showing as described later in this paper.

6 See Jimmy Carter, *Keeping Faith: Memoirs of a President* (New York: Bantam Books, 1982), 483.

7 Saddam Hussein, letter to President Rafsanjani of Iran, 15 August 1990. This letter, which revoked in a single stroke all of the war aims that Iraq had pursued during the eight years of conflict with Iran, was intended to secure Iraq's eastern border as its forces redeployed to Kuwait; or, as Saddam put it, "so as not to keep any of Iraq's potentials disrupted outside the field of the great battle." Foreign Broadcast Information Service, 16 August 1990.

8 Testimony of Alina L. Romanowski, Deputy Assistant Secretary of Defense for Near Eastern and South Asian Affairs, before the House Committee on International Relations, 23 March 2000, Federal News Service.

9 According to Hadi Qalamnevis, Director General of the Statistics and Information Department at the Islamic Revolution Martyrs Foundation, 204,795 Iranians lost their lives in the Iran-Iraq war, including 188,015 military and 16,780 civilians. Islamic Republic News Agency, 23 Sept. 2000, and *Iran Times*, 10 Nov. 2000, 4. Earlier estimates by Mohsen Rafiqdust, the former head of the Iranian Revolutionary Guard Force, had stated that 400,000 were wounded during the war. Robert Fisk, *The Independent*, 25 June 1995. According to Iranian health officials, about 60,000 Iranians were exposed to Iraqi chemical weapon attacks during the war. Agence France Press, 13 March 2000. Over 15,000 war veterans suffering from chemical weapons syndrome reportedly died in the twelve years after the end of the Iran-Iraq war, according to Abbas Khani, the head of the Legal Office for War Veterans. Islamic Republic News Agency, 13 Nov. 2000.

10 For an excellent synopsis of the issue see Richard Schofield, "Border Disputes: Past, Present, and Future," in *The Persian Gulf at the Millennium: Essays in Politics, Economy, Security, and Religion*, ed. Gary G. Sick and Lawrence G. Potter (New York; St. Martin's Press, 1997), 142–56.

11 This issue was debated at length in the Gulf/2000 conference on "Confidence-Building Measures in the Gulf," in Salalah, Oman, 9–12 Nov. 1999. This conference brought together about forty Arabs and Iranians, with a few Westerners, to address mutual security issues.

12 The Islamic Republic News Agency, 13 Oct. 1998, reported that the value of U.A.E. exports to Iran in 1996 stood at $1.080 billion and its imports at $330 million. Saudi Arabia and Indonesia followed Iran in the list of major trade partners to the U.A.E. in 1996. Much of this trade involved re-export of consumer goods to Iran via Dubai, often circumventing U.S. sanctions against direct sales to Iran.

13 See, for example, James Gavin, "Odd Man Out," *Middle East Economic Digest*, 7 April 2000, 5. For a report on Iran's adherence in practice, see Reuters wire service report, "Reuters Survey, OPEC Adds One Mbpd Oil Output in April," 8 May 2000.

14 Martin Indyk, "The Clinton Administration's Approach to the Middle East," Keynote Address to the Soref Symposium on "Challenges to US Interests in the Middle East: Obstacles and Opportunities," Proceedings of the Washington Institute for Near East Policy, 18–19 May 1993, 1–8.

15 Cable News Network, 7 Jan. 1998, "Transcript of interview with Iranian President Mohammad Khatami."

16 Secretary of State Madeleine K. Albright, "Remarks at 1998 Asia Society Dinner," 17 June 1998, as released by the Office of the Spokesman, U.S. Department of State, 18 June 1998.

17 Secretary of State Madeleine K. Albright, speech to the American-Iranian Council, Omni Shoreham Hotel, Washington, DC, 17 March 2000.

18 *The New York Times* subsequently published key CIA documents on the coup in its issue of 16 April 2000.

19 See "Khamene'i Address in Mashhad," Voice of the Islamic Republic of Iran Radio 1, 25 March 2000, as translated by the Foreign Broadcast Information Service.

20 Declaration of the Organization of the Mojahedin of the Islamic Revolution of Iran, 4 April 2000, published in *Asr-e Ma* 156, 6 April 2000, 1, 6, 8. Translated by the Foreign Broadcast Information Service.

21 After charges of irregularities and a lengthy recount of many voting boxes, including invalidation of 720,000 votes in the Tehran constituency by the Guardian Council, Rafsanjani was eventually identified as number 20 on the Tehran list. He aligned himself squarely with the conservative faction and emerged as the key strategist in efforts to unseat the reformers.

58

THE IRANIAN REVOLUTION

Its impact on economic relations with the United States

Khosrow Fatemi

Source: *International Journal of Middle East Studies* 12(3) (1980): 303–17.

> I, on this auspicious day ... announce the founding of the Islamic
> Republic of Iran. This day shall be known as the first day of rule of
> Allah in Iran.
>
> Ayatollah Rouhollah Khomaini April 1, 1979

The international political implications of the Iranian revolution will not be known for many years to come, and American foreign policy makers and pundits will debate the question of "who lost Iran" long after that. Even the international economic implications of the revolution will not be fully realized, or recognized, in the near future. It is, however, already amply clear that the fall of the Shah has had profound consequences on Iran's economic and trade relations with other countries, in general, and with the United States in particular. It is to the latter issue that this essay addresses itself.

It is generally believed that the climax of American economic involvement in Iran came in 1978 when:

American investments in Iran exceeded $682 million.

The number of Americans working and living in Iran approached 50,000.

The military purchase/commitments from U.S. manufacturers amounted to over $12 billion.

The United States became the second largest supplier of Iran's non-military imports totaling $12.7 billion.

Despite this logistic, even if imbalanced, entanglement of the economics of the two countries by 1978, all indications are that the incremental trend had not peaked; and, that in the coming decade we would have witnessed even further integration of the two countries, or, as some would maintain, greater submission of the Iranian economy to American interests.

Part of the phenomenal, if overburdening, growth in the relations between the two countries during the last few years was the result of the implementation, almost exclusively by Iran, of an agreement signed between the two countries in 1976 which projected an annual non-oil, non-military trade between the two nations of some $15 billion by 1981, nearly all of it in the form of U.S. exports to Iran.[1]

While American economic involvement in Iran was total, and included all aspects of the Iranian economy, the interrelationship was most conspicious in four sectors: the military, the oil industry, the banking industry, and the capital goods market. A fifth sector, agricultural and consumer goods, could be added to this list and will be treated accordingly. Owing to the nature of this sector, that is, the dominant global position of U.S. agricultural production, and Iran's heavy reliance on food imports, no major changes in this sector are anticipated.

The military

In the mid-1960s the British government, faced with severe economic problems, especially budgetary and balance-of-payments deficits, announced its intention to withdraw its military forces from east of Suez, including the Persian Gulf, by 1971. Following the announcement of the pending British withdrawal from the Persian Gulf, the Shah, probably with the dream of revival of the Persian Empire in the back of his mind, declared that the security of the Persian Gulf region was the responsibility of its littoral states and cautioned against any superpower attempts to fill the power vacuum to be created by the forthcoming British withdrawal. He, then, volunteered his armed forces as the new gendarme of the Persian Gulf. In this venture the Shah was not only supported by the United States and other Western countries who were, in effect, the benefactors of this new arrangement; but also, by the Soviet Union, potentially the greatest beneficiary of any instability in the region.

In the earlier stages, that is, until 1972, the raison d'etre of Iran's military buildup was to keep the crucial oil routes of the Persian Gulf free from any disruptions. Considering that over 20 million barrels of oil pass through the Persian Gulf every day, the West's willingness to support the Shah's efforts to keep the oil running was plausible; and, considering that oil was the backbone of Iran's economy, the Shah's endeavors to keep the Persian Gulf stable and under control were seemingly justifiable. Following the 1973–74 oil price increases, however, the picture changed drastically and the Shah began talking of grander designs including his plans to make Iran the world's strongest nonnuclear military power.[2]

The inventory of the Shah's arsenal which had begun in modest terms, soon began to look like the Jane's Directory of Modern Weapons (table 1). Iran's military budget registered astronomical increases reaching almost $10 billion by fiscal year 1978–79 (beginning on March 21) and the country's military purchases from the United States expanded even more rapidly reaching $5.8 billion by 1977 (table 2).

Table 1 A selected list of Iran's American-made arms

Quantity	Manufacturer and product	Delivery	Source[a]
Aircraft			
108	McD-D F4E Phantom fighters	1974–5	SIPRI 75/6
36	McD-D F-4E Phantom fighters	1976–7	SIPRI 75–7
12	McD-D RF-4E Phantom tactical reconnaissance	(1976)	SIPRI 77
141	Northrop F-5E Tiger II fighters	1974–76	SIPRI 75–7
28	Northrop F-5F trainers	1976	SIPRI 76–7
80	Grumman F-14 Tomcat fighters	1976–78	SIPRI 75–7
160	Gen. Dynamics F-16 fighters	(1979–)	AWST 6/13/77
6	Lockheed P-3C Orion anti-submarines	1975	SIPRI 75/6
3	Lockheed P-3C Orion anti-submarines	1977	SIPRI 77
12	Lockheed C-130 transports	1974	SIPRI 75
6	Lockheed KC-135 tankers	—	MB 75–6
6	Boeing 707-320-C tanker-transports	1974	SIPRI 75
7	Boeing 707-39JC tanker-transports	1976	SIPRI 77
7	Boeing E-3C Airborne Warning and Control aircraft	—	SIPRI 76
2	Airborne Reconnaissance and Ground Process Systems	—	OMC
31	Beech F33C Bonanza Light craft	1974–5	SIPRI 79
Helicopters			
202	Bell AH-1 J Sea Cobra gunships	1974–7	SIPRI 75
287	Bell 214 utility	1975–7	SIPRI 75/6
39	Bell 214C utility	1977–8	SIPRI 77
6	Sikorsky S-65As	1975	SIPRI 76
6	Sikorsky RH-53Ds	1976–7	SIPRI 77
50	Boeing CH-47s	—	MB 77–8
91	Bell-Agusta 206 Jet Rangers	—	SIPRI 75/6
6	Bell-Augusta 212s	1976–7	SIPRI 75/6
16	Boeing Meridionali CH-47C Chinooks	1974	SIPRI 75
22	Boeing Meridionali CH-47C Chinooks	—	SIPRI 75/6
Missiles			
280	Hughes AIM-54A Phoenix AS	1976–8	SIPRI 75/6
2,500+	Hughes AGM-65A Maverick AS	1974–5	SIPRI 75
754	Raytheon AIM-9J Sidewinder AA	1976–8	SIPRI 77
516	Raytheon AIM-7 Sparrow AA	1976–7	SIPRI 77
222	McD D AGM-84A Harpoon AS & ShS	—	SIPRI 75/6
6,200	Hughes BGM-71A TOW anti-tank	1974–7	SIPRI 75–7
300	Hughes TOW anti-tank (partial production in Iran)	—	OMC
634	McD-D FGM-77A Dragon anti-tank	(1977)	
—	Raytheon Improved HAWK Surface to Air system	—	MB 77–8
Naval			
6	Ex-US Navy destroyers	1978	SIPRI 76
3	Ex-US Navy submarines	1975–6	SIPRI 76
414	Mk. 46 torpedoes	—	SIPRI 76

[a] SIPRI, Stockholm International Peace Research Institute Yearbook; AWST, Aviation Week and Space Technology; MB, Military Balance (annual from International Institute for Strategic Studies, London; OMC, Office of Munitions Control, State Department). See *Middle East Research and Information Project (MERIP)* Report No. 71, p. 22.

Source: M. Klare and D. Volman, *Arms Trade Data* (Institute for Policy Studies, 1978), pp. 9–10.

Table 2 United States military sales to Iran, 1950–1979 (In thousands of dollars)

| Fiscal year | Government-to-government Foreign Military Sales (FMS) | | Commercial |
	Agreements	Deliveries	
1950–66	292,494	47,292	
1960–66			5,905
1967	143,873	38,866	2,022
1968	69,038	56,717	5,147
1969	251,573	94,881	10,084
1970	113,154	127,717	9,811
1971	396,841	79,352	27,059
1972	519,110	214,807	36,975
1973	2,157,355	238,633	19,421
1974	4,373,225	510,347	35,322
1975	3,020,979	956,372	49,410
1976	1,688,381	1,466,767	107,943
1977	5,803,079	2,245,899	121,500
1978 (est.)	3,000,000	—	131,000
1979 (est.)	2,625,000	—	141,000
Total	24,454,102	6,718,270	702,599

Sources: For 1950–1975, US Arms Policies in the Persian Gulf and Red Sea Areas, Report of Staff Survey Mission to Ethiopia, Iran and the Arabian Peninsula, House Committee on International Relations, Dec. 1977, pp. 135–136; For 1976–1979, Department of Defense, Security Assistance Program, Congressional Presentation Document FY 1979. See *Middle East Research and Information Project (MERIP)* Report No. 71, p. 23.

By mid-1978 it became abundantly clear that Iran was unable to meet its parallel budgetary increments in both economic development and military expenditures. Review of Iran's development plans, both military and economic, while under consideration earlier, became absolutely essential when Sharif-Emami's government adopted, and implemented, in September 1978, its appeasement policy of acceding to every economic demand of the striking government workers. Among the first projects to be in danger of curtailment were foreign military procurements and nuclear power plants. Several reports of cancellations surfaced during the ensuing months culminating in the announcement on February 4, 1979, of cancellation of orders for more than $7.0 billion in U.S. weapons.[3] The coup de grace, however, came after the revolution when Iran announced cancellation of the rest of the military purchases. This brought the total to about $12.5 billion (table 3).

No exact figures are available to indicate how much of this total figure involved lost sales, that is, cancellation of contractual orders that were in production; and how much of it was lost opportunity, that is, cancellation of agreed upon, but pending orders. In any event, one can surmise that the Iranian revolution resulted in a net loss of $12.5 billion in military hardware sales, plus a residual loss of approximately $1–2 billion in spare parts sales.

Table 3 Cancelled/defaulted military purchases by Iran, October 1978–June 1979

	Equipment	Manufacturer	Number	Price (*in millions of dollars*)
1.	F-16 Fighters	General Dynamics	140	2,500
2.	F-16 Fighters	General Dynamics	160	3,200
3.	F-4E Fighter-Bombers	McDonnell Douglas	31	350
4.	Shrike Air-to-Surface Missiles	Texas Instruments	1,000	105
5.	F-14 Fighters	Grumman	70	1,750
6.	Airborne Warning and Command System (AWACS)	Boeing	7	1,200
7.	Spruance Class Destroyers	Litton Industries	2	800
8.	Helicopter Production Plant	Textron Inc.	1	575
9.	Phoenix Air-to-Air Missiles	Hughes Aircraft	400	100
10.	RF4E Reconnaissance Planes	McDonnell Douglas	16	219
11.	M48M Tanks Reconstruction Plant	Harsco	1	80
12.	Miscellaneous Missiles, other weaponry and training	Different Companies	—	752
13.	Miscellaneous Naval Weaponry	Different Companies	—	350
14.	Naval Construction Project	Planning Research	1	30
15.	Construction Project	Harris Corp.	1	65
16.	747 Military Transport	Boeing Corp.	4 – 5	200
Total				12,476

Sources: Numbers 1, 3, and 4: *New York Times*, December 22, 1978.

Number 2, 6, and 7: *The Wall Street Journal*, February 5, 1979.

Number 5: *Los Angeles Times*, March 3, 1979, for the price, and November 3, 1978, for the quantity.

Number 8: *The Wall Street Journal*, December 28, 1978.

Number 9: *New York Times*, December 12, 1978, for the price, and *The Wall Street Journal*, February 6, 1979.

Number 10: *US News and World Report*, February 19, 1979.

Number 11: *The Wall Street Journal*, November 1, 1978.

Number 12, 13, and 16: *The Wall Street Journal*, November 3, 1978.

Number 14: *The Wall Street Journal*, March 14, 1979.

Number 16: Author's estimate.

Number 15: Author's estimate.

The oil industry

The oil industry has traditionally played a dominant position in the political and economic affairs of Iran. Furthermore, until recently, there has always been substantial foreign involvement in every phase of it. This unique position notwithstanding, the conclusions drawn in this section are generally applicable to all other industries as well.

Before the revolution

The West in general, and the United States in particular, profited from the Iranian oil industry in both tangible and intangible ways. The tangible benefits included, inter alia, employment and investment opportunities, and special discounts granted to the Consortium Members.[4] The intangible benefits of Iranian oil were the security of supply and the moderating behavior of the Shah within OPEC.

Foreign employment.   Foreign employment in the Iranian oil and related industries in the summer of 1978 was around 3,000, one-third of which were Americans.

Foreign investment.   According to U.S. Department of Commerce figures, total investment of American companies in the Iranian oil industry was $457 million.[5] American oil companies owned 40 percent of the Consortium and were partners in three other joint venture-producing companies.[6]

Special discounts.   The Sales-Purchase Agreement reached between Iran and the Consortium Members in 1972 included two provisions distinctly favorable to the latter. Under a revised version of one of these provisions, the Consortium Members were entitled to a discount of 22 cents for every barrel of Iranian oil exported by them.[7] The dollar value of this discount even during the glut of early 1978 – when companies were, to the utmost disdain of Iran, reducing their purchases of Iranian oil – was $770,000 per day or $280 million for the year, of which American companies received close to $120 million.[8] While not easily quantifiable in monetary terms, the intangible benefits of oil policies of prerevolution Iran, security of supply and moderating role in OPEC were substantial and indeed more significant than the tangible benefits.

Security of supply.   The Shah had repeatedly declared that his government would not use oil as a weapon and would not mix oil and politics. Events since his downfall have well illustrated the significance of this pledge. Iranian oil, once the most secure source of supply, has become a de facto tool of diplomacy. Also significant was the Shah's willingness to sell oil to Israel and South Africa.

The Shah's moderating role in OPEC.   While he was one of the main forces behind OPEC's price increases in the early 1970s, the Shah, probably realizing the dangers of haphazard and wreckless price increases, gradually became a moderating force within OPEC. His "indexation" system, had it not been rejected by the industrialized countries, would have given oil prices some degree of graduality.[9]

After the revolution

Very little information is available on the status of the oil industry in postrevolution Iran, and what is available is scattered and highly unreliable.[10] Iran's new oil "policies" as provided by various sources indicate the following changes since the revolution.

154

Foreign employment. Even though no reliable figures are available as to the number of expatriate employees of the Iranian oil industry, most likely, few of the 3,000 such employees are still in Iran.

Foreign investment. The status of foreign investors in the Iranian oil industry is very unusual.[11] Theoretically, in compliance with the most-favored-nation clause of the 1972 agreement, the Consortium Members were required to pay 40 percent of any investment in the Iranian exploration and production facilities. In reality, however, because of disagreements that developed between Iran and foreign oil companies, the latter, contending that the National Iranian Oil Company had negated the 1972 agreement by exporting more than the amount allocated to it by the agreement, refused to make any investment payments. The NIOC countered by making all the investment and charging the oil companies interest for their portion, 40 percent of the amount involved. As a result, the oil companies never had all the usual rights and privileges of an investor. They exercised their control not by equity but rather by virtue of their exclusive control of purchasing and monopoly of providing technical advice and assistance to NIOC.

Unrelated to the above, the oil companies began an acceleration process of amortization on their assets in Iran long before the revolution; to the extent that by 1978 their undepreciated investment in Iran was a very small percentage of the total value of Iran's oil industry assets, and an even smaller percentage of their revenues from their operations in Iran. Nevertheless, more than $400 million is involved and as of this writing no information is available as to the actual status of this investment.

Security of supply. Probably the sharpest contrast between pre- and post-revolution Iran is manifested in the area of supply, where Iran's position has been completely reversed. Not only has Iran repeatedly threatened to use the "oil weapon" itself, Mr. Khomaini has frequently urged other Muslim nations to do likewise and stand up against "western infidels." This is, of course, not taken very seriously at this early stage; but recent pro-Iran or anti-United States demonstrations in Saudi Arabia, Kuwait, and Libya, all major oil producing countries, should not go unnoticed. While it would be incorrect to assume that all these events are the result of Mr. Khomaini's success in converting his differences with the United States into an Islamic *jihad* against the Western powers, it would be as incorrect to assume that Mr. Khomaini does not have fanatic supporters outside Iran who view him as an Islamic Messiah or a modern day Robin Hood.

An additional complicating factor in the evaluation of security of supply of Iranian oil is the degree of control that the Tehran regime has over the actual implementation of any production policies it might have. There have been numerous reports of sabotage as well as labor unrest in the oil-producing regions.[12] From the little information available on the mood of the Iranian oil workers in Khuzistan, it seems that their position vis-à-vis oil production and marketing is even more radical than that of the Tehran regime.[13]

Should this be the case, the oil workers' support of the regime's noncompromising stand against the West would evaporate once economic realities in Iran force the government to take a more moderate – and rational – political stand. In this context different intervening variables such as active political, ideological, and racial groups, inter alia, Iran's communist party, the Tudeh, and Iranian Arabs should also be taken into consideration. While Tudeh's support in other parts of the country is sparse, some oil workers seem to have been attracted by its ideological doctrinaire. Moreover, many oil workers, particularly the unskilled, are of Arab origin and followers of the Sunni sect of Islam, and have always been unhappy over their political, social, and economic subservience to the Persians. Mr. Khomaini's new constitution adds religious inferiority to the Iranian Arab's causes of rebellion. Despite of, or maybe because of the above, the discontent among, and alignment of, Iranian oil workers has not thus far been a viable factor in determining Iran's oil production and marketing policies.

Iran's new position in OPEC. Iran's new position, while never formalized or stabilized, seems to be in line with those who advocate high price increases in every OPEC meeting. This has indeed shifted the power balance of OPEC against the moderates and has resulted, and will continue to result, in higher price increases than before.[14]

Probably more detrimental to the world's energy balance, however, has been Iran's sales in the volatile spot market. While price increases are indeed damaging to the international oil equation, they are usually infrequent and almost always predictable. Spot sales, on the other hand, are very erratic and spot market prices vary daily, thus making any planning by the consuming nations or the oil companies impractical.

Finally, it is very ironic that in the same context that the United States's inability to increase domestic production in the early 1970s furnished OPEC with the leverage it needed to dictate its oil policies to the consuming nations, Saudi Arabia's inability to increase its production but marginally in 1979 seemed to have provided Mr. Khomaini with the leverage he needed to try to dictate his policies to the consuming nations.[15] Through sheer naïveté or simple incompetence, however, the Tehran regime lost its strong position in OPEC when Iran's oil exports dwindled to less than one million barrels per day in the first half of 1980, down by more than 80 percent from the average level of the early and mid-1970s.

The banking system

The systematized relationship that existed between the United States and Iranian banking systems prior to the revolution is an example par excellence of the overall interdependence of the economics of the two countries and specifically of the logistical dependence of the Iranian economy on the United States. The significance of the association was not so much the billions of dollars involved and the income it generated for the American banking system, but the very important role it played in facilitating the growth of overall American economic involvement in Iran.

Capital exposure of American Banks in Iran

At the time of the Revolution, it was estimated that twelve major U.S. banks had a total capital exposure of $2.2 billion in Iran (table 4). Most of this was in the form of direct loans to Iranian government or semigovernment banks such as the Agriculture Development Bank of Iran or the Industrial and Mining Development Bank of Iran. Furthermore, most of these loans were either guaranteed by the Central Bank of Iran or had no guarantees at all. Had it not been for President Carter's decision on November 14, 1979, to freeze the assets of the Iranian government in the United States, the declaration on November 23, 1979, by Iran to default on its foreign commitments, including loans by the American banks, could have had serious repercussions for some U.S. banks. The President's decision provided the collateral to ascertain that Iran's debt to U.S. banks is not defaulted.

Direct investment by U.S. banks in Iranian banking institutions

Before the Revolution, there were thirty-seven banks in Iran, thirteen of which had foreign partners. The total book-value of foreign investment in the Iranian banks amounted to about $75 million, out of which a meager sum of $25 million was held by four American banks: Bank of America, Chase Manhattan Bank, Citibank, and the Continental Illinois Bank of Chicago.

Table 4 Credit exposure of American banks in Iran as of February 1979

Group A: $200 million or more
  Citibank, New York
  Chase Manhattan Bank, New York
Group B: Between $100 and 200 million
  Chemical Bank, New York
  First National Bank, Chicago
  Manufactureres Hanover Trust Company, New York
  Morgan Guaranty Trust Company, New York
  Bank of America, San Francisco
Group C: $100 million or less
  Wells Fargo Bank, San Francisco
  Security Pacific National Bank, Los Angeles
  First National Bank, Boston
  Western Bancorp., Los Angeles
  Crocker National Bank, San Francisco
Estimated Total: $2,200 million

Source: The Wall Street Journal, February 9, 1979.

U.S. banks' income from their operations in Iran

The income generated by U.S. banks in Iran came from three main sources:

Interest. Considering the magnitude of the loans involved ($2.2 billion) and assuming a 10 percent interest rate, this would amount to $220 million per year.

Banking services. The level of income generated from banking services such as money transfers and loan arrangements, while substantial, cannot be accurately determined.

Return on investment. Based on a 20 percent return on the book value of their investments in Iranian banks, this would amount to a nominal $5 million. The above monetary considerations notwithstanding, a macro-analysis of U.S.-Iranian relations would indicate a bifunctional role for the American banking institutions in Iran, that is, first to provide the Iranian banking system with the proper channels needed to "recycle" Iran's petrodollar billions; and second, to provide logistics for overall U.S. involvement in Iran.

The capital goods market

In October 1977, the U.S. Department of Commerce published a survey of U.S. business opportunities in Iran.[16] According to this survey:

> Iran's capital goods market was to grow at about 17 percent per year reaching $13.4 billion by 1980.
>
> While Iran's domestic production of capital goods was expected to grow at substantially higher rates, by 1980 only 30 percent of a total of about $4.0 billion could be locally produced.
>
> In 1975 the United States controlled 28 percent of Iran's capital goods market. Even though this ration was expected to decrease to 18 percent, in absolute terms U.S. exports of capital goods to Iran were to increase gradually to $1.66 billion in 1980.[17]
>
> The transportation and construction industries were to be the main contributors, together accounting for more than 60 percent of the total market.

The revolution has introduced some major conceptual changes in the structure of the Iranian economy. These revisions, along with modifications introduced in the implementation of remaining economic projects, have manifested themselves in many ways, including:

Resetting of development goals. The new regime's declared objective of making Iran agriculturally self-sufficient and its shelving of most of the Shah's industrial projects have had a great impact on the format of Iran's capital market. Some substantial losses notwithstanding, the United States seems to have been less affected in this area than many of its European competitors. This is because high on the list of scrapped projects were nuclear power plants at an estimated annual cost of $2.4–3.2 billion for the next 25 years and in which the United States was not a participant.

Reluctance of the private sector to make any commitment. The new regime's economic modus operandi, including the expropriation of assets of the country's fifty-one richest industrialists and nationalization of the country's banks and insurance companies, has all but eliminated any potential investments in the capital goods market by Iran's formerly prospering private sector. Construction is the most seriously affected industry, but others such as textiles, business services, and food processing are also in critical trouble.

Labor takeover of plants. Many manufacturing plants have, since the revolution, been taken over by labor councils. In the unlikely event that the legal owners of these plants are still in Iran and permitted to enter into what used to be their property, they will not be willing, and in many cases able to make any new investments.

Shortage of professionals. In the weeks that preceded or followed the revolution, Iran lost the elite, if not the majority of its professional technocrats and managers. Even though the impact of their loss will not be fully realized until Iran's ailing economy recovers; even under the present adverse circumstances, their absence is felt in both the public and private sectors.

The result of all the economic changes, conceptual as well as functional, that the revolutionary regime has introduced in Iran is to reduce Iran's forecasted $13.4 billion capital market in 1980 to a small fraction of that figure. In fact, despite the unavailability of any information, it is believed that Iran's net aggregate investment in 1979 was negative and all indications are that this will be repeated in 1980.

While economically, the American manufacturers and exporters were able to remain competitive in the Iranian market during most of 1979, the political realities of new Iran seem to dictate a turn for worse in 1980. It is improbable, if not impossible, that the United States will export to Iran even 10 percent of the $1,663 million forecasted only one year ago. That would indicate an annual loss of at least $1.5 billion in potential sales by U.S. manufacturers.

Consumer products

The revolution's impact on the consumer products sector will be minimal and, once revolutionary rhetorics give way to rational consideration of the problem, the net result of the revolution on U.S. exports of agricultural products and consumer goods to Iran might indeed be positive.[18] Despite repeated claims of "economic independence," in reality Iran's relative economic dependence on outside help for food and consumer goods has rarely been as high as it is today.[19] The Shah's overly ambitious economic development plans, and the "industrialization at any cost" philosophy of his regime, bear much of the fault for this situation. The unproductivity of postrevolution Iran, however, has done little to alleviate this problem and much to aggravate it. The reality of the Iranian economy is that mass immigration of Iranian farmers into cities and towns during the 1965–1975 period all but left Iranian villages uninhabited and agricultural production untenable. The immigration of the elite of Iran's professional managers and technocrats, in the months immediately preceding and succeeding the revolution, has all but brought the same fait accompli to the country's industries and mines and as well as to the governmental machinery. To aggravate the situation further, whatever is left of the country's labor force spends much of its time demonstrating for the revolution or against its enemies.[20] The Iranian economy simply is not, and judging by Mr. Khomaini's performance thus far, will not, in the predictable future be a self-sustaining entity.

Mr. Khomaini's solution to Iran's economic problems, such as scattered but frequent shortages of food and other essentials, has been to preach against their consumption. While the more fanatic elements of Iranian society might have accepted the philosophy that washing detergents or washing machines are "symbols of Western decadence" and thus to be rejected, this idea cannot be sold to the masses. Sooner or later Mr. Khomaini and his regime will have to come up with economically viable solutions to Iran's economic problems. Since a complete reestablishment of all production facilities is time-consuming and highly unlikely, importation seems to be the only short-term solution. Should this prophecy materialize, the United States would stand to gain. Total U.S. exports of consumer products, mostly food, to Iran in 1977 were estimated at over $1 billion. It was reduced during 1978 because of the strikes and civil strife which preceded the revolution, but increased to about $700 million in 1979. Iran used to purchase between 50 and 75 percent of its imported rice, wheat, and cereals from the United States, and despite mounting political problems between the two countries at the present time and repeated attempts by the Iranian authorities to permanently alter this relationship, evidence seems to suggest that, once the current political crisis is over, the dominant position of the United States in this market will be restored.

Conclusions

The quadrupling of oil prices in 1974 gave the Shah's grandiose objective of making Iran a regional military and industrial power some meaningful credence and respectability. It also provided Iran with an additional $17.0 billion to bring that goal to reality. In pursuing such objectives Iran needed a partner to supply it with technology, capital goods, know-how, and modern weapons to develop the country's economic and military infrastructure. For economic political, and geopolitical reasons the United States was the logical choice.

The benefits of this new relationship were substantial and, indeed, mutual, for:

Iran needed an industrial base to gradually supplement and eventually replace its oil revenues. The United States, on the other hand, needed a secure source of supply of oil;

Iran needed a powerful military to preserve its unity and protect its sovereignty.[21] The United States needed a strong ally in that strategically important region; and,

both Iran and the United States considered a strong and stable Iran a credible deterrent to Soviet penetration in, and domination of, the Persian Gulf.

During the latter years of his reign, the Shah hesitated little in spending the country's billions of petrodollars on sophisticated military weapons and the most advanced industrial equipment. From F-14s to the Concorde, from nuclear power generators to gas-injection steel plants, and from billion-dollar petrochemical complexes to manmade island terminals – all were on order or under construction for Iran. The Shah referred to his ideal as "the great civilization," one that would give Iran the same international prominence and wealth it once enjoyed under Cyrus the Great. Despite numerous planning problems and implementation shortfalls, Iran's macroeconomic performance during the 1970s was remarkable: From 1972 to 1977, the country's gross national product (GNP) registered a net gain of 16 percent per year, one of the highest in the world.

In retrospect, it now seems clear that the Shah and his advisors failed to see, or chose to ignore, the extent of disorientation that such forced, and at times artificial, economic development was generating in the Iranian society. The Iranian masses, not ready to accept the rapid transformation of their society, not able to digest it, and probably not capable of comprehending the reasons behind it, formed a gradual resentment against "alien incursions" into their culture. This indignation eventually manifested itself in the form of a strong and destructive reaction against change and all its symbols, most of all the Shah.[22]

The Shah's downfall drastically altered Iran's international posture vis-à-vis other nations and most notably the United States. Politically, the extent of anti-American sentiment in Iran has never been higher than today. Commercially, the United States has already severed economic relations with Iran and has frozen official holdings of the Iranian government in the U.S. banking system. Similarly, the Iranian authorities are doing all they can to reciprocate by limiting the indirect importation of as many U.S. products into Iran as possible. Militarily, Iran has stopped buying American weapons and the United States has stopped selling spare parts and training Iranian pilots. All in all, United States-Iranian relations are at the lowest level they have ever been. The seizure of the American Embassy in Tehran, and the subsequent and prolonged holding of the hostages has made meaningful relations between the two countries in the near future impractical, if not impossible. This predicament will probably be short-lived and transitional.

Much of the support that the Khomaini regime is currently receiving is a reaction against the excesses of the Shah's regime, including, but certainly not limited to, the unrealistic economic development goals and policies. Once emotions subside and logic prevails – and indications are that the process has already begun[23] – Iranian authorities will have to rely on outside help to rebuild a faltering economy. Political differences notwithstanding, and considering the structure of the Iranian economy, the United States might be the best alternative Iran has.

While it would be unrealistic to conclude that the United States will regain the predominant economic position it once enjoyed in Iran; it would be equally naive to suggest that Iran can get its economy functioning effectively without some U.S. involvement. Iran's reliance on American technology, equipment, and supplies is most pronounced in the military and oil sectors, but some degree of dependence on the United States is shared by almost every sector of the Iranian economy. It can, therefore, be concluded that while the Shah might be gone, the remnants of his policies, are, and for many years will be, present in the foundations of the Iranian economy, and that an inseparable part of the Shah's economic development planning route to a "great civilization" was, indeed, his American connection.

Notes

1 The United States' refusal to grant Iran most-favored-nation status or include Iranian non-oil export products in its General System of Preferences (GSP) limited, and in fact effectively eliminated, Iran's ability to penetrate the U.S. market. That notwithstanding, Iran's potential to expend its non-oil exports to any country was severely curtailed after the 1974 oil price increases by added consumption and hyper-inflation at home and by more intense competition from other countries in potential markets such as the United States.

2 While there were no indications that he was planning a nuclear capability, his insistence on nuclear power plants for Iran seemed highly precarious. Why would a country with the world's second largest reservoirs of natural gas and while exporting more than five million barrels a day of oil want to build more than 20 nuclear power plants at an estimated cost of $60–80 billion? Even politically this did not seem justified because Iran does not have any uranium deposits and such a reliance on nuclear energy would have made Iran dependent on other countries for raw material for a very large percentage of its energy production. Considering that the Shah was not politically naïve, it could be argued that his long-range plans did indeed include a nuclear capability. In doing so, one could not think of a better way of obtaining both the enrichment plants and the technology needed for nuclear weapons than having 20 nuclear plants in Iran.

3 *The Wall Street Journal*, February 5, 1979.

4 The breakdown of ownership in the Iranian Oil Participants, Ltd., commonly known as the Consortium, was as follows:

British Petroleum (British)	40%
Royal Dutch Shell (Dutch/British)	14%
Exxon (American)	7%
Texaco (American)	7%
Mobil (American)	7%
Standard of California (American)	7%

Gulf (American)	7%
C.F.P. (French)	6%
Iricon Group of Companies (American)	5%

5 *Los Angeles Times*, January 1, 1979.

6 Joint ventures with American companies in the Iranian oil industry were: (1) Iran-Pan American Oil Company (IPAC), a venture with Pan American Oil Company, a subsidiary of Standard Oil Company of Indiana; (2) Iranian Marine International Oil (IMINOCO), an international joint venture including $16\frac{2}{3}$ percent by Phillips Petroleum Company; (3) Lavan Petroleum Company (LAPCO), a 50–50 joint agreement between Iran and four American oil companies: Atlantic Richfield Oil Company, Murphy Oil Company, Sun Oil Company, and Union Oil of California.

7 The revisions came after the 1974 Abu Dhabi meeting of OPEC Oil Ministers and was in fact an implementation of an OPEC decision in the framework of the 1972 agreement.

8 Based on an average lifting by Consortium Members of 3.5 million barrels per day National Iranian Oil Company's direct exports accounted for another 1.5–2 million barrels per day.

9 Indexation would have made the price of oil dependent on the price increases in the West as indicated by either consumer price indexes of industrial countries or an index of import prices of OPEC countries.

10 A possible exception is "Iran's Energy Picture after the Revolution" by Dr. Feraidon Fesharaki, a former Energy Advisor to Iran's Prime Minister. In *Petroleum Intelligence weekly*, special supplement, September 24, 1979.

11 This discussion only deals with the Consortium area (which accounts for more than 90 percent of total production) and does not include joint ventures.

12 During a visit to the Abadan Refinery in September 1979, the oil minister was so severely beaten up by oil workers that he had to be hospitalized for several days.

13 Even during the Shah's regime many Iranian oil specialists, myself included, expressed the view that, for technical and economical reasons, Iran's production should be curtailed to about 3 million barrels per day. While highly unlikely under the present Iranian circumstances, it is entirely possible that on this issue the professionals have won over bureaucrats and politicians.

14 OPEC's traditional "moderates" have been Saudi Arabia, Kuwait, the United Arab Emirates and Qatar – all Persian Gulf producers. Consistent price "hawks" on the other hand, have been Irag, Algeria, and Libya. Iran's move has clearly shifted the balance in favor of the latter group.

15 Saudi Arabia's production in 1979 was 9.2 million barrels per day, up by 14.8 percent or 1.2 million barrels per day over 1978.

16 U.S. Department of Commerce, *Iran: A Survey of U.S. Business Opportunities* (1977).

17 Most of the drop was due to the reluctance or inefficiency of the U.S. government to reach an agreement with the Atomic Energy Organization of Iran for the sale of American nuclear power plants to Iran. Of an estimated $2.0 billion market for electrical generators, the U.S. was expected to capture $53 million, a mere 3 percent. Excluding this industry, the American share in Iran's capital goods market would have been 22 percent.

18 Assuming, of course, no further deterioration of the relations between the two countries and a peaceful solution to the embassy seige.

19 Before the revolution, even while factories in Iran were operating at capacity, the country had to import consumer goods. Today the same plants are operating at an estimated 40 percent capacity, in effect reducing local production by 60 percent. Much of this reduced supply is counterbalanced by diminished demand caused by unemployment and revolutionary rhetoric, but the rest – a much higher percentage of the total than in

prerevolution days – will have to be met by imports. Failing that, shortages, already reported in some sectors, will become widespread and more frequent.

20 This was repeatedly illustrated before an international television audience during the seige of the American Embassy in Tehran.

21 Even though some of the most severe criticisms of the Shah were directed against his military build-up, events since his downfall have given credibility to this argument.

22 For a more comprehensive discussion of the casual factors of the Iranian Revolution see Khosrow Fatemi and Ralph Salmi, *Iran in Revolution: A Multidisiciplinary Analysis*, forthcoming in 1981.

23 Many analysts believe that the seizure of the American Embassy in Tehran and particularly the prolonged holding of hostages is a diversionary attempt by Mr. Khomaini and his aides to save their faltering revolution.

59

MYTHS OF SOVIET-IRANIAN RELATIONS

Muriel Atkin

Source: N. R. Kaddie and M. J. Gasiorowski (eds) *Neither East nor West: Iran, the Soviet Union, and the United States*, New Haven and London: Yale University Press, 1990, pp. 100–14.

A recurrent theme in discussions of the turmoil in Iran since 1978 has been the question of how the Soviet Union could benefit from the collapse of American influence there. Estimates of Soviet intentions in Iran often cite the history of tsarist and earlier Soviet relations with Iran to explain the present and predict the future. Unfortunately, some of these appeals to history are ahistorical. This misunderstanding of history takes two forms. One is ordinary factual inaccuracy. The other stems from a fundamental conceptual error in the study of tsarist and Soviet foreign policy: the assumption that policy is made largely on the basis of compulsions that hold sway over the centuries, transcending political changes and unaffected by the mundane political processes and personal strengths and weaknesses that influence the making of foreign policy in other countries. These mistaken approaches also reflect, in some cases, a cavalier attitude toward the significance of history—namely, that it is sufficient to cite something that happened, or allegedly happened, in the past, perhaps out of context, perhaps inaccurately, to prove one's interpretation of current events. The problem is not the occasional slip that can happen to anyone but rather a questionable process of inquiry itself. Soviet foreign policy expert Keith Dunn justly warns that "we should avoid believing that an assumption stated at least three times by three different people is no longer an assumption but a proven fact."[1]

In a sense, the heart of the issue is whether one regards tsarist or Soviet foreign policy–making as fundamentally rational or irrational. "Rational" in this context does not mean wise or admirable. What it does mean is that those who make foreign policy at least attempt to assess pragmatically the conditions under which they must operate and on that basis determine what is in the best interests of the country or, less loftily, that particular faction of policymakers. It is an approach encapsulated in a remark attributed to A. M. Gorchakov, Russia's foreign minister for most of the reign of Alexander II. Gorchakov considered Russia a "great, powerless country" and observed that "one can always dress up finely but one needs to know that one is dressing up."[2] In contrast, to believe in the myths about Russian or Soviet foreign policy is to treat this policy as irrational by ascribing powerful influence to instinctual drives or ambitious grand designs that influence the judgment of generation after generation of policymakers far more than a given era's actual conditions. Many a country's foreign policy may be irrational on occasion. But irrationality is credited too often with too much influence in tsarist and Soviet foreign policy either because evidence to explain the real motives is scarce or because belief in certain irrational motives is viewed as a criterion for disapproval of the policies themselves.

This chapter will examine a few of the historical myths that have been revived in recent years to "explain" Soviet relations with revolutionary Iran. The first category is the conceptual myth, as manifested by the Testament of Peter the Great and the drive to warm-water ports. The second deals with inaccurate understandings of real events, namely, the 1921 Soviet-Iranian treaty and the 1940 Nazi-Soviet negotiations on the division of the postwar world.

Before proceeding, there are two points that require clarification. A critique of misconceptions about tsarist or Soviet ambitions regarding Iran is not at all the equivalent of an endorsement of any policy that St. Petersburg or Moscow actually followed. Nor is it a contention that tsarist or Soviet rulers have never had expansionist ambitions toward Iran. Rather, the issue is that one prerequisite for a sound assessment of such policies must be the rejection of spurious evidence.[3] Even someone like Sir Henry Rawlinson, who in the 1860s and 1870s wrote repeatedly to warn of what he perceived to be a Russian threat to the British position in India, rejected the notion that the motives of Russian foreign policy were inherently different from and less rational than those of other countries. He argued that Russia's early nineteenth-century conquests in Iran, the Caucasus, and the Ottoman Empire were not the result of an "insatiate thirst for conquest" but rather were "amply paralleled by our own annexations in India during the same period."[4] When he speculated about the motives for Russia's pursuit in his own day of increased influence or outright rule in Iran, Afghanistan, and Central Asia, he regarded the truth as difficult to discern but suggested causes that depended not on irrational drives but on the kinds of political and military concerns of ordinary statecraft.[5]

The second point is that scholarly works of high quality have already addressed many of the concerns this chapter discusses.[6] It is a sad reflection on the nature of expertise that some of the people who have sought to explain the current and future state of Soviet-Iranian relations have not benefited from these works.

One of the canards most resistant to the weight of evidence is the belief that there is a grand design for Russian expansion formulated in the Testament of Peter the Great and followed by all his successors, including the modern Soviet leadership. Peter the Great wrote no such plan; the Testament exists in several versions, all forgeries, dating from the eighteenth and nineteenth centuries. Scholars have been demonstrating its fraudulence for more than a century.[7] Despite these valiant efforts, belief in the Testament survives. The *Christian Science Monitor* reacted to the Soviet invasion of Afghanistan by stating that "Peter the Great would be proud of his commissar successors in the Kremlin.... He would see [them] ... acting in accordance with the injunction given in his will.... Whoever succeeded him, Peter said, should move southward to Constantinople and India, for 'whoever governs there will be true sovereign of the world.'"[8]

Another version of this point in the Testament includes an explicitly Iranian dimension—namely, Russia should make war on Iran and advance to the Persian Gulf in order to gain control over East-West commerce and, on that basis, to dominate Europe.[9] This was the version that *Time* cited when assessing the situation in Iran on the eve of the late Shah's departure into exile. The *Time* article introduced this provision of the Testament with an observation that reflects the belief in inherited drives that transcend normal political considerations: "Things have not changed much since czarist times."[10] A recent account of Soviet-Iranian relations cites the same provision of the Testament to argue that in it Peter "first formulated the guidelines" for Russian attempts to conquer northern Iran from his own day to the end of the second Russo-Iranian war in 1828.[11]

An even more popular legend about Russian intentions toward Iran deals with the quest for warm-water ports. This is not synonymous with a quest for access to the high seas, which many observers have also attributed to St. Petersburg and Moscow. Although some interpretations combine the two presumed motives, high-seas navigation is not contingent upon the acquisition of warm-water ports, as the modern use of icebreakers demonstrates. Alfred Thayer Mahan, whose turn-of-the-century writings on the importance of sea power enjoyed international influence, believed that Russia pursued territorial expansion in order to gain openings to the sea. He included Iran's Persian Gulf coast and the coast of China among the main targets, but did not cast the issue in terms of a quest for warm water. As a fervent believer in the importance of sea power, he concluded that Russia's leaders saw their country as having too small a coastline relative to its large land mass. He further contended that the pursuit of wealth through East-West trade, which he ascribed to Russia, required the acquisition of water routes, which he regarded as inherently superior to land-based means of transportation, including railroads.[12] In general, the access-to-the-high-seas interpretation is more likely to consider the nature of the objectives and pragmatic concerns than the warm-water-ports interpretation, which assumes that invoking the words "warm water" explains all.

The origins of the warm-water-ports theory blur with other European fears of Russian expansion in the direction of the Straits and India. By 1869, it had become an issue in its own right, as indicated when Germany's representative in St. Petersburg explained Russian expansion in Asia in terms not of conscious policy but rather of a force of nature drawn to warm-water ports and fertile southern lands.[13] My unscientific survey of various college-educated Iranians born since World War II is that the legend retains a following, at least among Iranians of that social milieu. It is also widely believed in the West.[14] For example, Alvin Cottrell, a veteran American specialist on Gulf affairs, used this to help explain the presence of the Soviet navy in the Indian Ocean in the 1970s: "Many writers have commented upon the historical continuity between Soviet and Czarist imperialism. The drive for warm water ports and an outlet to the great oceans of the world can be traced back to the days of Peter the Great and Catherine."[15]

The legend has been cited many times since the Iranian Revolution raised the possibility of a shift in Iran's orientation not only away from cooperation with the United States but also toward improved relations with the Soviet Union. During the final days of the Shah's regime, the *Wall Street Journal* identified a "warm-water port on the Persian Gulf" as one of Russia's longstanding objectives in Iran.[16] To some, the Soviet invasion of Afghanistan was especially significant because it brought the Soviet Union "closer to achieving an objective that eluded czars for more than a century ... [territorial advance] that eventually could yield Moscow direct access to warm-water ports" on the coast of Iran and Pakistan.[17] During 1987 some observers greatly exaggerated the extent to which Iran warmed toward the Soviets. In anticipation of the signing of a Soviet-Iranian friendship treaty in 1987, an event that did not occur, a historian and a journalist predicted that "the new accord could give Moscow what it has wanted since the days of the czars: a strategic corridor to the warm waters of the Indian Ocean" via Iran.[18]

In fact, Russia's rulers never looked at Iran in terms of a route toward warm-water ports. That various Russian rulers had ambitions regarding Iran has been amply documented; but this does not mean that one may ascribe any motive one chooses to those ambitions. The pursuit of warm-water ports was not a Russian ambition with respect to Iran.

The assertion quoted above that this alleged quest dates from the reigns of Peter and Catherine is simply erroneous. Peter's ambitions in Iran centered on the coast of the Caspian Sea. He hoped to trade with Iran and India but expected to do so from this northerly location, not by obtaining direct access to the Persian Gulf. Similarly, Catherine the Great's Iranian ambitions focused on the North— the Caspian coast and Transcaucasia. Only at the end of her reign, when she made war against Iran's new ruler because of competing claims to suzerainty over the Kingdom of Georgia, did she try to conquer more southerly parts of Iran. Even then, the prime objective was not the Gulf coast but Isfahan, the old royal capital on the central Iranian plateau. In any event, the campaign was canceled by Catherine's successor soon after her death, without her troops reaching any part of the Iranian plateau.[19]

Subsequent tsars lacked the naval resources and the serious intention of gaining a port on Iran's southern coast. One of the authors long consulted on Anglo-Russian competition over Iran, Lord Curzon, argued differently. In fact his warning against such aspirations by Russia was cited approvingly in the *Washington Post* article quoted above. Yet Curzon is hardly convincing on this point. He claimed that Russia "yearns for an outlet upon the Persian Gulf and in the Indian Ocean."[20] He offered no substantiation for this assertion, however. Moreover, he himself did not always take this threat seriously. When he discussed this possibility in the first volume of *Persia and the Persian Question*, he added that no British government would allow Russia such an outlet and that the prospect of Russia obtaining one was too unlikely to be worth discussing.[21] Only when he returned to the subject, in the second volume, did he omit his earlier dismissal of this coming to pass. In general, Curzon's depiction of the Russian menace is based on speculation, rumor, and the quotation of the most intemperate statements in the Russian press. The fact that many intemperate statements could indeed be found in the press does not prove that the people who made them determined Russia's policy.

On the rare occasions when Russian officials contemplated their country's prospects in the Gulf, a fair amount of probity colored their judgments. On these occasions, an obsession with warm-water ports was conspicuous by its absence. By the end of the nineteenth century, Russia had agents in various parts of Iran, including the southeastern province of Seistan, much to the chagrin of the British. These agents gathered intelligence and tried to increase Russia's influence. Although such activities may legitimately be deemed unwelcome by other parties, they are not in themselves proof that St. Petersburg had decided to escalate its involvement in Iran by launching a bold drive beyond the northern provinces, where its influence was already considerable, toward Iran's southern coast. Nor do they constitute motives for such a drive.

In 1890, a time when some Russian businessmen and officials were interested in building a railroad across Iran to the Gulf coast, the head of the Foreign Ministry's Asiatic Department, I. A. Zinov'ev, himself no friend of Britain, argued forcefully against attempting to establish a Russian presence in the Gulf. His position was that while Russia was weak in that region Britain was strong and would surely oppose a Russian attempt to gain a foothold there. The establishment of a naval facility in the Gulf to strengthen Russia's position against the British would be fraught with difficulties, which were, by implication, not worth the cost.[22] In the end, Zinov'ev won the policy debate.

A decade later, Britain's discomfiture in the Boer War encouraged Tsar Nicholas II and some of his officials to look for ways to overcome what they saw as Britain's constant obstruction of Russia's right to pursue imperial grandeur. The solution they envisaged was to profit from Britain's preoccupation elsewhere to enhance Russia's position in Asia, including its position in the Persian Gulf. Thus, new initiatives were contemplated not as the result of some irrational preoccupation with the region but rather as the result of a fortuitous opportunity in a particular historical context.

At that time, Russia sent a small number of ships, both naval and merchant, to Iran's Gulf coast. Russian publications urged the acquisition of a port there. Although that did not happen, two consulates were set up in the region and a shipping line between the Black Sea and the Gulf began operation. Nonetheless, the foreign minister, Count Murav'ev, although in favor of increasing Russian influence in Iran, argued against taking control of a Gulf port on the grounds that the British were too determined to be masters there and Russia lacked the means to defend such an acquisition. According to Murav'ev, the burdens of a

Russian foothold on the Gulf would outweigh the benefits because it would cost too much, overextend the government's resources, and be too far from Russia's base of strength. The part of Iran with which Murav'ev favored the development of sea and land communications routes was the North, not the southern coast. The ministers of war and the navy agreed with the gist of Murav'ev's argument about the Gulf.[23] Despite the alarm among some British officials, notably Lord Curzon, then viceroy of India, over Russia's appearance in the Gulf, that presence amounted to very little.[24]

During the same period, the tsar's powerful minister of finance, S. Iu. Witte, advocated ensuring strong Russian influence in Iran and even eventual territorial annexation. But the specific region he valued was the North, which he considered the most attractive on the grounds that it possessed Iran's best economic assets.[25] When Witte became interested in establishing a presence on Iran's southern coast, he was prompted by the same kinds of economic concerns that underlay his attitude toward foreign policy in general—the desire to develop Russia's economy by promoting exports, including exports to Asian markets. This had nothing to do with primeval instincts. Rather, it was an attitude that many of his Western contemporaries shared. His most ambitious plan regarding southern Iran was to build a pipeline from the Baku oil fields in Russia's Transcaucasia to some unspecified place on Iran's Gulf coast.[26] The aim was to give Russia a less costly route to deliver its own oil to Asian markets,[27] thus making its price more competitive, and also to open the door for Russia to compete with Britain for Gulf commerce. In the end, Witte reluctantly abandoned the plan because it interfered with a higher priority, the conclusion of a loan agreement with Iran, which promised to increase Russia's influence over the Tehran government.[28]

In any event, Russia had barely begun to expand its influence in the Gulf when the Russo-Japanese war began in 1904, bringing Russia immense problems, including naval catastrophe and an attempted revolution. These events ended any prospect of further Russian activity in the Gulf, for whatever motive, for the remainder of the tsarist era.

With the establishment of Communist rule in Soviet Russia, the new regime also developed ambitions in Iran. However, these ambitions were motivated by rational, though not necessarily wise or admirable, assessments of the international politics of the day. Soviet leaders tried to establish a modus vivendi with their comparatively weak southern neighbors, to end their own diplomatic isolation, and to revive the waning prospects for revolution in Europe by fomenting anticolonial unrest in Asia; they did not inherit an obsession with warm-water ports. In fact, until the late 1930s, Soviet naval thought focused on the defense of Soviet coastal waters. Through the end of World War II, coastal defense was the most the Soviet Union could have aspired to, given its limited naval resources.[29]

When the Soviet military formulated a contingency plan for an invasion of Iran during World War II (probably in the first half of 1941), the Gulf coast was not a serious target. The plan focused on northern Iran for defensive as well as offensive reasons. Considerations included the risk of an attack on the Baku oil fields from Iranian territory, the possibility of fighting a British force advancing toward Soviet territory via Iraq or northeastern Iran, the attractiveness of Iran's northern provinces as the most economically developed parts of the country, and the significance to the British of northeastern Iran for the defense of India. The plan provided extremely detailed information on routes the Red Army could take into Iran from the northwest, the Caspian coast, and the northeast. The Persian Gulf coast ranked as a minor consideration in this discussion; in a study that runs to 243 pages in the English translation, the total coverage of the route to the Gulf occupies only a handful of pages. Moreover, this study is vague about objectives on the Gulf coast. All it says is that, in the event of an advance to that region, the Red Army should aim for some town in Khuzistan, rather than another point on the Gulf, but does not specify an objective; it notes that there is oil in the area but does not identify where the main oil installations are or what might be done with them. The generality of this brief section contrasts sharply with the attention to minute detail in the rest of the plan.[30]

Since the 1950s, the Soviet Union has developed a navy that operates in many regions of the globe, including the Persian Gulf. It may be appropriate for the United States to regard this in a negative light, but that does not change the fact that the growth of Soviet naval power is the result not of some age-old drive but rather of specific developments in a particular historical context. These developments include the Soviet determination to acquire the kind of navy that befits a great power, to develop the capacity to strike foreign naval vessels capable of launching an attack on Soviet territory from great distances, to deny unchallenged dominance of the seas to an enemy in time of war, and to use naval forces for purposes that are not only military but also political, such as supporting client states and influencing other countries.[31]

So far is a preoccupation with warm-water ports from being the keystone of Soviet naval policy in the postwar era that one of the major routes the Soviets have developed since the 1960s is an Arctic passage to Siberia and East Asia. By using icebreakers, the Soviets can keep the route open for about one hundred days a year and save time in comparison with the Suez Canal route.[32] Of course, this does not mean that the Soviet navy prefers icy waters, but rather that it readily uses them and is not constantly preoccupied with finding warm-water routes as an end in itself.

In addition to the spurious motives that have been attributed to tsarist and Soviet foreign policy, certain events in Soviet-Iranian relations that have indeed occurred have been mythologized in the sense that they have been expanded to mean more than they really do and have been relied upon to explain too much. Two major examples of this are the 1921 Soviet-Iranian treaty and the 1940 Soviet-German talks about territorial claims in the postwar world.

The belief is widespread that the 1921 treaty, particularly its sixth article, permits the Soviets to send troops into Iran whenever they consider their security threatened from that direction. Typical of this view is the assertion that "relations between the two countries have been bedeviled by the ghost of the 1921 treaty ... which allowed the Soviet Union to intervene in Iran in the event of a threat against Soviet territory."[33] The *Wall Street Journal's* interpretation of the treaty presumed even greater latitude for intervention by claiming that the treaty permitted the Soviets to call a domestic attempt to topple the Iranian government a threat to Soviet security and send in troops on that basis.[34] A still broader interpretation, offered during the hostage crisis, posited that the Soviets might send troops into Iran to help that country repulse a hostage rescue operation by the United States and that "in accordance with the 1921 Soviet-Iranian treaty, they [Soviet troops] might continue to stay there after that help was no longer needed."[35]

All of these interpretations of the treaty are inaccurate. The treaty as ratified restricts the conditions for intervention in a way that has long since rendered the relevant provisions obsolete. Moreover, the government of the Islamic Republic of Iran may have a strong case under international law to support its abrogation of those provisions.

The controversial points of the treaty are Articles 5 and 6. Article 5 commits each signatory to ban from its territory "any organizations or groups of persons ... whose object is to engage in acts of hostility against Persia [Iran] or Russia, or against the allies of Russia [that is, the other Soviet republics]." Article 6 is even more important. It states that if some third party or foreign country should establish a military presence in Iran in order to strike at Soviet Russia and if the Iranian government could not stop such activities, then "Russia shall have the right to advance her troops into the Persian interior for the purpose of carrying out the military operations necessary for its defense."[36]

The Iranian legislature, the Majles, voiced serious misgivings about various provisions of the new treaty, including Article 6, as well as the general status of Soviet-Iranian relations. Therefore the Majles did not ratify the treaty soon after its signing in February 1921 but instead continued to ponder it for the rest of the year. To encourage ratification, and in response to a direct request from the Iranian government for clarification, the Soviets provided a note that sharply restricted the conditions under which Article 6 might be invoked.[37] The note specified that the relevant treaty provisions were "intended to apply only to cases in which preparations have been made for a considerable armed attack upon Russia ... by the *partisans of the regime which has been overthrown* or by its supporters among those foreign Powers which are in a position to assist the enemies of" Soviet Russia (emphasis added).[38]

The Soviet note met a condition set by the Iranian government for ratification of the treaty. That in itself would give it significance under international law. Moreover, the note became a revision added to the treaty itself.[39] Thus, the restricted definition of the permissible conditions for intervention is the valid one under international law. Since the prospect of armed intervention in the Soviet Union by supporters of the Romanov dynasty or the Provisional Government of March to November 1917, with or without foreign assistance, has long since ceased to be a realistic possibility, Article 6 no longer has any legitimate standing in the conduct of Soviet-Iranian relations.

Furthermore, the government of the Islamic Republic abrogated Articles 5 and 6 in November 1979. Ordinarily one party to a bilateral treaty cannot abrogate any part of the treaty unless the other signatory agrees, which, in this case, the Soviet Union has not done; but an argument can be made for the legitimacy of this particular abrogation. According to the Vienna Convention on the Law of Treaties, there are some occasions when changing circumstances are so at variance with a treaty's original intent and so alter what is required of the signatories that abrogation is permissible. The absence of any credible prospect for restoring Russia's old regime meets the criterion for drastically altered circumstances. In addition, the United Nations Charter prohibits any member from threatening or using force to interfere with a state's sovereignty or territorial integrity and ascribes to the charter precedence over other treaties conflicting with it that have been signed by members of the United Nations. By this standard, too, Article 6 could legitimately be abrogated.[40]

Nonetheless, the Soviet Union has invoked the provision several times since 1921, and the note of clarification has not been cited in response. The most dramatic occasion was in 1941, when it was one of the reasons used to justify the Soviet invasion of northern Iran.[41] The invasion was conducted in concert with Britain, for which the defeat of Nazi Germany was of vastly greater importance than Iranian sovereignty. If British diplomats were aware that Article 6 offered inadequate justification, they would hardly have considered it beneficial to Britain's interests at the time to raise that objection to a joint military action intended to aid the war effort. The Soviets have occasionally referred to Article 6 directly or indirectly since then, from the Azerbaijani crisis of 1945–46 to the era of the Islamic Republic. Moscow set the tone for contemporary allusions to the treaty even before the fall of the Shah. In November 1978, Leonid Brezhnev declared that the Soviet Union would regard foreign intervention in Iran as a threat to Soviet security and coupled that with a reference to the long border between the two countries.[42] Despite the implied threat in this statement and the episodes of mutual recrimination between the Soviet Union and the Islamic Republic since 1979, there have also been important occasions when each country has cultivated good relations with the other, even though they continue to disagree on the status of the 1921 treaty.

The other real event in Soviet-Iranian relations that has been extensively mythologized is the Soviet-German discussion in November 1940 about territorial claims in Eastern Europe and Asia. According to the mythic interpretation of these negotiations, "the Soviets revealed their vast ambitions" in the Persian Gulf.[43] Another commentator warned that in these talks, the Soviet representative, V. M. Molotov, declared that the Persian Gulf was the "focal point of the aspirations of the Soviet Union," which, wrote the commentator, remains the case today. "Any understanding," he added, "of what is happening in Iran today ... must begin with the historical record."[44]

German records of the negotiations, which have been available in published form in English for forty years,[45] present a different picture altogether, in which

Soviet attention was focused on Eastern Europe while Germany tried to deflect that focus to Southern and Central Asia, far from Germany's own expansionist targets in Europe.[46]

By the summer of 1940, Soviet-German relations were showing signs of strain, particularly over the war with Finland, competing interests in Romania, and the Soviet annexation of Lithuania. In November 1940, Molotov traveled to Berlin for talks with Ribbentrop and Hitler. Germany's aim was to persuade the Soviet Union to endorse the Tripartite Pact among Germany, Italy, and Japan and to lure the Soviets into concentrating on the Middle East while Germany strengthened its position in Europe.

Ribbentrop opened the talks by stating that Britain's defeat was assured and that Hitler advocated the rough delineation of postwar spheres of influence for Germany, the Soviet Union, Italy, and Japan. The German sphere was to include Western Europe, those parts of Eastern Europe already assigned to it by prior Soviet-German agreement, and parts of central Africa. Ribbentrop then asked Molotov "whether Russia in the long run would not also turn to the South for the natural outlet to the open sea that was so important."[47] Molotov's nonchalant response was to ask which sea. Again, it was Ribbentrop who demonstrated enthusiasm for Soviet expansion into Iran by advising Molotov that the best access to the sea for the Soviet Union would be "in the direction of the Persian Gulf and the Arabian Sea."[48] Thus, it was Ribbentrop who broached the idea in the first place and who coined the phrase that has been used to symbolize Soviet designs on the Gulf states.

Molotov did not object to letting Ribbentrop offer the Soviet Union a free hand in the Gulf, but neither was he distracted from far higher priorities elsewhere. When he met with Hitler, the points he pressed included Soviet interests in Bulgaria, Romania, and Turkey, the limits of the Japanese sphere in East Asia, and the status of Finland. The tone of the discussion showed signs of displeasure on both sides over these issues.[49] Molotov did not bother to raise the Gulf question at all.

At the final meeting, Ribbentrop offered Molotov encouragement for a new agreement with Turkey on navigation of the Straits and again tried to shift his attention far away, not only in the direction of the Gulf, but also toward the Indian Ocean, India itself, China's Sinkiang Province, and Outer Mongolia. Molotov still refused to be diverted. He used the opening Ribbentrop had given him on the status of the Straits to insist that Soviet security interests required much more than a new navigation agreement with Turkey and then pressed Ribbentrop to clarify Germany's position on all of Eastern Europe from the Baltic to Greece, thus broadening the discussion of that region far beyond its earlier bounds. Ribbentrop questioned Molotov on having said nothing about Soviet expansion southward to the Gulf. Molotov's response combined evasiveness with skepticism and wariness. He replied that spheres of influence would have to be specified but that he could say nothing binding on the subject without consulting Moscow. He further implied that Ribbentrop was offering vague promises that hinged on future developments that might not come to pass, like the defeat of England.[50] In summation, he stated that "all these great issues of tomorrow could not be separated from the issues of today and the fulfillment of existing agreements. The things that were started must first be completed before they proceeded to new tasks."[51]

Thus, the November 1940 talks do not provide an unusually frank admission of Soviet determination to take control of Iran and neighboring countries. What the talks do show is that two antagonists who were temporarily allies distrusted each other, were close to open rivalry in Eastern Europe, and wanted to use these talks to manipulate each other. Part of that manipulation was Berlin's attempt to distract Moscow from Germany's pursuit of European domination by proffering an adventuresome scheme for Soviet expansion in Asia. Not only were the Soviets not fooled, but the Germans did not take the scheme seriously either. A month after the talks ended, Hitler began to contemplate the invasion of the Soviet Union.

Difficulty in understanding the intentions of foreign countries' policymakers is a common enough problem in the history of international relations. It is an especially serious problem for those who have tried to deal with tsarist or Soviet Russia because of the sheer scarcity of accurate information. Under these conditions, history has often been used to fill in the gaps in the hope that it will reveal general patterns and long-term trends. But that is sometimes done in a way that mythologizes the history of tsarist and Soviet foreign relations. It is a disservice not only to Clio but also to other countries' diplomats because it restricts their own policy options. The mythic version of this history gives great weight to the role of quasi-instinctual obsessions. By their very nature, such irrational drives are not readily modified by the ordinary tools of conventional diplomacy.

Notes

1 K. A. Dunn, "'Mysteries' about the Soviet Union," *Orbis* 26 (Summer 1982): 361–62.

2 D. C. B. Lieven, *Russia and the Origins of the First World War* (New York: St. Martin's Press, 1983), 23–24.

3 For all the folly of the Iran-Contra imbroglio, the popular myths about Soviet designs on Iran seem not to have influenced those who supported the venture, at least as reflected by the information that has been made public thus far. Yet the perception of the Soviet role in Iran exhibited by two CIA documents used by advocates of the venture to support their case is just as disquieting as if ahistorical myths had guided the decision. At least the myths *attempt* to explain Soviet intentions and objectives. The CIA's "Special National Intelligence Estimate" and National Security Decision Directive on Iran (both of 1985), which policymakers used as part of their rationale for the dealings with Iran, do not consider such issues. This approach proceeds from the axiom that the Soviets pose the greatest danger to U.S. interests in Iran and that the Soviet threat is the most important reason for the United States to take an active interest in Iranian affairs. ("Special National Intelligence Estimate" by Graham E. Fuller, 17 May 1985, *Report of the Congressional Committees Investigating the Iran-Contra Affair* [Washington, D.C.: N.p., 1988], Appendix A, vol. I: 968; National Security Decision Directive [draft], ibid., 982, 986.) Ironically, within months of writing the pivotal "Special National Intelligence Estimate," Graham Fuller revised his interpretation, concluding that there was no pressing threat of Iranian domestic instability or extensive Soviet meddling.

However, this view did not become widely known in government circles. (*New York Times*, 20 Mar. 1987, A12.) (The author would like to thank Dr. Eric Hooglund and Mr. Malcom Byrne, both of the National Security Archive, for their help in exploring the documents of the Iran-Contra investigation.)

4 H. Rawlinson, *England and Russia in the East* (London: John Murray, 1875), 145.

5 These included the need to expand further in order to secure territory previously conquered, fear of British competition for Central Asian trade, expansion toward India until stopped by some insurmountable obstacle, the influence of the military on government policy, and the use of increased strength in Asia to gain more influence in Europe. Ibid., 191–92, 197–98, 338–39.

6 Among the valuable modern works in English dealing with Russian and Soviet intentions toward Iran are F. Kazemzadeh, *Russia and Britain in Persia, 1864–1914* (New Haven: Yale University Press, 1968), and J. C. Campbell, "The Soviet Union and the Middle East 'In the General Direction of the Persian Gulf,'" *Russian Review*, in two parts: 29 (April 1970): 143–53; (July 1970): 247–61. M. E. Yapp's *Strategies of British India* (Oxford: Clarendon Press, 1980), examines the varied assessments of British officials of the possibility of a Russian threat to British India via Iran and Afghanistan. D. Geyer's 1977 study, *Der Russische Imperialisms*, now available in English as *Russian Imperialism*, trans. B. Little (New Haven: Yale University Press, 1987), discusses the motives for Russia's expansion in various quarters and the practical limits to its ambitions in the period from the reign of Alexander II to the outbreak of World War I. E. Sarkizyanz's "Russian Imperialism Reconsidered," in *Russian Imperialism from Ivan the Great to the Revolution*, ed. T. Hunczak (New Brunswick, N.J.: Rutgers University Press, 1974), 45–59, debunks several major Russophobic myths. In addition to these works, Muriel Atkin, *Russia and Iran, 1780–1828* (Minneapolis: University of Minnesota Press, 1980), chs. 3 and 4, discusses the objectives of Russian policy toward Iran in the late eighteenth and early nineteenth centuries. Professors Hugh Ragsdale and Hans Rogger have works in progress that look at different aspects of Western misperceptions of tsarist foreign policy.

7 Among the modern works in English on the subject are L. Lockhart, "The 'Political Testament' of Peter the Great," *Slavonic and East European Review* 14 (1935–36): 438–41; D. V. Lehovich, "The Testament of Peter the Great," *American Slavic and East European Review* 7 (April 1948): 111–24; O. Subtelny, "'Peter I's Testament': A Reassessment," *Slavic Review* 33 (December 1974): 663–78; H. Ragsdale, *Détente in the Napoleonic Era* (Lawrence: Regents Press of Kansas, 1980), 16–17, 20–21, 109–10; and A. Resis, "Russophobia and the 'Testament' of Peter the Great, 1812–1980," *Slavic Review* 44 (Winter 1985): 681–93. Professor Rogger has also debunked the Testament as part of a larger study of diplomatic Russophobia in "Origin of the Concept of the 'Russian Menace'" (paper presented at the Kennan Institute of the Woodrow Wilson Center on 7 Dec. 1987).

8 *Christian Science Monitor*, 31 Dec. 1979, 1.

9 Resis, "Russophobia and the 'Testament,'" 684.

10 *Time*, 15 Jan. 1979, 23n.

11 M. Rezun, *The Soviet Union and Iran* (Boulder, Colo.: Westview Press, 1988), 2.

12 A. T. Mahan, *The Problem of Asia* (Port Washington, N.Y.: Kennikat Press, 1970), 25–26, 42–45, 56–57, 117–19.

13 O. Hoetzsch, *Russland in Asien* (Stuttgart: Deutsche Verlags-Anstalt, 1966), 26–27.

14 R. J. Kerner's *The Urge to the Sea* (Berkeley: University of California Press, 1946) is a particularly well known exposition of the argument that Russian expansion has been linked historically to water routes. However, Kerner was not concerned with the question of warm-water ports per se. Rather, he focused on river routes leading to the Baltic, Black, and Caspian seas. In any event, Kerner makes two fundamental

conceptual errors. By emphasizing the river system to the exclusion of all else as a factor in medieval Russian expansion, he came to the conclusion that the rivers were centrally important and that they were not only a means but also an end in themselves. He also treated river routes as uniquely important in the Russian context, without taking account of the great importance of riverine transportation in many parts of Europe before the development of the railroad.

15 A. J. Cottrell, "The Soviet Navy and the Indian Ocean," in *The Persian Gulf and Indian Ocean in International Politics*, ed. A. Amirie (Tehran: Institute for International Political and Economic Studies, 1975), 112.

16 *Wall Street Journal*, 4 Jan. 1979, 21.

17 *Washington Post*, 30 Dec. 1979, A16.

18 M. Hauner and J. Roberts, "Moscow's Iran Gambit: Railroading a Friendship," *Washington Post*, 16 Aug. 1987, D1.

19 Atkin, *Russia and Iran*, 4, 32–34, 37–40, 42.

20 G. N. Curzon, *Persia and the Persian Question* (London: Longmans, Green, 1892), 2:597.

21 Ibid., 1:236–37.

22 Zhurnal osobogo soveshchanie, *Krasnyi Arkhiv* 1, no. 56 (1922): 46.

23 Foreign minister [M. N. Murav'ev] to Nicholas II, *Krasnyi Arkhiv* 5, no. 18 (1926): 4–6, 9, 12–14; A. Kuropatkin [minister of war] to the minister of foreign affairs, 16 February 1900, ibid., 22; P. Tyrtov [naval minister] to the foreign minister, 14 February 1900, ibid., 19; Kazemzadeh, *Russia and Britain*, 334–39, 352, 436–40.

24 Kazemzadeh, *Russia and Britain*, 439–40.

25 S. Iu. Witte, *The Memoirs of Count Witte*, trans. and ed. A. Yarmolinsky (Garden City, N.Y.: Doubleday, Page, 1921), 433.

26 A similar proposal had been made in 1883 by a nobleman involved in the Baku oil industry. His motive, like Witte's, was competition with foreign oil companies in Asian markets. The government was completely uninterested in the plan. Kazemzadeh, *Russia and Britain*, 201.

27 The existing route, across Transcaucasia to the Black Sea port of Batum, already used a warm-water route, so the quest for one was not at issue in the pipeline project.

28 Kazemzadeh, *Russia and Britain*, 359–60, 378–84.

29 D. W. Mitchell, *A History of Russian and Soviet Sea Power* (New York: Macmillan Publishing, 1974), 373–75, 381–82, 408–10, 442, 469.

30 G. Guensberg, trans., *Soviet Command Study of Iran* (Moscow, 1941) (Washington, D.C.: Office of the Secretary of Defense, 1980). Almost all of the discussion of an invasion of Iran's Gulf coast is on pp. 190–93.

31 M. MccGwire, "The Turning Points in Soviet Naval Policy," in *Soviet Naval Developments*. Ed. M. MccGwire (New York: Praeger Publishers, 1913), 195, 197, 202–04; G. E. Hudson, "Soviet Naval Doctrine, 1953–72," ibid., 285–87; R. G. Weinland, "The Changing Mission Structures of the Soviet Navy," ibid., 299–301; I. M. McConnell, "Doctrine and Capabilities," in *Soviet Naval Diplomacy*, ed. B, Dismukes and I. M. McConnell (New York: Pergamon Press, 1979), 1–29; C. C. Petersen, "Trends in Soviet Naval Operations," ibid., 38, 41, 45, 47; idem, "Showing the Flag," ibid., 89, 91; Mitchell, *A History of Russian and Soviet Sea Power*, 470; K. A. Dunn, "Constraints of the USSR in Southwest Asia: A Military Analysis," *Orbis* 25 (Fall 1981): 616.

32 Mitchell, *A History of Russian and Soviet Sea Power*, 583.

33 Hauner and Roberts, "Moscow's Iran Gambit," D1.

34 *Wall Street Journal*, 4 Jan. 1979, 21.

35 A. Y. Yodfat, *The Soviet Union and Revolutionary Iran* (London; Croom Helm, 1984), 68.

36 "Treaty of Friendship of December 1921 between Soviet Russia and Iran," in *Diplomacy in the Near and Middle East*, ed. J. C. Hurewitz (Princeton: D. Van Nostrand, 1956), 2:91.

37 R. K. Ramazani, *The Foreign Policy of Iran, 1500–1941* (Charlottesville: University Press of Virginia, 1966), 190, 236; Kazemzadeh, "Russia and the Middle East," in *Russian Foreign Policy*, ed. I. V. Lederer (New Haven: Yale University Press, 1962), 523.

38 "Note to the Iranian Foreign Minister from the Russian Representative in Tehran (12 December 1921)," in *Diplomacy in the Near and Middle East*, 2:94.

39 W. M. Reisman, "Termination of the USSR's Treaty Right of Intervention in Iran," *American Journal of International Law 14*, no. 1 (January 1980): 145, 148.

40 Ibid., 145, 149–53.

41 Ramazani, *Iran's Foreign Policy, 1941–1973* (Charlottesville: University Press of Virginia, 1975), 33–34.

42 *Pravda*, 19 Nov. 1978, 5.

43 R. G. Neumann, "Moscow's New Role as Mideast Broker," *Washington Post*, 25 Oct. 1987, C4.

44 C. M. Roberts, "Iran: In the Historical Middle," *Washington Post*, 16 Dec. 1979, B7.

45 Germany, Auswärtiges Amt, *Nazi-Soviet Relations, 1939–1941*, ed. R. J. Sontag and J. S. Beddie (New York: Didier, 1948).

46 This was shown clearly by J. C. Campbell in "The Soviet Union and the Middle East," pt. 1, 149–51; Alexander Werth also gave a vivid, accurate account in his well-known book on the Soviet role in World War II, *Russia at War, 1941–1945* (New York: E. P. Dutton, 1964), 105–06.

47 Memorandum of Ribbentrop-Molotov talks in Berlin, 12 November 1940 (dated 13 November 1940), in Germany, Auswärtiges Amt, *Nazi-Soviet Relations*, 218–21.

48 Ibid., 221–22.

49 Memoranda of meetings between Hitler and Molotov, 12 November 1940 (dated 16 November 1940), and 13 November 3940 (dated 15 November 1940), in ibid., 228–33, 238–45.

50 Memorandum of meeting between Ribbentrop and Molotov on 13 November 1940 (dated 18 November 1940), in ibid., 247–52.

51 Ibid., 252.

60

NARRATIVES OF MODERNITY

Perspective of an Oriental despot

Abbas Milani

Source: M. J. Shapiro and H. R. Alker (eds) *Challenging Boundaries: Global Flows, Territorial Identities*, Minneapolis and London: University of Minnesota Press, 1996, pp. 219–32.

"Writing," according to Claude Lévi-Strauss, is a means "to facilitate the enslavement of other human beings."[1] In their interrogation of the genealogies of "the Barbaric Despotic Machine," Gilles Deleuze and Félix Guattari proclaim that "it is the despot who establishes the practice of writing."[2] Evidence for these claims can be found not just in the forests of Brazil or the intellectual salons of Paris but also in Nasir al-Din Shah's narratives of his travels to Europe.

Nasir al-Din Shah ruled Iran for nearly half a century. He came to power in 1848, when he was only seventeen years old. An assassin's bullet ended his reign in 1896. Iran's first, serious encounters with modernity began under his rule. His coterie of courtiers included both reformist zealots and incorrigible despots. The tremors that ultimately erupted into Iran's Constitutional Revolution (1905–07) began under his reign.

The onslaught of modernity shook to the core the existing Iranian sense of cultural identity and community. With the "overlap and displacement of domains of difference," what Homi Bhabha calls "the fixity and fetishism"[3] of cultural identities began to crack. A new "cultural hybridity"[4] seemed all but imminent.

In this context, new competing and conflicting cultural "strategies of selfhood"[5] began to emerge. Religious forces, reticent of change, advocated social and spiritual autarky. Only a culture enveloped in divine wisdom, they argued, can survive the Satanic verses of modernity. Comprador modernists, those advocates of "cultural transubstantiation," encouraged a total submersion of Iranian culture into the "Paradise of European civilization."

And thus, the primitive despotic machine of Nasir al-Din Shah was "forced into a bottleneck." It felt what Deleuze and Guattari call "the dread of flows of desire that would resist coding"; it recognized the necessity for the "establishment of inscriptions … that makes desire into the property of the sovereign."[6]

179

Nasir al-Din Shah's travelogues are an early testimony to this desperate attempt at an "inscriptional" process.

The king's idle curiosities, his insatiable desire for frivolities, his "addiction"[7] to travel, his attempt to consolidate his relationship with European powers, his greed for gold, hand in hand with the designs of his reformist courtiers to "enlighten"[8] the king, and finally the colonialists' attempts to enlist his favors led to his decision to travel to Europe and shaped the rubrics of the new "coding" regime. Out of a labyrinth of conflicting desires and designs came a project that laundered a quixotic narrative of despotism as a journey of discovery.

On three occasions, in 1873, 1878, and 1889, each time for about four to five months, the king, along with nearly all of the country's political elite, traveled to Europe. All the customary pomp surrounding an exotic "Oriental" surrounded his entourage.[9]

As was his habit in nearly all his trips, Nasir al-Din Shah decided to write an account of his travels.[10] In the genealogy of their form and the morphology of their content, these travelogues are a fascinating arena in which different cultures and sensibilities, competing orders of "coding" and "overcoding" cohabit and contradict one another.[11] The tensions and pretensions of the text are a metaphor for the historical dilemma of modernity in Iran. Indeed, the texts of the travelogues, as well as the context and the subtext of their production and dissemination betray a fierce battle between competing centers of political power and their incumbent discourses.

In a sense, every political discourse is ultimately also an attempt to "discourse" alternative claims (or structures) of power. It is, to use Fredric Jameson's words, a narrative in the service of "an imaginary resolution of a real contradiction."[12] In other words, like all other cultural objects, it "brings into being that very situation to which it is also, at one and the same time, a reaction."[13] Nasir al-Din Shah's narrative is no exception. The "political Unconscious" of his texts betrays a desire to domesticate aspects of modernity amenable to the needs of his despotic rule and subvert those he finds dangerous. To use Mary Louise Pratt's apt metaphor, Iran was then a "contact zone,"[14] a social space where "asymmetrical relations of domination and subordination"[15] between the colonized and the colonizer, as well as between the despot and his subjects, raged on. The narrative of the royal sojourn to Europe was part of his strategy to maintain hegemony in this "contact zone."

Confounding the battle was the peculiar problematic of modernity in Iran. If in the West the battle between the ancients and the moderns was in a sense a bipolar problematic, in Iran the fight was, every step of the way, overshadowed by the enormous complexities of the colonial question. Russia and England fought for hegemony, while lesser European powers each struggled for a smaller piece of the pie. On the one hand, the ferocity of this colonial fight ensured at least the nominal independence of Iran. On the other hand, all aspects of what Hannah Arendt calls "the Social Question"[16]—all the social issues modernity hurls into the public domain—were invariably ensnared with colonial politics. In Naser al-Din Shah's convoluted vision of Europe, in his mutilated narrative of discovery, in his peculiar acts of omission and commission, we see all the perils and the paradoxes of this entanglement.

In the place of the will to know, or possess—the engines of modernity's discourse of discovery[17]—here we find the will to pleasure and the will to contain. Instead of "theoretical curiosity," which in Hans Blumenberg's view is a cardinal element of modernity's epistemology,[18] we have here at best a politically neutered and often frivolous inquisitiveness. Throughout its tropes of concealment and containment, the royal text tries to subvert the subversive potentialities of modernity's discourse by appropriating some of its formal characteristics. The narrative's manner of production and dissemination is also emblematic of modern Oriental despots' elective affinities with modernity.

Before Nasir al-Din Shah, Iran's despots were often oblivious if not in fact haughtily disdainful of the West. In annals of history we read of Iranian kings who, less than one hundred years before Nasir al-Din Shah, received Western envoys in their pyjamas and showed a defiant, if not quixotic, haughtiness in their dealing with the West.[19] With Nasir al-Din Shah, the tide began to turn. Colonial hegemony was beginning to bloom. Henceforth Iranian despots were in awe of the West; their sense of political security was more dependent on the pulse of Western powers and public opinion than on the opinions of their own "subjects." At great cost, they tried to cultivate a "modern image" of themselves in the eyes of the West. Early signs of this development can be seen in the fate of Nasir al-Din Shah's royal narrative.[20] Their Ecoian "model reader"[21] seemed as much European as Iranian. In fact, the travelogues were immediately ordered by the king to be translated and published in English. Throughout the last decade of the nineteenth century, they were read and discussed in English intellectual circles.[22]

Of course, every narrative is, in the words of Hayden White, "not merely a neutral discursive form ... but rather, entails ontological and epistemic choices with distinct ideological and even specifically political implications."[23] What then is the way of political life insinuated in the Shah's narrative?

To begin, the privileged position of writing over orality and the nearly fetishistic preoccupation with memory[24] are of course both important signs of modernity in the West. The dearth of autobiographies and travelogues and the near complete absence of official records from Iran's past contrast sharply with the Shah's desire to write and record. At the same time we can speak of Nasir al-Din Shah as the author of these logs only in a Foucauldian sense. In other words, he was not "an individual who pronounced or wrote a text" but rather embodied "a principle of groupings of discourse."[25] The texts he authored were only in a *formal* sense a replica of modernity's privileged attitude toward writing. For him the act of writing was more royal theater than a simple individual discursive practice; it embodied what Certeau calls "scriptural operations" wherein words are orally performed in the "presence of officially sanctioned recorders."[26] Such is the king's description of one of these "scriptural operations":

> Bashi was holding the inkwell; Akbari the candelabra; Amin Khabar holding a notebook, ready to write; Etemad-Al Saltaneh holding a Western newspaper, ready to read; Mirza Muhamad Khan holding a candelabra for him; Majd-l Dowleh, Abbol Hassa Khan, Mardak, Mohhamad Al Khan, Muhamad Hassan Miraza, Adib Joojeh, Karim Khan, Agha Dai all standing, Taghi Khan holding water.[27]

With such a large constellation of courtiers in attendance, some enjoying their aristocratic titles (like *Eteme al Sataneh*, "the trustee of the king"), others suffering belittling, diminutive labels (like *Mardak*, "little man" or *Akbar Joojeh*, "Akbar the chicken"), the king trotted around dictating entries that he expected supplicant scribes would accurately transcribe into a text. If it can be said that the notion of an individual author only rose on the ruins of the idea of God as the master narrator, here we have a godlike distance from the act of creation comingled with authorial pretensions. On rare occasions, the Shah would deign to jot down a few words himself. Textual differences between different "editions" of the logs indicate a certain degree of expected scribal corruption.

The king not only had peculiar notions about the value of writing, but his sense of the mimetic principle implied by the travelogue as a genre is equally ambivalent. For instance, we read, "I said my prayers in the Kremlin, then I had the photographer take a portrait of me, then we went and visited the museum. Now that Abul Hassan Khan is writing these words, I haven't taken any pictures yet, nor have I visited the museum. Maybe there won't even be a picture-taking or a visit to the museum."[28]

The epistemic contract implied in this passage, with repercussions for the whole of the text, seems at once unusually avant-garde and dangerously despotic. The form of the narrative is in some complex and confusing way "modern." It resembles moments in modern novels when the novelist, in the process of writing, engages in a deconstructive act by exposing the fictive nature of the narrative. Like Chaucer's Pardoner, the king exposes the tricks of his narrative, yet unlike the modern novelist, he expects us to suspend disbelief. Whereas in the hands of novelists the deconstructive act serves to demonstrate the permeable boundaries between what Vladimir-Nabokov calls "the facts of fiction and the fiction of facts," the tone of the king's narrative leaves no doubt that he expects the reader never to doubt the facticity of his fiction.

From what the narrative betrays, the king travels not just to discover the West as the dreaded and desired "Other," but also to reinvigorate his own waning powers at home. In almost every page, we are treated to elaborate, repetitious details about the pageantry of his visit, the power of his presence among powerful Western politicians and kings, and the "unbelievable, uncontrollable" surge of popular enthusiasm for His Majesty. On all such occasions, the narrative is suffused with the kind of familiar honorifics that Iranian courtly discourse was commonly studded with, if in the Shklovskian trope of "defamiliarization,"[29] the familiar is rendered strange, the Shah's linguistic tropes try to tame and familiarize the unfamiliar. Repeatedly, the king insinuates the vocabulary of despotic power and traditional forms of authority into descriptions of what would have been an unfamiliar world of Western European politics.

The point is nowhere more evident than in the king's narrative of his trip to England. Queen Victoria was the monarch then. In spite of common diplomatic rules of decorum, the queen did not go to meet the visiting king at the port of entry, but forced the Shah to travel to Windsor Palace. Not only does the king make absolutely no mention of this clear diplomatic slight, but he instead waxes eloquent about all the respect afforded him during the visit.

But there was an even more serious problem. Victoria was a woman. To circumvent what the Shah felt to be the embarrassing and potentially dangerous idea of a ruling woman monarch, he chose to essentially hide from any but his most astute readers the gender of Victoria.[30] Throughout the text he repeatedly refers to her using the Persian word *Padshah*, a word that clearly implies the idea of a male ruler. He thus eschews another clearly understood and commonly used word *Malekeh*, which in Persian signifies a woman ruler. When referring to the safe distance of the sixteenth century, the Shah had no compunction about referring to Elizabeth as *Malekeh*. His linguistic preferences here are a fascinating example of the kind of ambivalence of language that Bhabha calls the "language of archaic belonging," a language that attempts to "marginalize" the "present of Modernity."[31]

In fact, the "woman question" permeates, often in a tragicomical manner, much of the fiber of the text. The king was renowned for his insatiable desire for women. By the time he died, he had legally wed eighty-five women. To be bereft of female companionship for the duration of the trip was of course unthinkable. To take all (or even some of) his *harem* proved logistically impossible, and politically embarrassing. Improvisation was in order.

On one trip, he took along a young boy with whom he had fallen in love. Throughout the three logs, the only time the language of the text becomes emotionally charged and resonates with human passion is when the king discusses his young beloved. At the same time, during the same trip, he ordered his ambassador to the Ottoman court to dispatch for the king a fourteen-year-old white slave girl.[32] With the arrival of the girl, the scene of the entourage seems nothing short of a Shakespearean comedy of errors.

The king's description of the affair is at the same time poignantly revealing of his own disturbed sense of self. In these descriptions, we get a rare glimpse of the rather mutilated sense of self, of that Fanonesque masque[33] of a pompous political persona behind which hides a man of pitiable insecurity. In describing the girl, he writes:

> I had asked for a girl from Istanbul. Last night when we were asleep, she arrived. Agha [the eunuch of the entourage] broke the good news of

her arrival. We had ordered that her hair be cut so that she could look like a man.

When I saw her today, she smiled. From her laughter, I gathered that when they told the girl that We were taking you for the Persian King she must have had strange ideas in her mind. She must have thought: What kind of a creature is this King of Persia? Does he have horns? In her mind, she conjured the image of a man with heavy, long pointed beard, with seven manes reaching the earth, a thick moustache curled around his head, a lanky jaundiced face, shining, bulging yellow eyes, big mouth, rotten teeth, with a couple of ugly canine teeth protruding, a foul-smelling mouth, long hat on his head, and so short-tempered that whomsoever he meets he slaps so hard that blood gushes from their nostrils.[34]

Aside from the fact that the depicted image bears a frightening resemblance to actual pictures of the Shah's father and grandfather, the passage is particularly significant for what it reveals about the fractured identity the king harbored beneath the facade of royal grandeur. This ambivalence of identity is, I think, at the core of the problematic relationship of many Iranians with Western powers. Whereas xenophobic nationalists and religious fundamentalists harbor narcissistic illusions of ethnic or religious grandeur and perfection, comprador modernists foster a cult of self-denigration and illusory notions about the "perfect West." To fashion a self free from both delusions and abnegations is one of the most central and daunting tasks facing the once colonized peoples of the world today.

Of course none of these competing narratives of submission or segregation, or conflicting tropes of "encoding," have ever succeeded in becoming a totalizing narrative, leaving a window of opportunity for other, more autonomous cultural strategies for selfhood.

As despots are wont to do, the Shah tried to turn necessity into virtue and to launder his constant preoccupation with women as sexual objects into a positive quality. In fact, he claims to have discovered the key to Europe's success, for he writes, "I met the Foreign Secretary of Holland. It has become apparent to me that all these Westerners are whoremongers and lechers. The Foreign Secretary was constantly looking at women. The reason the Westerners are so powerful is that they are constantly in pursuit of pleasure."[35]

Delusive distortions are not of course the only revealing textual strategy employed by the monarch. Implicit in every text is an epistemic hierarchy that helps categorize certain facts as relevant and important, and thus a necessary part of the narrative, and dismisses others as irrelevant. A crucial element of this implicit taxonomy is the presumed boundaries between the realm of the public and the private.[36] If we accept the notion that modernity transforms politics from the private arena monopolized by the elite to the public theater wherein the masses are legitimate players, then the Shah's narrative of discovery seems archaically premodern. Pages after pages of the text are given to descriptions of zoos and hunting trips, with scant allusion to the political structure of Europe.

He writes repeatedly of his desire "to buy" the beautiful women he meets.[37] His crude flirtations with a Russian woman—whom he has to give up because she, he finds out, is a Jew[38]—is treated with far more fanfare and in far more detail than the famous London, Paris, and Moscow world exhibits he visits. Indeed, in writing about the exhibit in Moscow, he comments only on "the beautiful women visiting the exhibit," lamenting the fact that he could not get his hand on any of them.[39]

Every day's entry begins with a repetitious reference to the fact that His Majesty woke up, ate, and went out, but there is hardly any allusion to any of the political discussions he engaged in throughout his trip. Nearly all references to such discussions are limited to a curt refrain to the tune of "Some good discussions were held."[40] In all such cases, the implicit tone is one of disdain. It exudes a sense of dismissiveness toward the reader. It implies in no uncertain terms that politics is not the business of the public, and, by extension, we the readers.

Ironically, although the king insists on preserving for himself the privileged monopoly of politics, he accepts no responsibility for the consequences of his own past political decisions. In parts of these three narratives, he uses an eerily cold and distant language to describe the miseries he witnesses in Iranian cities and villages. With no sense of shame, remorse, or responsibility, he writes of emaciated, hungry faces, derelict buildings, and bad roads. In one instance, traveling through one of the villages of his domain, he muses, "it is as if the Mongol hordes have ravaged the land."[41] The tone resembles one of an innocent traveler to a benighted land, not of its absolute ruler, who with his dynasty had by then ruled Iran for nearly a century.

By the third trip the king had also become overtly disdainful of the political atmosphere of Europe. Describing a meeting with Bismarck and the kaiser, he writes:

> I came down into the room and sat down. The Kaiser came too. We would sit, stand up, walk around, eat something, sit down again. The generals were also walking around. Some sat down. There was freedom. There stood one general, smoking, with his ass to the Emperor. Another was sitting yonder with his ass also to the Emperor. One of them had his ass toward me. In a word, there was freedom.[42]

Not all aspects of modernity were of course as disturbing to the king. His eclectic affinity with certain aspects of what he saw in Europe seems emblematic of many other "third-world" leaders' piecemeal appropriation of modernity. Modernity's never-ending fever for exchange fit perfectly with Nasir-al-Din Shah's insatiable personal greed.[43] He was more than willing to auction off Iran's sovereignty for paltry personal gains. Indeed during his reign, eighty-three concession treaties and economic pacts were signed with European powers. Of these, thirty-five were signed by the king before even looking at the details. As a recompense for his blind trust, he received payoffs from European powers.[44]

For a while, after his first two trips, he went into a frantic, often crazy search for gold in Iran. He also appreciated Europe's system of tax collection. With glee he writes about the system of income and property taxes he saw there and adds that "even animals are taxed separately."[45] He approved of the militarist air of Bismarckian Prussia. There even children, he reports, wear military uniforms and learn the habits of army life.[46] He relished the stores filled with commodities—and the enormously long list of his purchases is as impressive in its size as it is embarrassing in its kitsch quality. He liked Western guns. But most of all, he liked modernity's system of social control.

During his first visit, he hired an Austrian count to establish a modern police force for Iran. The blueprint the count—who had by then become Tehran's chief of police—prepared[47] reads like pages from Foucault's *Discipline and Punish*. He suggests a new regime of surveillance, based not only on the panoptic principle but also on permanent registration of the population, standardization of weights, and crowd-control techniques. Every teahouse, the traditional hub of neighborhood life and political gossip, was to have a police detachment. The Shah immediately approved the blueprints and ordered their implementation. They heralded the dawn of a new age that is, in a sense, shared by most third-world countries in their early encounters with modernity. It is an age where the despotism of individualized, tyrannical authority combines with the hegemonic force of panoptic surveillance.

There is yet another gradual change evident in the progression of the three narratives. Between the first and third logs, a definite linguistic change creeps into the texts. When talking about Iran, the king uses increasingly more hostile and disparaging adjectives and metaphors. To him Iran had come to look more arid, faces more vacuous, cities more decrepit. On the other hand, descriptions of European nature are more ebullient. On all too numerous occasions, the metaphor of "paradise" is invoked to describe a European garden or a forest. In fact, by the third trip, the word *Farangi*, the Persian word for the "Franks" or Europeans, had become for the king synonymous with higher and more noble qualities. On the eve of his third trip, Tehran, the capital city, was decorated with lights and flags. In praise of the city, Nasir-al-Din Shah writes, "the streets had so much glamour that they hardly looked like Tehran. They looked like European cities. There was grandeur to them."[48]

The royal lexicon is also transformed in the course of the three travelogues. In later writings, the king peppers his discourse with French words. Sometimes these words are by necessity used to refer to concepts still then alien to the Persian language. Oftentimes, however, he seems to derive a sense of personal pride in his newfound linguistic prowess. His linguistic proclivity has all the characteristics of what Pratt calls "autoethnography," or more specifically a "partial collaboration with and appropriation of the idioms of the conqueror."[49] Other accounts left by his courtiers support this perception. The king was always wont to pretend more comprehension of foreign languages than was warranted by his abilities.

Colonial hegemony is always interlaced with the waning aura of the native tongue and a near magical legitimization afforded to the colonizing language. What usually further complicates the picture is that inevitably in the marketplace of ideas and knowledge, these colonial languages are the common currency of exchange. Thus not only comprador modernists but genuine modernists as well have become party to this auratic transformation. And this transformation is a key ingredient in the sense of undermined cultural sovereignty and damaged self-esteem so often found in colonized lands. In terms of the royal texts, these transformations reflected, as well as reinforced, the kind of social and psychological changes that ultimately shaped the Iranian Constitutional Revolution.

Sometimes metaphors of reality are more powerful than any aesthetic construct. At the end of his first trip, in spite of his fear of the open seas, the Shah boards a ship on the Russian side of the Caspian Sea and heads home. If the sea is to be mythically understood as the metaphor of utopia and change, then the Shah's fear of the sea poetically fits his aversion to social change. Near the Iranian port, a storm sets in. He writes, "I descended from the deck. It was impossible to stand there. I went to my room, took off my clothes, and in melancholy, waited to see what Fate had in store for Us."[50] At the end of the second trip, once again near the same port, another storm threatens: "The horizons are bleak, winds are blowing, dark clouds appear. A storm seems imminent."[51] As Fate would have it, history, the Machiavellian *Fortuna* of modern times, had social revolution in store. The "inscriptional overcoding" proved ineffective. Desire for change would not remain "the property of the sovereign" and tore through the "nets of the despotic state."[52] Not long after the sea storms ended, political storms began at home.

Notes

I am grateful to Jean Nyland, Parvis Shokat, Farzaneh Milani, and Kamal Azari, who read and commented on early drafts of this essay. The idea for the essay came out of a discussion with Mike Shapiro some three years ago. But my debt to him is far greater than his role in the genealogy of this essay. In a sense, there is a bit of him in everything I have written over the past twenty years.

1 Claude Lévi-Strauss, *Tristes Tropiques*, trans. John Russell (New York: Viking Penguin, 1991), p. 192.
2 Gilles Deleuze and Félix Guattari, *Anti-Oedipus: Capitalism and Schizophrenia*, trans. Robert Hurley, Mark Seem, and Helen R. Lane (Minneapolis: University of Minnesota Press, 1993), p. 202.
3 Homi K, Bhabha, *The Location of Culture* (New York: Routledge, 1994), p. 9.
4 Ibid., p. 4.
5 Ibid., p. 1.
6 Deleuze and Guattari, *Anti-Oedipus*, p. 199.
7 Ehsan Yarshater, "Observations on Nasir-al-Din Shah," in *Qajar Iran: Political, Social and Cultural Change*, ed. Edmund Bosworth and Carole Hellenbrand (Edinburgh: University of Edinburgh Press, 1983), p. 8.
8 Fereydoun Adamiyat, *Andisheye Taragui* (Tehran: Kharazmi, 1972), p. 259.

9 Vita Sackville-West describes how Nasir-al-Din Shah "used to startle Europe by his arrival in her capital with his Oriental accoutrements and the black moustachios like a scimitar across his face." See Vita Sackville-West, *Passenger to Tehran* (New York: Harper Perennial, 1992), p. 138. See also Zeynek Celik, *Displaying the Orient: Architecture of Islam at Nineteenth Century World's Fairs* (Berkeley: University of California Press, 1992), pp. 34–36 and pp. 120–22.

10 In spite of their singular significance in understanding Iran's encounter with modernity, no scholarly edition of these texts has yet been published. Except for parts of the logs for the third trip, recently reissued in a critical, annotated edition, I have relied on reproductions of the handwritten originals. See Nasir-al-Din Shah, *Safar Nameye Nasir-al-Din Shah* (Tehran: Charg, 1964); Nasir-al-Din Shah, *Safar Nameye Farangstan* (Tehran: Charg, 1963); Nasir-Ai-Din Shah, *Rooznameye Khaterat Nasir-Al-Din Shaha Dar Safar Sevum Farang* (Tehran: Resa, 1990).

   Parts of each of these travelogues were published in English almost immediately after the trips. They were part of the king's attempt to forge a "modern" image for himself. Many oriental despots at the turn of the last century were caught in the frenzy of appearing modern (See Edward Said, *Culture and Imperialism* [New York: Alfred A. Knopf, 1993], pp. 110–35).

11 Deleuze and Guattari, *Anti-Oedipus*, pp. 199–224.

12 Fredric Jameson, *The Political Unconscious; Narrative as a Socially Symbolic Act* (Ithaca: Cornell University Press, 1981), p. 77.

13 Ibid., p. 82.

14 Mary Louise Pratt, *Imperial Eyes: Travel Writing and Transculturation* (New York: Routledge, 1992), p. 4.

15 Ibid., p. 4.

16 Hannah Arendt, *Between Past and Future: Eight Exercises in Political Thought* (New York: Penguin, 1983), pp. 41–80.

17 Stephen Greenblatt's *Marvelous Possessions* is an insightful look into the two types of medieval and modern curiosities, or "wonders," and their corresponding representational practices (see Stephen Greenblatt, *Marvelous Possessions: The Wonder of the New World* [Berkeley: University of California Press, 1991]). For a broader articulation of modernity's "regime of truth," see Michel Foucault, *The Archeology of Knowledge and the Discourse on Language*, trans. A. M. Sheridan Smith (New York: Pantheon, 1982).

18 For a dazzling discourse on modernity's "theoretical curiosity," see Hans Blumenberg, *The Legitimacy of the Modern Age*, trans. Robert M. Wallace (Cambridge: MIT Press, 1983), pp. 229–437.

19 Rustam-al-Hokama, *Rustam-al-Tavarikh* (Tehran: Amir Kabir, 1972).

20 Said, *Culture and Imperialism*, pp. 110–15.

21 Every text, Eco reminds us, has at the moment of its inception a "model reader" in mind. The relationship between the text and this reader is reciprocal. The text at once shapes and is shaped by the model reader. Eco writes that "every text is a syntactic-semantical-pragmatic device, whose foreseen interpretation is part of its generative process." See Umberto Eco, *The Role of the Reader: Explorations in the Semiotics of Text* (Bloomington: Indiana University Press, 1979), p. 11.

22 Sackville-West, *Passenger to Tehran*, pp. 130–40.

23 Hayden White, *The Content of the Form: Narrative Discourse and Historical Representation* (Baltimore: Johns Hopkins University Press, 1987), p. ix.

24 Michel de Certeau, *The Writing of History*, trans. Tom Conley (New York: Columbia University Press, 1988), p. 210.

25 Michel Foucault, "What Is an Author?" in D. F. Boncard, ed., *Language, Counter-Memory, Practice* (Ithaca, N.Y.: Cornell University Press, 1977), pp. 125–27.

26 Certeau, *The Writing of History*, p. 212.
27 Nasir-al-Din Shah, *Rooznameye Khaterat*, p. 17.
28 Ibid., p. 138.
29 Victor Shklovsky, "Art as Technique," in *Russian Formalist Criticism*, trans. Lee T. Lemon Maron (Lincoln: University of Nebraska Press, 1965), p. 13.
30 It is only many pages after recounting the meeting that the king, in passing, mentions the fact that the British monarch had had a husband. Reference to this fact is the only clue to Victoria's gender.
31 Homi K. Bhabha, "Dis-semination: Time, Narrative, and the Margins of the Modern Nation," in *Nation and Narration*, ed. Homi K. Bhabha (London: Routledge, 1990), p. 317.
32 For a discussion of this episode, see Yarshater, "Observations of Nasir-al-Din Shah," pp. 6–9.
33 For a discussion of the impact of the colonial experience on the psyche of the colonized people, see Franz Fanon, *Black Skin, White Masks* (London: Pluto, 1986); and Franz Fanon, *The Wretched of the Earth* (Harmondsworth: Penguin, 1967).
34 Nasir-al-Din Shah, *Rooznameye Khaterat*, p. 17.
35 Ibid., p. 286.
36 For a discussion of the dialectics of the public and the private, see Richard Rorty, *Contingency, Irony, and Solidarity* (Cambridge: Cambridge University Press, 1989), pp. 1–95.
37 Nasir-al-Din Shah, *Rooznameye Khaterat*, p. 130.
38 Ibid., p. 128.
39 Ibid., p. 162.
40 Ibid., p. 17.
41 Ibid., p. 70.
42 Ibid., p. 220.
43 For a discussion of the dialectics of sovereignty and exchange, see Michael J. Shapiro, "Sovereignty and Exchange in the Orders of Modernity," *Alternatives* 16 (1991), pp. 447–75.
44 Nazem Al-Islam Kermani, *Tarikh Bidari Iranian* (Tehran: Agah, 1970), p. 143.
45 Nasir-al-Din Shah, *Safar Nameye Farangstan*, pp. 190–91.
46 Nasir-al-Din Shah, *Safar Nameye Nasir-al-Din Shah*, p. 75.
47 For a detailed account of this blueprint, see Morteza Tafrashi, *Nazm va Nazmiyeh Dar Doreye Ghajar* (Tehran: Neghah, 1973), pp. 53–90.
48 Nasir-al-Din Shah, *Rooznameye Khaterat*, p. 18.
49 Pratt, *Imperial Eyes*, p. 7.
50 Nasir-al-Din Shah, *Safar Nameye Nasir-al-Din Shah*, p. 250.
51 Nasir-al-Din Shah, *Safar Nameye Farangstan*, p. 257.
52 Deleuze and Guatrari, *Anti-Oedipus*, p. 224.

61

THE LAST PHASE OF THE
IRAN–IRAQ WAR

From stalemate to ceasefire

Shahram Chubin

Source: *Third World Quarterly* 11(2) (1989): 1–14.

The Iran–Iraq war is unusual among conflicts in the Third World in several respects. Most commonly cited are the costs in human life and economic resources, and its inordinate length. Less often remarked is the genre of conflict that it has represented, being untypical of the prevailing pattern in non-industrial areas, where the tendency has been for internal or civil wars. In contrast this was a relatively rare case of interstate conflict. It was a war in the classic mould in that it represented not simply a dispute about territory but also about power and ideas.

The war, which ended one month short of its eighth anniversary, had throughout the 1980s become part of the political and strategic landscape of the Middle East, establishing or accelerating new alignments and forcing new priorities. Because of its durability, its bouts of intense clashes alternating with seasonal lulls, and the impenetrability of the Iranian Islamic revolution, it had by the middle of the decade given rise to a host of assumptions, *bons mots* and clichés among observers that substituted for informed analysis. No part of the war, I believe, came as a greater surprise to such spectators (as well as to others) than the way the war ended, and it is on this phase in particular that this article is concentrated.

The onset of the war at least should not have come as a surprise. The relationship between revolution and war is a close one, as history has often shown. In this case, as in others, the advent of a cataclysmic change in a major state and its replacement by a revolutionary 'order' that made claims on its neighbours was bound to cause instability. The revolution in Iran upset the balance in two ways: first militarily, by replacing the Shah's army with what seemed to be a revolutionary rabble; and second, politically, by making a conservative and satisfied Iran into a revolutionary power intent on the quasi-universal mission of spreading its version of true Islam and hence destabilising its neighbours. What made war likely—even inevitable— was not simply Iran's provocation but also its neglect of, and disdain for, the traditional military balance between the two countries. (It had been this balance—in Iran's favour—that had secured the 1975 Algiers Agreement and sustained the new relationship of respect and reciprocity that had followed it.) Iran's rhetorical excesses and claims and inattention to the military balance were matched on the Iraqi side by a compound of fear and ambition: fear about Iran's goals if the revolution were to become entrenched, and ambition to achieve a position of regional supremacy while Iran was preoccupied and Iraq was in a relative position of unmatched military and economic strength. From Iraq's perspective the time to strike (preventively perhaps) was unlikely to be better than in 1980, before the revolution put down its roots, while its forces were in disarray, and while its relationship with both superpowers and most regional states was at best strained.[1]

Iraq's miscalculation was severe in that it overestimated its own capabilities while misconstruing the nature of its adversary and the sources of power at Iran's disposal. For while revolutionary Iran was deficient in the traditional or quantitative indices of military power, it made up for this, to a certain extent, by reliance on the superior commitment of its populace to the regime and hence the war. Indeed so eagerly did the revolutionary regime embrace the war as a 'blessing', label it as a struggle between 'Islam and blasphemy', define its war aims as the overthrow of the Baathist regime in Baghdad, and use the war to suppress its enemies at home, that Iraq's leaders might well have wondered what Iran would have done in the absence of such an external diversion.

Iraq's inability to use surprise to military effect in the early weeks of the war was not as serious as its failure to fashion a clear political objective. It seems to have expected either a quick collapse of Iran's regime, or a willingness to sue for peace, based on limited losses. However, Iraq completely misjudged the nature of revolutionary systems which traditionally neither understand nor wage limited wars (let alone a revolution based on the Shii emphasis on the positive value of martyrdom and sacrifice). Martin Wight commented on this general phenomenon:

> International revolution … transforms the character of war. It blurs the distinction between war and peace, international war and civil war, war and revolution … International revolutions generate revolutionary wars, in the sense that their wars are tinged with a doctrinal ferocity, and have unlimited aims. They tend to be not wars for defined objectives but crusades or wars for righteousness. They aim not at a negotiated peace but at a 'Carthiginian peace' or unconditional surrender.[2]

Iran stumbled into a war which it did much to provoke but was ill prepared for. Once embarked upon the 'imposed war', which it embraced with characteristic ardour and militancy, Iran used it to harness the energies of the mobilised revolutionary rank and file, settle domestic scores, consolidate power and focus on the mission of the revolution abroad. The latter was less controversial than the events of the revolution at home, which remained contentious. The war thus came to represent a test for the revolution—its capacity for commitment and sacrifice, as well as its ingenuity and self-reliance. It came gradually to epitomise all the themes of suffering and martyrdom that the leadership seemed determined to cultivate. In time it simply displaced any other item on the agenda of the revolution. The war and the revolution had merged; support for the two had become so intertwined as to make them virtually indistinguishable.

If Iran's revolution and its claims helped to precipitate the conflict, its definition of the absolute stakes that the war represented helped fuel it long after it had stopped making any sense. Iran's expulsion of Iraqi forces from its territory had been effected by mid-1982, yet the momentum of war and the drive to extend the sway of the Islamic revolution throughout the region prevailed over a more sober assessment of Iran's military capabilities. A series of costly offensives led by revolutionary guards and volunteers (*Basijis*) failed. In the next two years the war settled down into a pattern of reckless Iranian attacks on Iraqi forces dug in behind water and earth obstacles, and defended by a network of mines, artillery and automatic weapons. Iran's attacks at Majnoon and Howeizah in the spring of 1984 and 1985 respectively, demonstrated Iran's ingenuity and tolerance for punishment but also an inability to hold the territory it had captured.

Iraq seemed unwilling to resort to counter-offensives or to take casualties; consequently it let Iran dictate the tempo of the war. Iraq also relied on superior weapon-systems because of its continued access to friendly governments (especially the USSR and France after 1982), but otherwise resorted to universal conscription. The morale of its forces appeared suspect if only because it had lost three times as many prisoners of war to Iran as its adversary had lost.

Iran by contrast relied heavily on the superior commitment of its forces. It constantly affirmed, and came to believe, the slogan articulated by Rafsanjani in 1984 that 'The faith of the Islamic troops is stronger than Iraq's superior firepower.' As a consequence Iran's leaders really believed that they could demonstrate the vitality of the revolution and affirm its message and validity by confronting and overcoming adversity through self-reliance. They were in no mood for lessons from the West or the professional military; their war, like their revolution, was to be an experience unique in the annals of war, unsullied by practical considerations or constraints.

If Iran's military successes between 1982 and 1986 were ephemeral and costly, with long gaps between major offensives from 1984–86, the problem stemmed as much from deficiencies in strategy as from logistics. Alternating between frontal offensives and attrition along the length of the frontier ('defensive *jihad*'), between enthusiasm for the daring of the revolutionary guard and the more sober appraisals of the professional military, Iran's leaders were unable to frame a strategy that tied their war aims—the overthrow of the enemy—to their military capabilities, which in terms of equipment dwindled with each offensive. To achieve their war aims (which were 'total' in Clausewitzian terms), Iran needed either to defeat the enemy's forces decisively, or to capture a major strategic asset, thus precipitating their surrender (for example, the southern port city of Basra, which was predominantly Shii). The problem was that Iraq's forces would not venture out into the field to fight and risk defeat while the capture of Basra or Baghdad remained increasingly difficult because of their redundant defence lines.[3] This gap between aims and capabilities was to widen and precipitate the process that led to the end of the war.

Iran fought the war with both hands tied; without dependable or rich allies, without access to weapons systems compatible with those in its inventory, and without the benefit of its own best-trained minds. Iran's leadership revelled in this, insisting, as Khomeini said in 1984, that 'Those who think that the Koran does not say "war until victory" are mistaken.' If self-sufficiency was the goal, then improvisation, self-reliance and a refusal to be bound by conventional approaches had to be the means. At times the war appeared to be merely a vehicle for consciousness-raising, rather than a deadly serious business. It was 'a continuation of politics with the admixture of other means' in a sense that Clausewitz had surely not meant or intended.

Even so, Iran seemed to be winning the war. The breakthrough at Fao in February 1986 seemed to confirm that an Iranian victory was only a matter of time. Jeffrey Record's analysis was typical of this conventional wisdom:

> The longer the war lasts, the greater the prospects for a decisive Iranian victory. Iran has three times the population of Iraq, and Iranian forces, though less well-equipped, appear to be much more highly motivated than those of Iraq. In February 1986 Iran launched a series of offensives that succeeded in gaining firm control of the Shatt-al Arab waterway. Iraqi counterattacks, which deliberately sought to avoid high casualty rates for fear of undermining already tepid popular support for the war, relied primarily upon artillery fire and failed to dislodge Iranian forces. According to some Western observers of the conflict, Iraqi military leadership borders on the incompetent, and Iraqi troops, especially infantry, have little motivation.[4]

By February 1986 a number of clichés had achieved widespread currency. One was that 'peace was only possible with the removal or disappearance of one or both of the two leaders, Saddam Hussein and Ayatollah Khomeini', implying that compromise short of victory (for Iran) would be unimaginable and tantamount to political suicide. Another was that 'Iran could not lose the war nor Iraq win it', implying that time was on Iran's side. For the Iranian leadership the lesson drawn from Fao had been that a military solution to the war *was* now indeed possible, contrary to the cautious (and possibly faint-hearted) advice of the professional military. One Fao followed by several other similar incidents could wrap up the war quickly. What was lacking was not material for the war effort but commitment and faith. Iran's political leaders began to unlearn what had been learned painfully on the battlefield, namely that incremental success was an inadequate basis for achieving the total victory required to attain Iran's ambitious war aims; and that only a smashing, devastating defeat of the enemy could possibly achieve this, and such a defeat was still unattainable. Now, after Fao, it seemed more attainable, and the Iranian leadership sought to capitalise on its success by proclaiming 'a year of decision'. Naturally, it again reverted to the style of war most suited to its forces, the frontal offensive.

In fact, paradoxically, Fao was to be the culminating point of Iran's success, the point at which it both over-reached itself and misled itself as to the implications.[5] Why was the prevailing wisdom regarding the likely outcome of the war, if it were to continue, so wrong? In war the relative positions of the two sides is in constant flux, and the longer the war the more fluid the picture and the more delicate the assessment of the relative balances on various levels between the two adversaries. To take but one element in relative strengths: Iran's superior commitment, its principal asset, was neither indefinitely sustainable nor by itself an adequate substitute for access to weapons systems, spares and training. While 'final offensives' gave at least a semblance of momentum to Iran's war effort, so necessary to stimulate the 'bandwagon effect' on the popular forces of the revolution, they also ate up trained manpower and hard-to-replace equipment. And the prospect of breakthrough seemed to recede with each effort. Yet at the same time, recourse to a strategy of attrition held obvious drawbacks: it could not deliver the decisive victory essential for the achievement of Iran's war aims; it was uncongenial to the revolutionary spirit nurtured on *élan*, and it was a two-edged sword in that it could wear down Iran's will to fight as much as Iraq's, with quite devastating consequences because of the importance of commitment in Iran's limited inventory of assets. The superior commitment of Iran's troops, and Iran's will to continue the war could suffer from a strategy of attrition that relied on incremental progress without the dynamic momentum of battlefield success.

On the other hand, the instruments of war were dwindling; Iraqi air attacks and the sharp drop in the price of oil in 1986 made the replacement of weapons more economically onerous. At the same time the inventory of arms inherited from the Shah's day was a finite resource; at some point it could no longer be cannibalised and would need to be replaced. Furthermore Operation Staunch, in existence since 1984, was being taken more seriously by the US which appeared to be in a vengeful mood after the Irangate revelations. European governments also began to take the issue more seriously. Thus Iran's access to arms was being curtailed at precisely the time when its strategy called for more resources and when existing stocks could no longer be raided to serve as improvised replacements.

The gap between Iran's military capabilities and its political aims widened as the war went on. On every quantitative indicator of power, Iraq's position improved year by year, compared with that of Iran. To take a few illustrative examples: in terms of arms purchases (from all sources expressed in dollar terms), Iraq spent more than Iran every year between 1981 and 1985, in ratios varying between 6:1 and 3:1.[6] Iraq consistently exceeded Iran in military expenditure, maintaining a constant annual rate of $12–14 billion in 1984–87, while Iran's expenditure plunged and dipped from $14 billion in 1985–86 to $5.89 billion the next year to between $6–8 billion in the succeeding years. As the war dragged on, Iraq's access to superior sources of arms became increasingly pronounced. In 1984 Iraq could 'only' manage a 2.5:1 superiority in tanks, 4:1 in aircraft and APC and had a 3:4 inferiority in artillery.[7] This had widened by 1988 to 4:1 superiority in tanks, 10:1 in aircraft and 3:1 in artillery. The commander of the Revolutionary Guard, Mohsen Rezai, was to say after the war: 'They had armour and we did not. If our circumstances in the war are not taken into account when comparisons are made with classical warfare, it will be a major error on the part of the analysts. We were unarmed infantrymen against the enemy's cavalry. There are few instances in the history of Islam of such a war.'[8]

Even Iran's much vaunted numerical advantage of 3:1 in terms of population was not much in evidence on the battlefield towards the end of the war. Whereas between 1986 and 1988 Iraq was able to increase its manpower by some 150,000 men, and reorganise and expand its forces from thirty to thirty-nine infantry divisions, Iran's manpower fell in the same period by 100,000 men.[9]

Not only did the declining pool of volunteers necessitate greater reliance on conscripts who could not match the former in zeal, but Iran's war effort was also clearly hampered by logistical difficulties. These stemmed partly from political decisions such as the fielding of two sets of armed forces, the regular military and Revolutionary Guard, who duplicated each other and did not always work harmoniously. The problems were no doubt compounded by the difficulties of supplying troops with an astonishing variety of ammunition and spare parts, some of Western origin, some bought and captured in the Soviet bloc, some from Third World sources and some of indigenous manufacture. It would have been surprising if under these conditions Iran could have obtained a 'teeth to tail' ratio anywhere near that of Iraq.

As Iran launched what were to be the last major offensives of the war at Basra and in the central sector between 24 December 1986 and mid-March 1987, the attacks took on the semblance of a last gasp—a make or break attempt to force a military decision. Even the limited advance toward Basra was revealing, for it demonstrated not the workings of an unstoppable, dynamic force, but proved to be a strenuous and costly effort barely adequate to sustain itself. As such, Iran could scarcely count on Iraq's collapse even in the unlikely event of the capture of Basra.

If the war was becoming harder for Iran to conduct militarily due to the demand for greater resources, it was also becoming more politically onerous in two ways. The strategy begun by Iraq in 1984 of internationalising the conflict was beginning to bear fruit. In 1986 the 'tanker war' had expanded, with more shipping hit and more casualties than the cumulative total of the preceding years. Iraq's aircraft with new missiles and air-refuelling capabilities were now ranging as far south as the Larak and Lavan terminals, putting at risk all Iran's oil terminals in the Persian Gulf.

In response Iran had threatened *in extremis* to close the straits of Hormuz, and in the meantime had targeted those Gulf states known to be actively supporting Iraq's war effort, particularly Kuwait. Iran's accusation that Kuwait served as a trans-shipment point for arms destined for Iraq and that the sheikhdom with its financial subsidies and anti-Iranian policies was in effect an undeclared belligerent, was not seriously contested. But neither the superpowers nor the Gulf Corporation Council states were prepared to condone Iran's targeting shipping destined for the Gulf sheikhdoms as a legitimate response to Iraq's attacks on Iran's shipping. This ran counter to the outside powers' policy of containing the Gulf war (as it had by now become) and defending the other Gulf states.

The more sustained Iraq's attacks on shipping serving Iran became, the more acute was the pressure on Iran to submit passively or to exert military pressure on the Gulf states. The dilemma posed did not admit of a solution; unable to find Iraqi targets in the waterway, Iran attacked the next best thing and found itself playing into Iraq's hands by antagonising both its immediate neighbours and the superpowers. (Iran's retaliation against third party shipping as a result of attacks sustained from Iraq thus played into Iraqi hands by bringing in outside powers against Iran.)

By mid-1987 the result of this was seen on two levels: a virtual schism between Persian and Arab states in the Gulf after the Mecca incident in July 1987, which was symbolised by the Arab summit conference in Amman in November 1987. At the insistence of Saudi Arabia, priority was given at the conference for the first time to the Gulf war in Arab councils. The formation of Security Council resolution 598 by the United Nations was another indicator of the degree to which Iran's conduct in the war had aroused international concern and even stimulated a parallel response. The resolution, for all its apparently neutral terminology, was manifestly aimed at arresting Iran's continuation of the war, threatening mandatory sanctions (in the form of an arms embargo) if a ceasefire was not accepted.

This is not the place to discuss Iran's relations with the superpowers except to note that by mid-1987 it had done little to cultivate the friendship of either, and much to push the two together in order to contain and end the war. Soviet leaders, particularly Andrei Gromyko, repeatedly counselled Iranian officials that 'three years of negotiation are better than one day of war'. In December 1987 Gromyko told the Iranian ambassador prophetically that 'the later Iran's leaders reach the conclusion that it needs to end the war, the less favourable it will be for Iran'.[10] Iranian leaders consistently overestimated their own centrality in international affairs and the importance of oil, while being insensitive to the changing nature of relations between the superpowers. At the same time they were unable to improve their margin for manoeuvre between the superpowers simply because Iran's ideological inflexibility shackled its diplomacy and prevented credible threats to ally with either the East or the West.

If the internationalisation of the war, regional isolation and the threat of a future comprehensive arms embargo increased the psychological pressure on Iran, the lack of success since the breakthrough at Fao had also begun to diminish the domestic enthusiasm for the war, even among the die-hard *hezbollah* (party of God) and the *mustazefin* (oppressed) class. Thus in the second arena, domestic politics, the cost of continuing the war without any decisive result was beginning to be felt.

There were several indications that Iranian leaders were at least reassessing their approach to the war as of mid-1987.

1. Iran's willingness to take up the gauntlet of the superpowers' decision to escort Kuwaiti shipping suggested that Iran somehow welcomed the diversion of a sideshow in the war.
2. Iran's unwillingness to reject the Security Council resolution outright but to seek modifications was also indicative of a change in attitude.
3. Iran's war aims, although still ambiguous, had nonetheless been modified over previous months; the demand for the removal of Saddam Hussein still stood, but the insistence on the removal of the Baath party, reparations, and the installation of an Islamic republic had disappeared.
4. The stream of volunteers for the front had dwindled and Iran's leaders, notably Rafsanjani, had begun to talk publicly in mid-1987 of continuing the war *unless* (or until) it began to interfere with the political administration of society.[11]

By the autumn of 1987 Iran's leadership had begun to despair of a military solution to the conflict, but was still far from devising a diplomatic strategy for Iran's extrication from the war. For one thing, the war, whose importance had been repeatedly and irresponsibly inflated, and equated with 'Islam' and 'our life', was clearly becoming costly to continue, but who could guess what the political costs of ending it ignominiously—in failure—would be? And who would be the courageous soul willing to convince Khomeini of the need for an end to the war, and of the change in the cost-calculus of protracted war versus negotiations? This was not made any easier by the fact that Iran's sense of aggrievement about the origins of (and hence blame for) the start of the war was not shared by many permanent members of the Security Council, in part because of Iran's prolongation of the conflict since mid-1982. And the political collapse of Iraq now seemed more remote and a less likely source of salvation. Furthermore, the US fleet (aided by five European allies) had taken on the appearance of a permanent fixture, less vulnerable and therefore less susceptible to political intimidation than the land presence in Lebanon in 1982–83, to which Iranian leaders erroneously compared it.

However, it was one thing for Iran's war effort to be running out of steam and quite another for it to collapse outright, precipitating the difficult if unavoidable decision to sue for peace. The elements squeezing Iran's war effort were not on their own enough to galvanise its leaders into making such a momentous decision in favour of peace. Only a perception that the continuation of the war would threaten the very existence of the Islamic republic, Khomeini's legacy, could have done so. Simply stated, two sets of events catalysed Iran into the decision to seek a quick ceasefire in mid-1988: the intensive use by Iraq of long-range missiles on cities and chemical weapons on the front; and a consequent change in the balance of power on the ground, particularly the shattering of the morale of Iranian forces.

Although Iran and Iraq had been trading attacks on each other's city centres since 1984, they had not reached the intensity of the exchanges witnessed in the revived 'war of the cities' in early 1988. In earlier years Iraq had used its air superiority to take the war home to Iran by bombing Tehran (for example, in the spring of 1985), in order to raise the political and economic costs of continuing the war. This had had some political effect, but not enough to produce more than occasional panic and resentment. Iran had responded by proclaiming a programme for building air-shelters and by acquiring Soviet bloc SSMS from Syria, Libya and possibly China. These missiles, together with artillery, were to counter Iraq's air threat to Iran's inland cities, for Iran had the advantage of being within shelling range of Iraq's principal cities. The situation of mutual vulnerability might have been expected to produce an end to these exchanges, were it not for Iraq's perception in late 1987 of the need to intensify the war against Iran at the period of its maximum vulnerability.

Reference has already been made to the widening gap between the two adversaries' military equipment. Nowhere was this more evident than in the next phase of the war, when Iraq launched 150 SCUD-B missiles (allegedly modified by East German technicians for extended range at the cost of reduced payload)[12] in a period of five weeks starting from the end of February 1988. In the same period Iran fired one-third the number. Less significant than the ratio was the fact that Iraq felt confident enough of the numbers at its disposal to loose off such barrages, and it was indicative also that Iraq, with uncontested advantage in fixed-wing aircraft, was now being supplied with apparently unlimited numbers of SSMS as well. The effect of these indiscriminate terror attacks was to instil panic in the urban populations. (It may be that the attempts of Iranian leaders to publicise these attacks for propaganda advantage inadvertently led to the amplification of their terror effect.) After the war, Rafsanjani was to claim that of a total of 133,000 Iranians killed, 10–11,000 deaths were attributable to air and missile attacks on cities.[13]

The effect of this was doubled by Iraq's resumed use of chemical weapons at the front, notably in the attack on the town of Halabja in the north. Again, the effects may have been greater psychologically than they were militarily. But it did not escape notice in Iran that the international outcry at documented uses of these banned substances was relatively restrained when they fell on Iranian soldiers or villages. Rafsanjani was later to tell the Revolutionary Guards that the war had shown chemical and biological weapons to be 'very decisive', and that 'all the moral teachings of the world are not very effective when war reaches a serious position'.[14]

The turning point in the war came, I believe, shortly after this with the double blow sustained by Iran on 17–18 April 1988, when Fao was lost to Iraq and several boats to the US navy. Fao, of course, was politically and psychologically significant, being the major tangible symbol of Iranian success in the war, whose loss would leave Iran virtually empty-handed after six years of prolonging the war.

But more important still was what Iraq's recapture of Fao signalled in terms of the shift that had taken place in the psychological balance; Iraq had dumped its 'defence only' policy of leaving the initiative to Iran, hiding behind static defences and seeking to limit casualties in engagements. By seizing the initiative and striking out with counter-offensives, Iraq not only complicated Iran's defence planning but showed evidence of a new and unsuspected confidence.

Certainly Iraq's new-found confidence and belligerence on the battlefield came as a surprise to the Iranians, who were used to dictating rather than reacting to the timing and location of engagements. A week before Iraq's recapture of Fao, President Khamenei was depicting the 'war of the cities' as a logical outgrowth of Iraq's incapacity to do anything else militarily: 'The Iraqi regime lacks the power even to defend itself. For years it had lost the power to mount an offensive on the battlefield. Today it does not even command defensive forces, as is evidenced by Halabja.'[15] In Iranian eyes, the double blow was too suspiciously coincidental in timing to have happened accidentally. After all, it was generally known (and admitted) that the US was already providing Iraq with detailed intelligence data to aid Iraqi bombing runs on Iranian targets. Furthermore, both the range of Iraqi aircraft and the accuracy of their bombing against Iran's oil refineries and terminals had improved suspiciously of late. It was but a short step from there to seeing the actions on 17–18 April 1988 as being coordinated and even jointly planned. Rafsanjani accordingly depicted them as a plot.[16]

Nonetheless the fact remained that Iraqi troops had wrestled the initiative away from Iran (which had been unable to mount an offensive in the appropriate period for the first time since the start of the war) and forced its troops to flee. Coming on the heels of the missiles and chemical weapons, it was evident that Iranian morale had finally cracked.

The one asset on which Iran had relied to compensate for inferiority in every other area had simply dissolved. This was of decisive importance because morale, commitment, zeal, dedication—whatever its label—could not, by its very nature, be reconstituted overnight. Unlike a shortage of aircraft or spare parts, it could not be made good or topped-up by outside suppliers.

Indicative of this shift in the respective motivation of the two sides were the tremors of discontent that were again emanating from within Iranian society. In May 1988 Mehdi Bazargan, the head of the Liberation Movement of Iran (the only 'opposition' party allowed by the Islamic republic), made public a scathing criticism of the government's policy of continuing the war. What distinguished this from earlier criticisms from the same source were the echoes it now audibly evoked in many sectors of society. For the stoical populace of the Islamic republic, economic hardship and other privations such as fuel rationing and electricity cuts were tolerable in the cause of victory, but not otherwise. Now there was precious little optimism about this goal evident even among the high priests of the war.

The scene was now set for a radical rethinking of policy. What lent it urgency was the evidence that Iran's soldiers were unwilling to continue the fight. Even in those cases where impending Iraqi attacks were publicised, as in Majnoon, the Iranian troops' commitment to defence was a shadow of their earlier performance. The string of Iraqi military victories after Fao—Shalamcheh, Mehran and Majnoon among others—only hastened Rafsanjani's determination to get Khomeini's approval for Iran's acceptance of a ceasefire.

The destruction of an Iran-Air airbus by a missile of a US naval vessel in early July 1988 provided a convenient occasion for the announcement of this decision. It gave Iran's leaders precisely the moral cover of martyrdom and suffering in the face of an unjust superior force they needed to camouflage the comprehensive defeat of their political goals. Khomeini, at least, could not dissemble the depth of the defeat.

If the war and the revolution had imperceptibly merged into one, and the war had proven virtually the only achievement of the revolution in nine years, what possible verdict on the revolution could now be passed? Judged from the standpoint of traditional diplomacy, Iran's war effort had been a valiant but pointless exercise. Having elevated self-reliance to an absolute goal, Iran had found through its own immoderation that it was no longer just a goal, but a reality and a constraint with which its war effort had to struggle. The concepts of self-reliance, self-sufficiency, a nation tempered and forged in war and similar such romantic notions were the most that could be salvaged from a war that should never have occurred. Iran's inattention to the military balance had made war attractive to its rival neighbour. Similar inattention to the business of making peace at the optimum time ensured that Iran was to reach the conference table at the point of its maximum weakness. The major casualty of the war has been the credibility of the Islamic republic among its own rank and file. It will no longer be able to call effectively upon its populace for crusades and sacrifices, but will have to act more like a traditional state. It is for this reason that Hashemi Rafsanjani has indulged in preemptive self-criticism of past policies. It is for this reason too that reconstruction policies are particularly important. A peace dividend must be found for the supporters of the revolution if the virus of discontent is not to spread and affect the very legitimacy of the revolution. Whether or not future generations will commemorate the war as a glorious chapter in the revolution, the present generation may be forgiven for not doing so.

Notes

1 For a more detailed discussion see Chubīn and Tripp, *Iran and Iraq at War*, London: I B Tauris, 1988.

2 M Wight, *Power Politics* (edited by H Bull and C Holbraad), London: Penguin/RIIA, 1979, pp 89–90, 91–2.

3 See my longer discussion of this problem in 'Les conduites de opérations militaires', *Politique Etrangère*, 2, 1987 (special issue on *Iran–Irak: La diplomatie du conflit*), pp 303–17.

4 J Record, 'The US central command: toward what purpose?', *Strategic Review*, spring 1986, p 44, fn 4.

5 See E Luttwak, *Strategy: the logic of war and peace*, Cambridge, Massachusetts: Belknap Press, Harvard University, 1987.

6 Figures can be consulted in: *World Military Expenditures and Arms Transfers 1986*, quoted in 'Overview of the situation in the Persian Gulf', Hearings and Markup before the Committee on Foreign Affairs, May/June 1987, pp 230–1.

7 See 'War in the Gulf', a staff report prepared for the US Committee on Foreign Relations, Senate (Committee Print), Washington DC: USGPO, August 1984.

8 Tehran television, 22 September 1988, in BBC summary of world broadcasts ME/0267/ A/3, 27 September 1988.

9 Unless otherwise stated these figures are all derived from the annual IISS *Military Balance*, 1984–1988. Saddam Hussein recently boasted about this; 'Our people who began with 12 divisions at the beginning of the war, now have about 70 divisions at the end of the war. The entire world has never seen such a development.' Baghdad Home Service, 14 November 1988, in BBC summary of world broadcasts ME/0311/A/9, 17 November 1988.

10 *Pravda*, 5 December 1987; *Izvestiya*, 8 December 1987.

11 Chubin and Tripp, *Iran and Iraq at War*, pp 73–4 and citations therein.

12 See *The Independent* 22 March 1988 and *Washington Post* 10 March 1988.

13 See Rafsanjani's speech in *Qom*, 24 September 1988, broadcast by Tehran radio on 25 September and excerpted in BBC/ME/0267/A/4, 27 September 1988.

14 Tehran home service, 6 October 1988, excerpted in BBC/ME/0277/A/2, 8 October 1988.

15 President Khamenei, sermon, Tehran University, 8 April 1988, excerpted in BBC/ME/ 0122/A/3, 11 April 1988.

16 See his interview with Tehran television 18 April 1988 in BBC/ME/0130/A/6, 20 April 1988.

62

MILITARY POWER AND
FOREIGN POLICY GOALS

The Iran–Iraq war revisited*

Efraim Karsh

Source: *International Affairs* 64(1) (1987–88): 83–95.

For every state there exists an interrelationship between the availability of military power and the setting of foreign policy goals. The nature and scope of the quest for military power is a direct consequence of the world view held by a state's leadership, which is in turn translated into national goals. At the same time a state's military capabilities at any given moment can determine the limits of a forceful foreign policy. Any successful pursuit of foreign policy goals depends to a considerable extent on the state's assessment of its military power in relation to its external environment. Since the assessment of military power and the perception of external threats are as much subjective as objective, any state can commit one of two errors in evaluation. It can set itself goals which are beyond its military power to achieve; or it can underestimate its power and pursue policies and goals that are narrower or more limited than its 'objective' power base might make possible.

Though most would agree that setting sights too low can be just as harmful to a state's interests as setting them too high, it is the latter kind of error that generally attracts the attention of analysts. Setting sights too low is usually read as a sign of inactivity, passivity, lack of initiative and missed opportunities. But once a state undertakes concrete action in pursuit of its foreign policy course and fails, the failure is usually attributed to an overestimation of its relative power.

This is the line of thought that has been applied to the decision by Iraq in 1980 to invade Iran, a decision which is commonly explained by what may be called the *grand design* theory. According to this theory, the Iraqi invasion in September 1980 reflected President Saddam Hussein's ambitions—which ranged from the occupation of Iranian territories (the Shatt al-Arab and Khuzestan), through the overthrow of the Khomeini regime, to the desire to assert Iraq as the pre-eminent Arab and Gulf state. It has even been suggested that, by defeating Iran, Saddam Hussein hoped to become the most influential leader of the Non-Aligned Movement.[1]

On this line of argument, Iraq's inability to bring the war to a swift conclusion is attributed to the wide gap between these very ambitious goals and the limitations of Iraqi military power. Iraq, so it is said, has committed the common mistake of trying to bite off more than it can chew, having overestimated its own power and underestimated that of its opponent.

The present article is inclined to reject this analysis. It will present three interconnected arguments. First, the Iraqi invasion of Iran did not emanate from a premeditated 'grand design' but was a pre-emptive move, intended to forestall the Iranian threat to the existence of the Baath regime by destroying opposing forces and denying territory. Secondly, Iraq cannot be said to have overestimated its relative military power, for in the summer of 1980 it enjoyed an undeniable military edge over its rival. Thirdly and finally, Iraq's crucial mistake was that it did not use its advantage decisively. Iraq's grand strategy failed, therefore, not because it was too ambitious, but because it was too narrow; not because Iraq lacked the military power to attain its national goals, but because it assigned its forces too limited objectives.

Towards the Pax Irana

Much has been written about the ambitions of Iraq's Baath regime to win regional and Pan-Arab pre-eminence. Its vocal adherence to the precepts of Arab unity and its record of interference in the affairs of its Arab neighbours, combined with the country's increasing prosperity in the late 1970s (as well as Egypt's departure from Arab forums), led many observers to view Iraq as the coming power in the region. It is not surprising, then, that the Iraqi invasion of Iran was interpreted in most quarters as a calculated step in the direction of regional primacy.

The events of the 1970s belie such an interpretation. Its 'revolutionary' ideology and far-reaching ambitions in the Arab world notwithstanding, the Baath regime was throughout this period fully aware of Iraq's demographic and geostrategic inferiority in relation to Iran. Iraq refrained from competing with Iran for strategic mastery, and concentrated on developing its defensive capabilities. By and large the course of the Iran–Iraq strategic relationship in the decade leading up to the war was dominated by Shah Mohamad Reza Pahlavi's persistent thrust for regional hegemony. Iraq played a reactive and defensive role.

Alarmed by Britain's pronounced intention to withdraw from its military bases east of Suez in 1968 on the one hand and encouraged by rising oil revenues in the middle and late 1960s on the other, the Shah was determined to establish Iran as the dominant power in the Gulf. This aspiration manifested itself in an impressive expansion of Iran's military capabilities during the 1970s. By the time of the Shah's overthrow in January 1979, the Iranian armed forces had grown from a modest force of some 161,000 in 1970 to approximately 415,000 troops, employing some 1,735 tanks and 447 combat aircraft (compared to 860 and 140 in 1970).[2]

The Shah's Gulf policy, which was received very favourably by the West, did not fail to make its impact on Iraq. In an attempt to match the Iranian arms build-up Iraq concentrated first and foremost on developing its ground forces. This is turn led to a threefold increase in the number of major weapons systems at their disposal: from 600 tanks and 600 armoured fighting vehicles in 1970 to 1,800 of each in 1979. The rate of growth of the air force was less impressive (from 229 to 339 aircraft). The navy hardly grew at all in this period.

The differing patterns of military expansion in Iran and Iraq were the result of the two countries' contrasting perceptions of their regional roles. The more or less balanced and simultaneous growth of the Iranian forces was undoubtedly motivated in part by the traditional goals of securing the country's northern and western borders. But the impressive air and, particularly, naval build-up clearly indicated a shift of focus southwards towards the Gulf. Iraq's consuming interest in the development of its ground forces, on the other hand, reflected its essentially defensive posture, its preoccupation with domestic affairs (the Kurdish insurgency, the Baath regime's stability), and the need to deter its two hereditary enemies, Syria and Iran. The lack of any significant naval development would seem to indicate that Iraq was aware of its basic geostrategic inferiority in relation to Iran and its inability to compete with it for Gulf supremacy; while Iran has a Gulf coastline of about 2,000 km, Iraq is virtually land-locked, with a Gulf coastline only 15 km long. Consequently, whereas Iran has five naval bases along the Gulf coast, some of them beyond Iraq's operational reach, Iraq had to rely on two naval bases, Basra and Umm Qasr, which were extremely vulnerable and within range of Iranian artillery. These geostrategic facts explain the historical Iranian association with the Gulf and that of Iraq with the 'fertile crescent'. In a sense, then, the distinct patterns of the military expansion undertaken by Iran and Iraq during the 1970s can be seen as the natural continuation of long historical trends imposed by geography.

The contrasting perceptions of each country's regional role were illustrated further by their Gulf policies in the early 1970s. The increased confidence felt by the Shah in Iran's growing military power led him as early as 1971 to state that 'the Persian Gulf must always be kept open—under Iranian protection—for the benefit not only of my country but the other Gulf countries, and the world'.[3] This assertion of Iran as the sole guardian of Gulf security became a regular theme in the Shah's pronouncements in the following years,[4] and was highlighted in the early 1970s by a series of Iranian actions intended to signal both to the Gulf countries and to the great powers who had the final say in the region.

On 30 November 1971, Iranian forces occupied three strategically located islands near the strait of Hormuz—Abu Musa, and Greater and Lesser Tumbs— which were at the time under the sovereignty of the sheikhdoms of Sharja and Ras al-Khaima. Iran used its historical claims on these islands to gain international understanding for the seizure, but it also justified their capture in strategic terms, arguing that the smooth flow of oil to the West depended on Iranian control of the Hormuz Straits. The increased Iranian interest in the Gulf was further demon-strated by the shift in 1972 of the Iranian naval headquarters from Khorramshahr, at the head of the Gulf, to Bandar Abbas near the strait of Hormuz. Also in 1972 the Sultan of Oman, Qaboos, acknowledging Iran's growing power in the Gulf, sought Iranian assistance in suppressing the Dhofari rebels operating along Oman's border with South Yemen (and supported by the latter). The Shah was ready to provide support.

The Shah also challenged the prevailing *status quo* with Iraq. On 19 April 1969, following an attempt by Iraq to exercise its rights in the Shatt al-Arab according to the border agreement of 1937, the Shah announced the unilateral abrogation of this agreement.[5] The practical consequences of this declaration emerged very quickly. On 24 April an Iranian merchant ship, escorted by the Iranian navy and with cover provided by fighters, passed through the disputed waters of the Shatt al-Arab to Iranian ports and paid no toll to Iraq as required under the 1937 agreement. The Iranian show of force, to which Iraq did not respond, was followed by a series of Iranian moves in the early 1970s which served to exacerbate Iraq's feelings of vulnerability, hostility and resentment. Among these were attempts to isolate Iraq politically from other Arab Gulf states, Iran's plan for a regional defence organization comprising Iran, Saudi Arabia and Kuwait and, above all, the extensive economic and military assistance provided by Iran to the Kurdish rebels in northern Iraq. The growing hostility between the two countries erupted into violence in the winter of 1973–4, with fierce border clashes that involved tanks, heavy artillery and aircraft. The ceasefire of March 1974 did not in practice lead to the cessation of hostilities, which merged into the Kurdish war. Iran went so far as to deploy artillery and air-defence units on Iraqi territory.[6]

Unable to suppress an insurgency that was imposing an intolerable burden on its domestic system, Iraq had no alternative but to seek some kind of agreement with Iran that would lead to the withdrawal of Iranian support from the Kurds. This took the form of the Algiers Agreement of 6 March 1975, which provided for some territorial adjustments, including the demarcation of the Shatt al-Arab waterway's boundary on the basis of the *thalweg* (i.e. median) line.[7]

The Algiers Agreement constituted a formal Iraqi acquiescence in Iranian dominance. While Iraq went out of its way to placate Iran by granting it sovereignty over half of the Shatt al-Arab, Iran made no practical concessions—unless non-interference in the domestic affairs of other sovereign states can be considered a concession. In other words, in the Algiers Agreement Iraq 'bought' the inviolability of its frontier, a fundamental and self-evident attribute of statehood, at the high price of territorial concessions. The weight of the Iraqi concessions is further illustrated by the fact that the Shatt, Iraq's sole point of access to the Gulf, is supremely important for the country's political, strategic and economic needs. Iraq's willingness to make such far-reaching concessions on the Shatt reflected its painful awareness that the effective enforcement of its internal sovereignty depended on the goodwill of its neighbour to the east—and it implied also an Iraqi recognition of Iran's military superiority. For unlike the Iranian armed forces, which because of their expansion had been virtually unaffected by the confrontation with Iraq, those of Iraq were still distracted by the Kurds on the borders of northern Iraq and thus unable to organize, train effectively or absorb their new weapons systems. Iraq was in no position to compete with Iran for hegemony in the Gulf; at the time of the Algiers Agreement, the Iraqi armed forces were on the verge of total collapse. According to Saddam Hussein the Iraqi army had been suffering from 'a great shortage of ammunition' in the winter of 1975, which prevented it from carrying on the war against the Kurds. This shortage was kept secret lest it affect the morale of the army.[8]

The Algiers Agreement thus opened a new—if brief—era in Iran-Iraq relations, the era of Pax Irana. After almost a decade the Shah had managed to achieve his goal—the substitution of a relationship that presupposed unquestioned Iranian dominance for the old Iran-Iraq *status quo* based on the 1937 agreement. Having attained its goals, the Shah's Iran turned naturally from a revisionist into a *status quo* power and began to advocate the perpetuation of the situation in the Gulf. Iraq was neither in a position nor had it the inclination to undermine the newly established *status quo*. Rather the Baath preferred to turn inward, to put down the Kurdish insurgency, to reconstruct its armed forces and to stabilize Iraq's social, economic and political systems. Consequently the agreement was followed by a period of much-reduced tension between Iraq and Iran which lasted for four years—until the overthrow of the Shah.

After the revolution

Iraq's initial response to the Shah's overthrow and the emergence of the Ayatollah Ruhollah Khomeini was by and large positive. Not only did the Baath regime not attempt to take advantage of the civil strife in Iran to revise the Algiers Agreement, but it was quick to indicate its willingness to continue to observe the *status quo* between the two states: 'a regime which does not support the enemy against us and does not intervene in our affairs, and whose world policy corresponds to the interests of the Iranian and Iraqi people, will certainly receive our respect and appreciation'.[9]

This positive attitude towards the revolutionary regime in Tehran continued throughout the spring and summer of 1979. Thus, for example, the Iraqi government took the opportunity of Iran's formal withdrawal from the Central Treaty Organization (CENTO) to offer its good offices in case Iran should decide to join the Non-Aligned Movement; and as late as July/August 1979 Iraqi authorities extended an invitation to the Iranian premier, Mehdi Bazargan, to visit Iraq in order to improve relations between the two countries.[10] The Iraqi leaders at the time referred to Iran as a brotherly nation, linked to the Arab people of Iraq by 'strong ties of Islam, history and noble traditions', and praised the revolutionary regime in Tehran for pursuing a policy that underlined these 'deep historical relations'.[11]

Iraq's shows of goodwill were not reciprocated. In June 1979 the revolutionary regime began publicly urging the Iraqi population to rise up and overthrow the Baath regime.[12] This propaganda campaign was paralleled by widely spread anti-Baath demonstrations in Iran, some of them involving armed attacks on Iraqis and Iraqi installations. In late 1979 Iran escalated its anti-Baathist campaign by resuming its support for the Iraqi Kurds; it also began providing moral and material support to Shiite underground movements (in particular the Daawa Party) in Iraq; and, last but not least, the Iranian government initiated terrorist attacks on prominent Iraqi officials, the most significant of which was the failed attempt to assassinate the Iraqi Deputy Premier, Tariq Aziz, on 1 April 1980.

The Baath regime tried to check these Iranian pressures. In the domestic sphere, Iraq suppressed the Shiite underground organizations and expelled Iranian citizens. On the external level, Iraq tried to organize a united Arab front to oppose the export of the Iranian revolution; it countered the Iranian propaganda campaign by lauching a series of verbal attacks on the Islamic regime; and finally, it lent its support to Iranian separatist elements such as the Iranian Kurds and the Arabs in Khuzestan. These countermeasures failed to impress the revolutionary regime. Responding to Saddam Hussein's pledge to take revenge for the attempt on the life of Tariq Aziz, Khomeini called on the Iraqi Shiites on 9 June 1980 to overthrow 'Saddam's government'. Iran's Foreign Minister, Sadegh Ghotzbadegh, revealed on the same day that his government had taken the decision to topple the Baath regime. The same theme was repeated two days later by the Iranian President, Abolhassan Bani Sadr, who also warned that Iran would go to war in case of a further deterioration in the situation on the border.[13] In April 1980 the Iran–Iraq confrontation had entered a new phase with clashes on the border. These skirmishes, which took place along the whole frontier, continued intermittently until late August. At that point they escalated into heavy fighting, involving tank and artillery duels and air strikes.

Iran's subversive activities in general, and the protracted and escalating border fighting in particular, drove the Iraqi leadership to the conclusion that it had no alternative but to contain the Iranian threat by resorting to arms. With the bitter experiences of the 1974–5 armed confrontration with Iran still fresh in their minds, the Baath leaders had serious doubts whether the Iraqi political system could sustain another prolonged and exhausting confrontation with Iran. These doubts, which were clearly illustrated by reported purges against 'unreliable' elements in the armed forces and the Baath Party in early 1980,[14] were reinforced by the unique nature of the new theocratic Iranian regime.

Iraq had perceived the Shah, for all his military power and ambitious objectives, as rational, if unpleasant. Certainly the Shah's goals were opposed to Iraqi national interests, and they could only be satisfied at Iraq's expense. But the Shah had not sought to unseat the Baath regime, and his intervention in Iraq's domestic affairs had been limited and purely instrumental, designed to prevent Iraq from competing militarily with Iran. Once the Shah's aspirations for Gulf hegemony were recognized, a deal (disadvantageous as it was for Iraq) could be struck and both parties could be expected to live up to it. The revolutionary regime in Tehran was a completely different type of rival—an irrational actor motivated by an uncompromising ideology and pursuing goals which were wholly unacceptable to Iraq. Unlike the Shah, the revolutionary regime did not see its intervention in Iraq's domestic affairs as a means to an end. It actively sought to overthrow the secular Baath regime.

In the Iraqi view, then, the strategic relationship between the two countries had been transformed by the revolution from a *mixed-motive game* into a *zero-sum game*. Given the growing amount of evidence that the Iranian regime was set upon destabilizing the Baath, Iraq came gradually to the realization that the only way to contain the Iranian threat was to raise the stakes for both sides by resorting to armed force.

The balance of advantage

The preceding discussion has indicated that the Iraqi decision to go to war was not taken easily or enthusiastically. Iraq did not go to war in pursuit of some wider ambition but was pushed into it as a result of increasing anxiety. War, as argued above, was not Iraq's first choice, but rather an act of last resort taken only after all other methods of deflecting the Iranian threat had been exhausted. It was indeed a pre-emptive move, taken when Iraq realized that it could no longer live with Iranian superiority because of the simple fact that that superiority threatened to lead to the overthrow of the Baath regime. If the Baath entertained any hopes or aspirations beyond the containment of the Iranian danger—as they may have done—they did not constitute the reason for launching the war. Rather they represented possible gains.

Against this background the question whether Iraq overestimated its military power and underestimated its opponent's capabilities becomes irrelevant. Since the Iraqi leadership saw war as the country's only option, it had to be launched regardless of the actual balance of forces. True, Iraq's decision to go to war involved the *possibility* of a failure, or even of defeat; but the avoidance of war could only result in the overthrow of the Baath regime.

But even in these circumstances, where strong perceptions of threat outweighed comparisons of military capabilities, Iraq did not in fact overestimate its relative potential. Iraq *did* in fact enjoy a tangible military (and political) edge over Iran in the summer of 1980.

The dethronement of the Shah had thrown the Iranian armed forces into total disarray. Viewing them as the Shah's instrument of oppression and as the most dangerous potential source of counter-revolution, the Islamic regime was determined to emasculate the armed forces by systematic purges as well as by the establishment of a counterweight, the Pasdaran revolutionary guard militia.

The purges dealt a devastating blow to the operational capabilities of the Iranian armed forces.[15] The army apparently lost over half its officers in the ranks from major to colonel; the air force reportedly lost half its pilots and 15–20 per cent of its officers, non-commissioned officers and technicians. The navy suffered least from the purges, which appear to have affected only a few hundred of its personnel. Over and above the purges, about half of the regular servicemen deserted and many more had been killed during and after the revolution. Conscription was not enforced and some fighting formations were dissolved; others fell apart or were much reduced. Even though the revolutionary regime came to recognize the importance of the regular army, mainly because of its relative successes in handling the Kurdish insurgency (where the Pasdaran proved ineffective), and took some steps to enhance its capabilities (such as the reintroduction of conscription), the Iranian armed forces were well below their pre-revolutionary strength by the summer of 1980, with their overall effectiveness considerably reduced.

By the time of the outbreak of war, then, the size of the Iranian army had decreased significantly, from 285,000 to approximately 150,000 (six under-strength divisions), whereas the Iraqi army stood at 200,000 (twelve divisions). This in turn meant that while the Iraqi army could deploy almost all its major weapons systems (2,750 tanks, 2,500 armoured fighting vehicles and some 920 artillery pieces), the Iranian army could hardly deploy 50 per cent of its 1,735 tanks, 1,735 armoured fighting vehicles and 1,000 artillery pieces.

The balance of air forces was no more favourable to Iran. The procurement programmes which had been expected to enhance air force operational poten-tial (particularly the plan to buy 160 F-16 fighters) had been suspended; and the post-revolutionary air force also suffered from acute maintenance and logisti-cal problems. Consequently, by the outbreak of war the Iranian air force was unable to fly more than half of its 447 aircraft. The Iraqi air force, on the other hand, had modernized its front-line aircraft and maintained a high level of ser-viceability (about 80 per cent of its 337 aircraft were operational at the start of the war).

Only at sea was Iran's pre-1979 superiority maintained. Even though the navy did not completely escape the purges of the revolutionary regime and was suffering from maintenance and logistical problems, these things made less of an impact on its operational capabilities than on the air force. Iranian naval superiority was so pronounced that the navy was able to maintain it regardless of the deterioration in its operational strength.

But numbers do not tell the whole story. The quality of military leadership, combat experience, training and command-and-control also count. Indeed, it has been argued that the root of the failure of Iraq's war strategy lay in the incompetence of its military leadership.[16] But this assessment seems to be too harsh. Even though the high degree of politicization in the Iraqi armed forces and the influence of internal problems on their structure and organization cannot be denied, the impact of these factors on the Iran–Iraq balance of power is less clear-cut than is often asserted. Politicization and rigorous control over armed forces by ruling elites is by no means a problem unique to Iraq; the Iranian armed forces were just as tightly controlled, whether under the Shah or the mullahs. In the days of the Shah, for example, there was no Joint Chiefs of Staff organization, nor were the three services linked in any way except through the person of the Shah, who was commander-in-chief of all the armed forces. Every officer above the rank of colonel or its equivalent was personally appointed by the Shah, who employed four different intelligence services to carry out surveillance on the officer corps.[17] Like Iraq, therefore, Iran too had a 'politicized' military leadership, selected and promoted not on professional criteria but by virtue of loyalty to the regime.

The rapid force expansion and modernization programmes had a pronounced impact on the operational competence of the armed forces of both countries. Both Iran and Iraq found it extremely difficult to train, expand and modernize simultaneously. This process was further exacerbated by the poor quality of conscripts in both countries, who found it extraordinarily difficult to get used to handling the advanced weapons systems in a short space of time. As a result, despite the massive advisory assistance provided by the arms donors (mainly the United States and the Soviet Union), both armed forces were more or less incapable of maintaining their advanced major weapons systems. Thus, for example, even before the fall of the Shah the Iranian armed forces appear not to have been able to operate more than 80 per cent of their tanks.[18]

Besides their low technical skills, both forces had very modest combat experience. The Iranian combat experience was limited to the participation of six brigades, along with elements of the navy and the air force, in the suppression of the Dhofari rebellion between 1972 and 1975. But the intervention had been more of a show of force than real combat, since the total strength of the Dhofari rebels had never been more than 2,000, with perhaps 1,000 inside Oman at any one time. Moreover, the Shah's determination to give as many of his units as possible combat experience led to the rotation of the Iranian divisions in Oman every three months—too short a period of duty to allow them to make the best use of their involvement.

The Iraqi armed forces seemed, on the face of it, to have more combat experience than their Iranian opponents. Not only had Iraqi forces taken part in the October 1973 War, but the army had fought a counterinsurgency campaign in Kurdistan for over a decade. A closer examination of this combat experience, however, reveals its clear limitations. The tactics employed during the Kurdish campaign were hardly applicable to conventional wars. On the other hand, Iraq's preoccupation with the Kurdish insurgency interfered with its regular training programmes and thus served to constrain improvement of its operational capabilities. Iraq's experience in the October War was no more impressive: the Iraqi armoured division that arrived at the Golan front ten days after the war began was comprehensively ambushed by the Israelis and lost some 100 tanks within a few hours.

In the area of command and control it did seem that Iraq had an edge at the outbreak of the war. Whereas there was no Joint Staff on the Iranian side, Saddam Hussein, as commander-in-chief of the Iraqi armed forces, controlled the war from the Revolutionary Command Council where each of the three services was represented. The Iranian President, Abolhassan Bani Sadr, had tried in his capacity as commander-in-chief of the Iranian armed forces to strengthen the central command and coordinating staff structure, but his efforts were frustrated to a great extent by the power struggle between the Pasdaran and the armed forces. Consequently, at the outbreak of war, Iran had no central command-and-control system that could coordinate the execution of its war strategy.

In qualitative terms, therefore, the two armed forces could be judged to be more or less even. Both suffered to a comparable extent from problems of military leadership owing to the process of selection and promotion; both were poorly trained; and both had low technical skills to maintain and employ the modern weapons systems at their disposal. Combat experience was very limited, and both forces were saddled with inefficient command-and-control systems.

Against this background of approximate qualitative comparability, Iraq's—perhaps temporary—*quantitative* superiority became significant. Recognizing that this situation could not last because of its fundamental demographic inferiority to Iran, the Iraqi leadership hurried to take advantage of a unique opportunity to pre-empt and forestall the Iranian threat to the Baath regime. The means chosen to attain the Iraqi goal was a strategy of limited war. The choice of a strategy, however, reflected a gross misperception by Iraq of the interrelationship between its national goals and the means to be employed in their pursuit. This mistake turned out to be the principal reason for the failure of the Iraqi campaign.

The war

A *limited war* may be defined as one which does not demand the utmost military effort of which the belligerents are capable, leaving each side's civilian life and armed forces largely intact.[19] More specifically, limited wars involve a small portion of the local armies, are conducted within confined theatre boundaries, and are directed against counter-force rather than counter-value targets. A war which fails to meet any of these requirements is deemed to be a *general war*.

In the case of the Iran–Iraq war, there is little doubt that Iraq's initial war strategy was limited in all three respects mentioned above. Its territorial aims, as reflected in the general course of the war, did not go beyond the Shatt al-Arab region and a relatively small portion of Khuzestan (bounded by the Khorramshahr–Ahvaz–Susangerd–Messian line). The invasion of Iran was carried out by approximately half the Iraqi army—some five divisions. The initial strategy focused almost exclusively on counter-force targets, taking care to avoid targets of value. It was only *after* Iran had started to strike strategic non-military targets in the Iraqi hinterland that Iraq responded in kind.

More concretely, the Iraqi war plan stipulated three simultaneous thrusts along a front of approximately 700 km. The main axis of attack, involving the bulk of Iraqi forces, was made in Khuzestan and consisted of an armoured thrust aimed at disconnecting the Shatt al-Arab from the rest of Iran and establishing a territorial security belt along the southern frontier. The operations in the central (Mehran, Qasr-Shirin) and far northern (Panjwin) fronts were no more than secondary and supportive efforts, designed to secure Iraq's strategic assets against an Iranian counter-attack. The occupation of the Qasr-Shirin area, which dominated the traditional Tehran–Kermanshah–Baghdad invasion route, was intended to secure Baghdad, situated only 80 miles from the frontier. The operations in the northern front were meant to establish strong defence positions opposite Suleimaniya to protect the Kirkuk oil complex.

These limited objectives were in effect achieved within a few days of the onset of hostilities. In Khuzestan, the only positive goal of the invasion, the Iraqi army managed to sever the Shatt almost completely from the rest of Iran and to occupy the Khorramshahr–Ahvaz–Susangerd–Messian line; occupying also the Mehran and Qasr–Shirin areas, Iraq had secured the important road network linking Dezful with northern Iran west of the Zagros mountains, and forestalled potential threats to Baghdad. At this point Saddam Hussein ordered the halt of his forces, while they were still going forward, and publicly announced in an 'address to the nation' on 28 September, five days after the war began, that Iraq had achieved its territorial aims and that his country was willing to cease hostilities and to negotiate a settlement.[20]

This decision not to follow up Iraq's early military successes had a number of dire consequences which, it could be argued, led to the reversal of the course of the war. In the first place, the Iraqi decision saved the Iranian army from a major defeat and allowed it to remain largely intact. It also gave the Iranians the necessary breathing space to reorganize, regroup and move to the offensive. Last but not least, the voluntary surrender of the initiative to Iran had a devastating impact on the morale of the Iraqi army and therefore on its performance in combat. Finding themselves entrenched for months in hastily prepared defence positions, subjected to the hardships of the Iranian winter and the heat of the summer and engaged in a futile war of attrition, the Iraqi forces began to lose any sense of purpose. The Iraqi loss of will, which was reflected in reports of discipline problems and a growing number of defections as well as in the large numbers of prisoners taken and weapons abandoned, was exploited to the full by Iran in 1981–2.

Perhaps in recognition of his mistake, Saddam Hussein tried in late October/early November to reverse the tide of events by striking in the direction of Dezful and Ahvaz—only to discover that it was already too late. Had these two cities been attacked in September, Iranian resistance might have crumbled. By November, with the cities transformed into military strongholds and in the face of the winter rains, Iraq found their occupation beyond its power.

The seriousness of Saddam Hussein's mistake is further illustrated by the relatively satisfactory course of the Iraqi invasion. Certainly the Iraqi operation did not resemble Israel's 1967 campaign, nor even the Syrian and Egyptian attacks of October 1973: it lacked proper close air support and was conducted in a cautious, pedestrian and somewhat clumsy manner. Even so, despite the constraints imposed by the terrain (such as the numerous water obstacles in the southern and central fronts), the Iraqi army managed to drive back the Iranian forces and to reach its objectives; contrary to commonly held beliefs the Pasdaran, which took the lion's share of the Iranian defence, proved unable to halt the Iraqi army in open terrain. Not only did Iraq not face great difficulties in overcoming the uncoordinated Iranian resistance in those first days; it did not even use all the forces available within the immediate theatre of operations.

Limited and general wars

Failures in the implementation of national strategies are not necessarily, therefore, the consequence of over-confidence and overestimation of power. They can equally well arise from the employment of a foreign policy instrument—armed force—in *too limited* a way. Iraq did not grossly misjudge the balance of power between itself and Iran prior to the war, for in the summer of 1980 it enjoyed an undeniable military edge over its rival. Nor does it appear that it set its sights higher than its means permitted. Instead it set its military forces tasks that were too limited. By not destroying a significant fraction of the opposing forces, Iraq laid itself open to counterattack and was thus unable to maintain a hold on its limited territorial objectives. To put it another way, Iraq's grand strategy did not fail because its military power was insufficient to attain its national goals, but because it *did not make more* demands on it.

The Iraqi experience should also cast some doubt on the value of limited war as a foreign policy instrument. True, since wars are not waged for their own sake but in pursuit of political ends it is reasonable to expect a direct correlation between the scope and intensity of a given war on the one hand and the political goals it is intended to serve on the other: the less far-reaching the objectives, the more limited a war is likely to be. And yet there remains a great measure of uncertainty about the willingness of the victim of the attack to play 'according to the rules' and refrain from widening the war. Strategies of limited war try to evade this uncertainty by presupposing the existence of some kind of symmetry between the two belligerents in both capabilities and intentions. That is to say, both sides are assumed to have the same interest in keeping the war limited, so long as approximate equality in capabilities will tend to ensure that the outcome of a conflict is not a foregone conclusion.[21]

But the former assumption is questionable, and the latter liable to misjudgment. Symmetry in states' interests, stakes and perceptions is not at all common. There are few instances in which one may point to a more or less balanced relationship between pairs of actors in the international arena. As a result 'assured limited war' remains to a considerable extent the exclusive domain of the superpowers. An armed conflict at superpower level may well remain limited because of the fear of nuclear war arising. No such inhibitions affect other, non-nuclear powers. A war between a superpower and a minor power, on the other hand, is likely to be limited as the minor power will lack the means to turn it into a general war and the superpower will not devote all its resources to the achievement of victory. Thus the Korean and Vietnam wars were limited wars for the United States (and the other great powers involved) but a general war for the Koreans and Vietnamese.

Since the potential costs of Third World inter-state wars are significantly smaller than those incurred in a superpower nuclear war, and the ultimate outcome more ambiguous, accurate assessment of the adversary's inclination to widen the war becomes more complicated: what seems an unacceptable cost for one party may be perceived as affordable by the other, with all the subsequent ramifications of that disparity on the limitation of the war.

This was indeed the source of the Iraqi miscalculation. It would seem that Iraq's war strategy was based on the belief that the two states' interests were fundamentally symmetrical—that both sides recognized the undesirability of a general war because of the high long-term costs it would involve. As the Iraqi Deputy Premier, Tariq Aziz, put it: 'We want neither to destroy Iran nor to occupy it permanently because that country is a neighbour with which we will remain linked by geographical and historical bonds and common interests. Therefore we are determined to avoid taking any irrevocable steps.'[22]

This mode of reasoning, however blinkered, apparently led Iraq to conclude that a strategy of limited war would serve its national interest best—and be accepted by Iran for the same reason. The assumption was probably that a quick, limited but decisive blow would suffice to bring the revolutionary regime 'back to its senses'—that is, to make it realize the futility of the idea of trying to overthrow the Baath Party, without at the same time pushing the Iranians into a corner. By imposing self-restraint on the initial conduct of war, Iraq sought to signal to Iran its lack of interest in a general war in the hope that Iran would respond in kind, refrain from broadening the war and be willing to negotiate a settlement. The existence of such expectations is perhaps best illustrated by the fact that Iraq voluntarily halted its advance within a week and announced its willingness to negotiate an agreement.

It was not long before Iraq realized the fundamental asymmetry between its intentions and perceptions and those of Iran. Even though the limited scope of the Iraqi invasion did not place the revolutionary regime in imminent danger, it did not bring it round to moderation. Instead it enabled the revolutionary authorities in Tehran to capitalize on the Iraqi attack, to consolidate their legitimacy, to end (or at least significantly diminish) the power struggle within their ranks and to suppress the opposition to their regime.

Most states would normally react to an external armed interference in their affairs with all available means; but when the regime under attack is a revolutionary one which has not yet gained full legitimacy, it is likely to channel all its national fervour (and in this case religious fervour also) from the domestic to the external sphere. Saddam Hussein might well have benefited from President Sadat's warning at the beginning of the war that one should not make war on a revolution.

Conclusion

The general conclusion of the foregoing is obvious, but it is still worth restating. States should strive to keep the maximum degree of correspondence between their foreign policy goals and the instruments employed in their pursuit. More concretely, limited wars in the Third World remain to a large extent the prerogative of the strongest in their dealings with weaker states. In confronting a power with similar potential, a state can hardly expect its adversary to keep the war limited unless the interests at stake are very minor indeed. Instead it should opt to keep the widest possible security margins by preferring a strategy of general war in the pursuit of limited political goals (as with the Egyptian initiation of the October 1973 War) to one of limited war for the attainment of far-reaching political goals (as in the case of the 1982 Israeli invasion of Lebanon). In the case of Iraq this meant that in its attempts to contain the Iranian threat to the Baath regime the Iraqi leadership should have taken one of the following courses of action: either to avoid the war and try to forestall the Iranian pressures by other means (as indeed it did between the winter of 1979 and the summer of 1980); or to follow a strategy of general war in pursuit of limited aims. Such a strategy might still have failed, given the nature of the regime against which it was pursued. A strategy of limited war, as pursued by Iraq, could not but fail.

Notes

* This article draws on the author's larger study, *The Iran–Iraq war: a military analysis* (London: International Institute for Strategic Studies, Spring 1987, *Adelphi Paper* No. 220). He would like to thank Professors L. Freedman, F. Halliday, J. C. Hurewitz and R. K. Ramazani for their helpful comments on an earlier draft.

1 See for example A. Cordesman, *The Gulf and the search for strategic stability* (Boulder, Colo.: Westview, 1984), pp. 645–6; W. O. Staudenmaier, 'A strategic analysis', in S. Tahir-Kheli and S. Ayubi, eds., *The Iran–Iraq war* (New York: Praeger, 1983), p. 37.

2 *The military balance, 1979–1980* (London: International Institute for Strategic Studies, 1980). All data cited in this article on military procurement and armed forces are derived from various issues of the IISS *Military balance*.

3 *Guardian*, 9 Oct. 1971.

4 See for example *Financial Times*, 31 May 1973; *Christian Science Monitor*, 27 July 1973.

5 The 1937 agreement contained two major provisions: first, in designating the low-water-mark on the eastern bank of the Shatt al-Arab as the frontier, it gave Iraq control over the waterway except for the area adjacent to the Iranian ports of Abadan, Khorramshahr and Khosrowabad, where it was fixed at the *thalweg* (median line); and secondly, as a result of that demarcation, it provided that vessels on the Shatt should employ Iraqi pilots and fly the Iraqi flag (again with the exception of those three areas in which the boundary was determined by the *thalweg*).

6 J. M. Abdulghani, *Iraq and Iran: the years of crisis* (London: Croom Helm, 1984), p. 142.

7 The Algiers Agreement stipulated the following: (a) demarcation of the land frontier in accordance with the 1913 Protocol of Constantinople and the verbal accord of 1914; (b) agreement to demarcate the Shatt al-Arab waterway's boundary on the basis of the *thalweg* (median) line; (c) agreement to 're-establish security and mutual confidence along their common frontiers' and undertake to exercise a strict and effective control with the aim of finally putting an end to 'all infiltrations of a subversive character from either side'; (d) the pledge of both parties to regard the provisions negotiated at the 1975 OPEC meeting as indivisible elements of a comprehensive settlement, such that a breach of any one would be considered a violation of the spirit of the Algiers Agreement. For the English text of the agreement see *New York Times*, 8 Mar. 1975.

8 See Abdulghani, *Iraq and Iran*, pp. 156–7.

9 Iraqi News Agency, 14 Feb. 1979: see *Foreign Broadcast Information Service* (henceforth FBIS), *MEA*, 15 Feb. 1979.
10 R. K. Ramazani, *Revolutionary Iran: challenges and responses in the Middle East* (Baltimore, MD, London: Johns Hopkins University Press, 1986), pp. 58–61.
11 See for example interview with President Baqr, reproduced in *BBC Summary of world broadcasts* (henceforth *SWB*), ME/6122/A/1–2, 22 May 1979.
12 *SWB*, ME/6144/A5, 8 June 1979; *SWB*, ME/6145A7, 9 June 1979.
13 *Guardian*, 3 Apr. 1980; *Financial Times*, 12 Apr. 1980; *International Herald Tribune*, 10 Apr. 1980; *Daily Telegraph*, 9 Apr. 1980.
14 *Guardian*, 11 Apr. 1980; *Daily Telegraph*, 18 Apr. 1980.
15 For an excellent account of the purges of the Iranian armed forces see W. F. Hickman, *Ravaged and reborn: the Iranian army, 1982* (Washington, DC: Brookings, 1982), pp. 8–18.
16 Cordesman, *The Gulf*, p. 74–9.
17 R. Graham, *Iran: the illusion of power* (New York; St Martin's, 1980), pp. 182–4; D. D. Sargent, 'Iran's armed forces: 1972 and 1978', *The Army quarterly*, July 1979, pp. 277–8; F. Halliday, *Iran; dictatorship and development* (London: Penguin, 1979), pp. 64–71.
18 Author's own assessment based on the number and structure of Iranian fighting formations at the time.
19 This definition is based on the definitions offered by Robert Osgood. See R. Osgood, *Limited war: the challenge to American strategy* (Chicago, Ill., London: University of Chicago Press, 1957), p. 18; Osgood, *Limited war revisited* (Boulder, Colo.: Westview, 1979), p. 3.
20 In his 'Address to the Nation', Saddam Hussein also presented Iraq's conditions for a political settlement. They included; (a) Iran's recognition of Iraq's legitimate rights over its land and waters; (b) Iran's cessation of its 'racist, aggressive and expansionist' policies and the end of its interference in the internal affairs of Iraq and the Gulf states; (c) adherence to the principle of good-neighbourly relations; and (d) Iran's return of the three Arab islands to the United Arab Emirates. See *FBIS-MEA*, 29 Sept. 1980.
21 L. Freedman, *The evolution of nuclear strategy* (London: Macmillan, 1981), p. 103.
22 *FBIS-MEA*, 11 Sept. 1981.

INDEX